WARM WHITE BEAN SALAD WITH FRAGRANT GARLIC AND ROSEMARY (page 116)
Walnut raisin bread
GLASS OF ROUGH RED WINE

BIG TOMATO SWEET-SOUR SALAD (page 22)
Black Pepper–Honey Steak (page 252)
MELTING GREENS (page 268)
Garlic-Cauliflower "Mashed Potatoes" (page 274)
SALLY'S COCONUT MACAROONS (page 319)

RIBBONS OF GREENS AND GREEN APPLE SALAD (page 16)
Lynne's Retro Garlic Bread (page 179)
PILSNER OR PALE ALE

OVEN-ROASTED CHICKEN CACCIATORA (page 202)
Working Mother's Barley (page 294)
CRACKED NUTS AND DRIED FIGS WITH A GLASS OF PORT

DRESSING-IN-A-BOWL SIMPLE SALAD (page 9)
Almond-Turmeric Potatoes (page 289)
RUSTIC JAM SHORTBREAD TART (page 305)

CHEATER'S HOMEMADE BROTH (page 48)
Pan-Crisped Deviled Eggs on French Lettuces (page 93)
DARK ROAST COFFEE WITH FARMHOUSE PANNA COTTA (page 316)

SPRING GRILL OF ASPARAGUS AND SCALLION SALAD (page 31)
Baked potato
ICED GREEN TEA

SCANDINAVIAN SPICED MEATBALLS WITH CARAMELIZED APPLES (page 255)
Scallion-Dill Pilaf (page 298)
SLICED ORANGES WITH HONEY

PORK TENDERLOIN PAN ROAST WITH BLACK OLIVES AND ORANGE (page 244)
Three-Pea Toss (page 263)
Working Mother's Barley (page 294)
SALLY'S COCONUT MACAROONS (page 319)

EDAMAME AND SMOKED TOFU SUCCOTASH (page 139)
Dumbed-Down Rice (page 297)
FRESH MANGO

SWEET YAMS IN GINGER-STICK CURRY (page 281)
Dressing-in-a-Bowl Simple Salad (page 9)
ICED MANGO TEA

THE SPLENDID TABLE'S®
HOW TO EAT
SUPPER

THE SPLENDID TABLE'S®

HOW TO EAT
SUPPER

Recipes, Stories, and Opinions from Public Radio's
Award-Winning Food Show

Lynne Rossetto Kasper and Sally Swift

Clarkson Potter/Publishers
NEW YORK

Library of Congress Cataloging-in-Publication Data
Kasper, Lynne Rossetto.
   The Splendid table's How to eat supper: recipes, stories,
and opinions from public radio's award-winning food show /
Lynne Rossetto Kasper and Sally Swift.—1st ed.
      p.   cm
   Includes index.
   1. Suppers.   2. Cookery, American.   I. Swift, Sally.   II.
Splendid table (Radio program).
III. Title.   IV. Title: How to eat supper.
TX738.K38   2008
641.5'3—dc22
2007024749

ISBN 978-0-307-34671-1

Printed in U.S.A

Design by Wayne Wolf / Blue Cup Design
Photographs by Mette Nielsen/Tony Kubat Photography

10 9 8 7 6 5 4 3

First Edition

Grateful acknowledgment is made to the following for
permission to reprint previously published material:

Carl Fischer, LLC: Excerpt from "Hunger" by Peter
Schickele, copyright © 1985 by Elkan-Vogel, Inc., a
wholly owned subsidiary of Theodore Presser
Company. International copyright secured. All rights
reserved including performing rights. Reprinted by
permission of Carl Fischer, LLC.

Alfred A. Knopf: "Sugared Raspberries" from *The
Gift of Southern Cooking* by Edna Lewis and Scott
Peacock with David Nussbaum, copyright © 2003 by
Edna Lewis and Scott Peacock. Reprinted by
permission of Alfred A. Knopf, a division of Random
House, Inc.

McClelland & Stewart Ltd.: "Lettuce" and
"Cauliflower" from *The Blue Hour of the Day* by
Lorna Crozier, copyright © 2007 by Lorna Crozier.
Reprinted by permission of McClelland & Stewart
Ltd.

William Morrow: "Crisp Brick-Fried Chicken with
Rosemary and Whole Garlic Cloves" from *The
Improvisational Cook* by Sally Schneider, copyright ©
2006 by Sally Schneider. Reprinted by permission of
William Morrow, an imprint of HarperCollins
Publishers.

Scribner: "Tarragon Chicken Breasts" from *The
Herbfarm Cookbook* by Jerry Traunfeld, copyright ©
2000 by Jerry Traunfeld. All rights reserved.
Reprinted by permission of Scribner, an imprint of
Simon & Schuster Adult Publishing Group.

Jane and Michael Stern: "Mama Lo's Broccoli
Casserole" from *Blue Plate Special & Blue Ribbon
Chefs* by Jane and Michael Stern (Lebhar-Friedman
Books, 2001). Reprinted by permission of Jane and
Michael Stern.

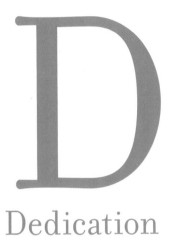

Dedication

This book is for Frank, who still makes me laugh at myself, and for Sally, for being the whirlwind and bright light I've come to hold dear. —**LRK**

For Tom, Ollie, and Lucy; there is no one I love to feed more, and for Lynne, my generous partner in crime. —**SS**

And especially for our listeners who continue to teach us so much.

CONTENTS

Introduction

The world is divided into two kinds of people: *those who wake up thinking about what they're going to eat for supper, and those who don't.* We are decidedly in the former camp; in fact, we wake up thinking about what we are going to *cook* for supper.

T his book is more than recipes.

When we declare How to Eat Supper, we intend two things. Of course we will provide recipes and cooking techniques that we hope will make the process more enjoyable. But this book is also a look at the world that surrounds the food that shows up on our plates.

We Americans don't eat, shop, or cook the way we used to. Our relationship with food has intensified, become more controversial, richer, more pleasurable, and more puzzling. The American food psyche is flourishing, and we're placing more value on food and its influences than ever before. To have a respectable cultural IQ these days, you must have some nimbleness with the language of food—even if you never cook.

How to Eat Supper is about those values, and about the discoveries we've made over the years on our public radio program, *The Splendid Table*®.

We do a national show about food, and while cooking is part of it, believe it or not, it is a relatively small one. Since 1995 *The Splendid Table* has taken radio audiences far beyond the recipe. We hope we've given voice to the dimensions of food rarely heard in media—from the quirky to the political, from the grassroots to the scholarly, from the high to the humble. And yes, we talk to cooks, too.

An experiment that yielded surprising results was the birthplace of this book. We and our associate, Judy Graham, wondered if listeners would find value in receiving a free e-newsletter each week with a tested work-night recipe. With hordes of recipes everywhere, we wondered if the idea would fly. We launched *Weeknight Kitchen* in December 2002, and if subscribers had actually shown up on our doorstep, the line would have stretched to the next county. Our collective curiosity is insatiable, and *Weeknight Kitchen* is still going strong, as the dishes between these covers attest.

You will hear two voices in these pages: that of Sally Swift, the show's producer and my partner in its creation, and mine. Sally cooks for necessity and pleasure; she has two children and a husband who travels, and she works long hours. Real-world work-night food is in her DNA. You should know, too, that Sally is the kind of person who gets up before the kids on Christmas morning so she can start hand-grinding her own Mexican mole sauce.

Long hours are part of my life and I cook nearly every night for my husband, both for play and as therapy. Walking into that kitchen closes the door on any of the day's downsides. Most nights my cooking is fast and simple. That said, I have been accused of putting many recipes into print that begin "On day one . . ."

Although my other books have focused on Italy, for much of my life I've cooked from around the world with a special affection for the flavors of India, the Middle East, North Africa, and Asia. In fact, years ago in New York City I started out teaching

Chinese cooking classes. Curiosity about how foods link from culture to culture drives my work. Sally shares that affection for and curiosity about those flavors and cultures, and consequently they show up in many of the recipes here.

Nowhere is it written that everyone should cook. Our judgment about what constitutes supper has changed. It can be take-out chicken with chutney and fresh herbs rolled up in lettuce leaves, a slice of bread spread with fresh cheese heaped with radishes eaten off a napkin at your laptop, or a salad piled high with the five-a-day you missed at lunch. But supper can also be a home-made oven roast of tandoori-spiced vegetables or a bowl of Cuban black bean soup. For the times when you do want to cook, the food in this book will serve you well.

The recipes in this book are hand-holders, built on the idea that if you've never seen the dish before, you need to know the details of how to cook it—the ideas behind the techniques, what to look for as the food cooks, what kind of pot ensures success, and where substitutions would work. We tell you how long it takes to get the food to the table, and how long it will keep.

All cooking breaks down into logical systems. Cooks call them techniques. Once you learn the technique, the possibilities are legion. Many of our recipes have variations; they start with the same technique you learn in the master recipe and then show you how to vary the theme with new ingredients to wind up with a whole new dish.

Curiously, never have we Americans worried more about eating for health, nor have we ever left so much of the cooking to entities that could care less.

—Anonymous

Politics drives a lot of what you'll find in our refrigerators and on these pages. We feel strongly about local, sustainable, and organic food. We are apt to change a dinner menu to pasta if organic chicken isn't to be had. This philosophy doesn't come solely from concerns over our well-being. It is larger than that. It is about ecology, the survival of rural life, and values.

Over the years we have met via our radio show some incredible people who have had a great influence, sometimes in unusual ways, on the world of food. Their thoughts, stories, and ideas are peppered throughout these pages, along with often unexpected stories behind the dishes. It's a reminder of how much more there is to food than simply lifting your fork to your mouth.

We hope you'll find as much pleasure in these pages as we have had in creating them for you and hope that you sit down to supper more often than not.

A SHOPPER'S
Manifesto

Supporting local, organic, and sustainable growers and producers isn't solely about us and our own well-being. It is about the large view—the environment, the community, the ethical treatment of people and animals, the value of the small and unique. And it's about feeding the people you care about as best you can.

If at all possible, please prepare these recipes with organic ingredients. We know that the sticker from the USDA, "Certified Organic," is not the perfect solution. But for now, it is one of the better options we have. In the best of all possible worlds, shop as close to the source as possible. We like handing our money over to the person who grows the lettuce.

Essential
EQUIPMENT

We share a theory: If you don't like to cook, you should have the very best

equipment. Non-cooks usually shortchange themselves in the equipment department, and that's a mistake. Having good equipment is like having a bunch of friends in the kitchen who always pitch in. Sound tools help ensure success and make cooking a lot easier. If you do like to cook, the best equipment will give you that much-needed leg up.

Pots and Pans

How do you know which pots you need or which ones are worth upgrading? Keep an eye on your kitchen sink. The pots and gadgets you see there all the time are your workhorses, and they should be of the highest quality you can afford.

I favor thick aluminum pots lined with stainless steel. They should have heat-conducting aluminum all the way up the sides of the pan, not just a thick disc on its base. Those discs have a nasty habit of giving you a burned ring around the pan's edge when you sauté.

Be sure to handle a pot before you buy it. Get its feel, and see if you are comfortable with its weight and balance. When you are tempted by that gorgeous 12-quart cast-iron casserole, remember it will be filled when you lift it, and most kitchens are not equipped with cranes.

A nonstick coating is handy for cooking eggs and fish, but these pans are not the all-purpose wonders that manufacturers claim, and they have some significant drawbacks. The finish is fragile and cannot take high heat. Additionally, a nonstick surface doesn't allow that essential flavor-packed brown glaze to develop on the pan's bottom as you brown.

- Straight-sided 12-inch sauté pan with lid and ovenproof handles. You'll find this pan called for in a majority of our recipes. Straight-sided sauté pans have nearly 30 percent more cooking surface than slope-sided skillets. Cook for two or eight in this pan. The 12-inch sauté pan doubles as a roasting pan; it can go straight into the oven.
- Slope-sided 10-inch nonstick skillet with lid and ovenproof handles. Use it for scrambling eggs, making frittatas, and fast sautés for two.
- One-, 2-, and 4-quart saucepans with lids.
- Six-quart pot with lid and ovenproof handles. Boil a pound of pasta, simmer soup for a gang, steam a bunch of broccoli, or bake a party casserole in this pot.
- Fourteen-inch wok with domed lid. Chinese cooks do everything in the wok—quick stir-fries, slow-cooked stews, steamed meals, and even soup. (See How to Buy a Wok, page 187.)
- Half-sheet or a large jelly-roll pan of thick aluminum with thick rolled edges. This is a double-duty pan. Upside down, it's a cookie sheet; right side up, its very low sides and good heat conduction make it an essential for roasting meats, vegetables, and whole fish, and for baking bread or pizza and anything that needs heat surrounding the food. Buy the largest pan your oven can accommodate.

Tools and Gadgets

Knives. Never buy a knife without handling it, and be warned: a knife that claims never to need sharpening will remain sharp for only a short while.

- **Paring knife.** You can do most slicing, paring, and even boning with this knife. Have at least two—a disposable one and a keeper. Look for the ridiculously inexpensive plastic-handled ones from Japan that are lethally sharp and can go in the dishwasher.

    The keeper should be about 4 inches long, have the shank of the knife running through the handle, and fit comfortably in your hand.
- **Six-inch utility/sandwich knife.** This is a step up in size from a parer. You'll find yourself using it for nearly every task short of chopping.
- **Eight-inch chef's knife.** This is the workhorse. Make sure it fits your hand and balances well, and buy the very best you can afford. As mentioned above, you want a knife with the shank of the blade running through the handle.

Oven thermometer. Oven temperatures are almost always off (it's not your fault your first roast chicken didn't come out right—it was the oven). If you tuck an accurate thermometer into your oven, all will be well. Just check the real temperature and adjust the heat as needed.

Instant-reading thermometer. Know immediately if the fish is done just right or the chop is cooked through by poking this into the center.

Heavy-duty spring-loaded tongs. One long, one short. These are invaluable for turning, lifting, tossing salads, and for retrieving things from under the couch.

Wooden spatulas. With their wide, flat bases these spatulas can do what a round spoon can't. In a stir or two they sweep the bottom of a pan clean or prevent the oatmeal from sticking. They are so inexpensive that you can put them in the dishwasher and throw them away when they crack.

Scoop-shaped plastic spatulas. We think Rubbermaid has nailed this gadget better than anyone else to date.

Microplane grater with a handle. Depending upon the size, you can use this to grate anything from a raw rutabaga to nutmeg.

Lemon reamer. A classic for juicing citrus fruits.

Pastry scraper. Sweep up piles of chopped vegetables or clean off your countertop with this handy tool.

Pepper mills. One for pepper, the other for whole spices (although nothing beats a Mexican stone grinder, called a molcajete).

Stainless-steel bowls, from smallest to biggest available. Ideally these have flat bottoms for stability and wide rolled edges for easy handling. And you can never have too many. Use for mixing, storing, serving, salads, and as a top of a double boiler (just set the bowl over a saucepan of bubbling water).

Large, thick hardwood cutting board. Get the largest your counter space can accommodate. Use for everything but meats, fish, and poultry (see below).

Small and large white plastic cutting boards. For meats, fish, and poultry. Clean them in the dishwasher or by hand with bleach.

Oversized stainless-steel colander. It should be big enough to hold a baby. Use this for draining everything from 2 pounds of pasta to a handful of green beans.

Palm-sized rock for crushing and peeling garlic. (See Sally's Garlic Rock, page 117.)

Asian drain strainers. Available in Asian groceries, these are strainers that fit into the drain of your kitchen sink to catch all the little bits. They actually do the job better than the stopper that came with your sink.

Salads

FEATURING

DRESSING-IN-A-BOWL SIMPLE SALAD

Dressing-in-a-Bowl Supper Salad

RIBBONS OF GREENS AND GREEN APPLE SALAD

Provençal Tuna Salad

BIG TOMATO SWEET-SOUR SALAD

Ripe Tomato Stack with Pine Nuts and Mozzarella

SPRING GRILL OF ASPARAGUS
AND SCALLION SALAD

Crisp Cucumber Shrimp in Retro Goddess Dressing

AVOCADO SEAFOOD COCKTAIL WITH
BITTERSWEET CHIPOTLE DRESSING

Asian-Style Chopped Salad on Lettuce Spears

THAI CANTALOUPE SALAD WITH CHILE

Cabbage Slaw with Orange–Pumpkin Seed Dressing

LETTUCE

Raised for one thing
and one only,
lettuce is a courtesan
in her salad days.
Under her fancy crinolines
her narrow feet are bound.

—Lorna Crozier, from The Blue Hour of the Day
(McClelland & Stewart, Ltd., 2007)

It was June 1988

and I hadn't seen a salad in eight days. I was traveling with several other journalists in then Czechoslovakia. Those were the grand old days of Communism, when meals were preprogrammed no matter where you went. There was cabbage, potatoes, and pork, or cabbage, potatoes, and goose. We saw green lettuce in the fields but not on our plates. The revolution finally came. As I recall it took the form of something like our declaring we'd march out of the dining room en masse singing "God Bless America" if we didn't get a salad. It worked.

Looking back on that trip, I realize that our salad revolt reflected how the American salad had gone through a seismic shift well before the late '80s. Salad used to be that mean-spirited little bowl to the left of your dinner plate until, one day, the salad was heaped right onto the dinner plate itself. It *was* the meal. As things stand now, Sally, me, and most of the country can't imagine life without salad, and for good or for ill, prebagged salad blends have turned on even the hesitant salad maker.

The recipes in this chapter embrace what salads have become and can be. No other part of the meal invites improvisation the way salads do, so we've tried to give you some basics—guides to dressings and greens—as well as some recipes that illustrate flavor combinations from around the globe.

DRESSING-IN-A-BOWL SIMPLE SALAD

Serves 4 as a side dish, and multiplies easily | *10 minutes prep time* | *Once the salad is dressed, serve immediately*

In the hodgepodge world of the salad bar and the multiple-personality Caesar, maybe we've forgotten the beauty of a simple bowl of greens. Glossed in a little good oil and vinegar, it can approach the transcendental.

Here is where you could start every night: salad greens (before buying, decide which kinds by tasting a tiny leaf tip), cleaned and pristine, that you dress right in the salad bowl.

No need to mess another bowl making the dressing; do it right over the salad. Trust yourself. Your eyes and your taste won't fail you. Begin with a little oil, barely coating the leaves, and then taste your way forward.

Some inspired blends are mild Bibb with baby spinach and the luxe winter splurge of Belgian endive with meaty yet delicate mâche. Take a look at the Taste Guide to Salad Greens (page 13) for more ideas.

1 big handful of your choice of **salad greens** for each serving (12 to 16 ounces for 4 salad lovers)
Light sprinklings of **coarse salt** and fresh-ground **black pepper**
2 to 4 tablespoons good-tasting **oil** (extra-virgin olive oil, or walnut, almond, or hazelnut oil)
1 to 3 tablespoons **vinegar** (red wine, white wine, cognac, sherry, or cider vinegar)

1. Wash and thoroughly spin-dry the greens. Tear them into bite-sized pieces, and pile into a big salad bowl.
2. Just before serving, sprinkle the greens with salt and pepper. Drizzle with 2 tablespoons of the oil, and toss to barely coat the leaves. Then toss with 1 tablespoon of the vinegar.
3. Taste for balance. Add more oil, vinegar, salt, or pepper as needed, but use a light hand; you should still be able to taste the greens.
4. Tossed salad waits for no man. Serve it while it's still standing up and saluting.

THE PURE AND THE VIRGINAL
An Olive Oil Guide

A frequent **question** we get from callers and readers is "Why should I spend the extra money on extra-virgin olive oil? Isn't pure good enough? Is there really a difference?"

The **answer** is always the same: "There is a big difference. 'Pure' is not pure."

All the reasons you buy olive oil—the nutrients, the absence of trans fats, and the flavor—are ensured only when olives are pressed right after picking with absolutely no heat or chemicals. This is where the word "virgin" comes in. That term on the label means the olives were pressed without heat and what the trade calls "solvents" (i.e., chemicals). Here is what the language on olive oil containers means:

Demystifying Olive Oil Labels

- **"Extra-Virgin"** contains less than 0.8 percent acidity, which makes it easy to digest, among other things. Extra-virgin is the purest expression of the olive in all its nutritional and sensual glory. There is no guarantee of taste here; each brand of extra-virgin will be different, but this is *the one truly pure olive oil.*
- **"Virgin"** olive oil can contain up to 2 percent acidity. You rarely see this oil, which is just as well.
- **"Pure," "Pomace,"** or simply **"Olive Oil"** on the label indicates an oil treated with chemicals and, in most cases, heat. These do not belong in anyone's kitchen.
- **"Light"** is marketing. This doesn't mean fewer calories. It does mean the oil is heavily filtered to remove flavor and color. Don't bother with these, either.
- **Spray Oils** and **Refillable Spray Containers:** Some spray oils are bolstered with chemicals and artificial flavors, and all contain alcohol or propane to create the spray effect. Aside from the issue of additives, every spray oil I have tasted leaves much to be desired. Simpler, and probably healthier, is to moisten a paper towel with good-tasting oil and wipe it onto the surface you want to cook on.

We don't recommend refillable oil spray containers either. They are difficult to clean thoroughly between refills, so you end up with rancid oil permeating your fresh additions. Keep life simple: stay with the bottle the oil comes in.

How to Buy and Use Olive Oils

Olive Oil Golden Rule #1: Older is never better; flavors fade in a year. Premium extra-virgins demand hefty prices, so don't put your money down unless the label bears a harvest date (*raccolta, annata di produzione* in Italian; *cosechar, recoger* in Spanish) and that date is less than a year ago. Most Northern Hemisphere olives are harvested between October and January. Lamentably, they are usually not available in stores until February or later.

South-of-the-equator olive oils are the lifesavers for us in the fall and winter months. It is ironic that at the very time we need to restock or find special oils for gifts and festive cooking, the Northern Hemisphere's oils are fading.

Olive Oil Golden Rule #2: Ignore rumors about not being able to cook with extra-virgin oil. It is true that heat will slightly diminish the oil's flavor, and that extra-virgin olive oil cannot tolerate extremely high temperatures for any length of time, but the entire Mediterranean has cooked with extra-virgin oils since before Christ. For health reasons alone, extra-virgin is the only olive oil that should pass your lips. Our only caveat is that premium extra-virgin olive oils are expensive. So you might want to save them for seasoning cooked dishes and use lower-priced extra-virgin oils for cooking.

Olive Oil Golden Rule #3: Light oxidizes olive oil, so buy dark bottles or boxed oils. Store your oil away from light and heat.

Olive Oil Golden Rule #4: Buy for flavor. If you don't like an oil, don't use it no matter how highly rated it may be.

Here are some oils we've enjoyed:

REASONABLY PRICED OLIVE OILS: These are good for cooking and for salads: Bella, Carapelli, Cost Plus, Crespi, Costco's Kirkland Toscano (a dated oil that changes in taste each year), Whole Foods 365, Carli, Fabri, Colavita, Spectrum Naturals blends, and Sciabica from California.

PREMIUM OLIVE OILS: Consider these seasonings as much as dressings and cooking oils. Use these oils as you would salt or pepper. They naturally break down into the following flavor categories.

Buttery and Gently Fruity: Spain's Dauro de Aubocassa. Italy's Roi Carte Noire, Ardoino "Fructus," Frantoio Borgomaro di Laura Marvaldi. And not as distinctive as the previous, but decent, are Rainieri and Isnardi.

Uses: Gentle oils shine with gentle dishes. Use these oils wherever you would routinely dip into the butter dish.

- Simple fish recipes (Flash-Roasted Trout on Green Herbs, page 222) and nearly any food that is poached or boiled.
- Bibb lettuce, steamed mild greens, sugar snap peas, green beans, and the naturally sweet waxy-style potatoes like Desiree, Yellow Finn, and Red Bliss take to these oils.
- Drizzle the oil over slices of young cheeses or on Belgian Beer Bar Tartine (page 119), or blend it with grated Parmigiano-Reggiano cheese and black pepper as a dip for spring vegetables.

- Dress the simplest of pastas with these oils, like a late-night garlic and pepper (*aglio olio*) or ricotta and walnut sauce.

The Pesto Oil: All the Italian oils in this category come from northern Italy's Liguria region, the home of pesto. These oils are made often from a single olive, the taggiasca, which is picked ripe; hence the buttery, soft quality. This is the olive oil that goes into the famous pesto because those qualities complement rather than overwhelm the young sweet basil that local cooks like to use. The Quintessential Pesto with Risotto recipe on page 149 will reveal all.

Fruity, Full-Flavored, with Some Pepper: Italy's Ravida, Laudemio Frescobaldi (both are favorite all-around oils), Pianogrillo Tonda Iblea, and Olio Verde of Gianfranco Becchina. Spain's Hermans Catalan 100% Arbequina, Pons Early Harvest, and Baena Nuñez de Prado. Portugal's Joana and João Oliveira High Ridge Orchard, California's Lila Jaeger, and Australia's Yellingbo.

Uses: These oils pair with foods that absorb flavors, like potatoes and the entire bean family. They stand up to grilled meats, seafood, and roasted vegetables. Italians love them drizzled over fresh cheeses and often finish simple tomato-sauced pastas with them.
- Fuller-flavored seafood dishes (see Salmon Pan Roast on page 217), straightforward grilled meats, and eggs like Pan-Crisped Deviled Eggs on French Lettuces (page 93).

- Vegetables—assertive greens, potatoes, yams, the entire bean family from fresh to canned. Look at Melting Greens (page 268), Wine-Braised Carrots (page 264), Green Beans with Lemon, Garlic, and Parmigiano Gremolata (page 270), and Warm White Bean Salad with Fragrant Garlic and Rosemary (page 116).
- Pastas, soups, grain and rice dishes—try with Chopping-Board Pistachio Pesto (page 176), whole-grain breads, Farmhouse Minestrone (page 56), and Garlic-Cauliflower "Mashed Potatoes" (page 274).

Robust, Peppery, and Aggressive: Italy's Castello di Ama, Capezzana, Castel di Lego, Trevi, Biondi Santi, Col d'Orcia, Laudemio Poppiano, and Magni. Spain's Almazara Luis Herrera, California's McEvoy Ranch, Australia's Lakelands Olives' "Frantoio" and their Special Reserve, New Zealand's Moutere Grove, and Argentina's Armando Mansur.

Uses: Think of these oils as the pepper and the snappy spice of the olive oil world. Use them where you want to give a dish some extra snap. Any dish with chiles, powerful wine sauces, and assertive vegetables takes to this oil as its final seasoning.
- Vegetables and salads—try finishing spicy pastas, rices and grains, Ripe Tomato Stack with Pine Nuts and Mozzarella (page 25), and Provençal Oven Onion Sauté (page 278).
- Meats—this is the style of oil to use on grilled meats and big-flavored seafoods.

A Taste Guide to Salad Greens

You can reshape supper from night to night solely with what is in your salad bowl. Knowing salad greens beyond iceberg, leaf lettuce, and romaine is akin to a do-it-yourselfer being handed a new set of power tools. **You gain so many options once you figure out what unfamiliar greens taste like.** Nibble on individual leaves in the bagged mixes and sample (discreetly) from the heads and bunches you see in the market.

For instance, bold greens cut through the richness of spice and fat. They pair well with things like barbecued ribs, vindaloo takeout, hot and sweet wings, short ribs, chili, and lasagne. The delicate ones are a foil for subtler dishes—roast chicken, vegetable stews, and grills. Greens are beautiful simply dressed and eaten all by themselves.

Here is a sampling of the familiar and unfamiliar. First, try the unfamiliars on their own to get a sense of what they are; then start mixing and matching.

Subtle

Bibb lettuce, butter lettuce, leaf lettuce, and iceberg (which is much maligned, but good for watery crunch).

Mild and Distinctive

Young beet greens, baby chard, romaine, Kentucky limestone lettuce, Lollo Rossa, mâche (corn salad), nasturtium leaves, lamb's quarters, Chinese or napa cabbage, and baby bok choy.

Standouts but Not Overpowering

Watercress, chickweed, deer tongue, oakleaf, baby mizuna, pea tops (also known as pea shoots or pea leaves), perilla (also known as shiso), young amaranth, spinach, purslane, water spinach, and arugula. (There are two types of arugula. The smaller, rougher-leaved "wild" or "wall rocket" is preferred for its more peppery, less medicinal character.)

Greens with Punch or Bite

Baby dandelion, young chrysanthemum leaves, Belgian endive, curly endive, escarole, frisée, young kale, mature mizuna, young mustard, sorrel, Tuscan kale (lacinato), and radicchio (small radicchio heads are particularly bitter, because they are actually older ones with the rotting leaves trimmed away).

DRESSING-IN-A-BOWL SUPPER SALAD

| Serves 4 | 15 minutes prep time | Once the salad is dressed, serve immediately |

Pristinely simple side salads secretly long to be wonderfully jumbled main-dish concoctions. Or at least it's fun to think so.

A supper salad can be a thoughtfully articulated bowl of restraint or a gloriously messy gathering of things you love. Think of the last few roasted vegetables or those lick-your-fingers-they're-so-good pan juices from the other night's chicken: Warm them up and add them to the dressing. Supper salads are blank canvases, and this recipe presents a flock of possible improvisations. Each one gives you a one-of-a-kind dinner.

Kosher and other coarse salts bring an accent and a crunch to salads that fine-ground salt cannot equal. Skip flavored oils and vinegars. Most are second-rate. It is much better to add fresh flavorings to the greens.

½ medium **red onion**, thin sliced

3 to 4 tablespoons good-tasting **vinegar**

Salt and fresh-ground **black pepper**

2 tablespoons dark grainy **mustard**

½ cup canned **chickpeas**, kidney beans, or black beans, rinsed and drained

About 2 cups **raw vegetables** (green tomatoes, cucumbers, broccoli, snow peas, corn, jicama, edamame, etc.), chopped into bite-sized pieces if large

2 tablespoons fresh mild **herbs** (basil, mint, coriander, parsley); *or* 1 to 2 teaspoons fresh assertive herbs (thyme, rosemary, sage, tarragon)

1 to 2 cups **soy foods** or cooked meat, seafood, or poultry, chopped into bite-sized pieces

2 heads **salad greens**; *or* 2 packages prewashed greens of your choice (12 to 16 ounces total)

4 to 6 tablespoons **extra-virgin olive oil** or almond, walnut, or hazelnut oil

1. In a large salad bowl, stir together the onion, 3 tablespoons of the vinegar, some salt and pepper, and the mustard. Add the chickpeas, moistening them with the mixture. Let it stand for about 30 minutes while you set the table.

2. When you are ready to serve, add the vegetables, herbs, soy foods or meat, and salad greens along with 4 tablespoons of the oil. Toss the salad together. Then taste, and adjust the seasoning as you like with more oil, vinegar, salt, and/or pepper. Serve the salad while it is still crisp.

Supper Salad IMPROVISATIONS

Begin improvising with the Dressing-in-a-Bowl Supper Salad proportions, substituting the following suggestions for the recipe's ingredients.

Cheddar/Craisin with Autumn Greens: Try shards of sharp cheddar and a handful each of Craisins (dried sweetened cranberries) and salted sunflower seeds, tossed with curly endive, baby spinach, and red-leaf lettuce. Apples are good in this mix, too.

Sweet and Hot Chicken Salad: Do an arranged salad by tossing 2 or 3 cups of cooked chicken with bottled Thai sweet/hot chile sauce and crushed peanuts. Heap the blend on top of a mix of romaine, bean sprouts, jicama chunks, and sliced scallions. Finish the salad with generous sprinkles of rice vinegar and a little Asian sesame oil.

Marseille Salad: Toss together mild and bold greens (see page 13), two 6-ounce cans of olive oil–packed tuna, and several tablespoons each of tapenade, chickpeas, pickled onions, and roasted peppers.

The Uptown Pear Salad: Show off a fruit balsamic vinegar like fig or apple, or a European sweet fruit vinegar, by taking the supper salad in a different direction. Rather than tossing every-thing together, slice 2 pears into long narrow wedges. Fan them out on a big platter, and put a bundle of frisée or curly endive at the base of the fan. Sprinkle everything lightly with the vinegar, a little olive oil, some coarse salt, and a few grindings of pepper.

Goat cheese, shavings of Gruyère or young sheep cheese, or salted almonds could finish the salad.

RIBBONS OF GREENS AND GREEN APPLE SALAD

Serves 4 to 6 | *20 minutes prep time* | *Once it is dressed, serve the salad immediately*

Chiffonade—a fussy concept, but it's amazing how slicing lettuce into thin strips impresses. People think you have worked for hours. The trick is to stack the leaves, roll them into a tight cylinder, and cut them all at once.

The combination of crunch, sweet, and tart gives this salad its distinction. Picky little eaters in the house? This one will win them over. For grown-ups, an addition of fresh goat cheese would move this into the main dish category.

1 medium **red onion**, cut into thin rings
Pale green inner leaves from 1 large head **curly endive**,
    frisée, or other tangy lettuce
Pale green inner leaves from 1 large head **escarole**; *or*
    1 small head oak-leaf lettuce or green radicchio
1 small head **red-leaf or Bibb lettuce**
1 crisp **apple**, such as Granny Smith, Fuji, Pink Lady, or
    Braeburn, quartered, cored (not peeled), and thin sliced
⅓ cup whole **salted almonds**, coarse crushed
Salt and fresh-ground **black pepper**
½ teaspoon **dried basil**
2 to 3 tablespoons peppery **extra-virgin olive oil**
1 to 2 tablespoons **red wine or cider vinegar**

1. Place the onion in a bowl, add ice water to cover, and refrigerate for 30 minutes.

2. Wash and thoroughly dry the greens. Stack 4 leaves, roll them up into a tight cylinder, and thin-slice crossways. Repeat with the remaining leaves. You'll have fine ribbons of salad. Put them in a large salad bowl, and add the apple slices and almonds.

3. Just before serving, drain the onion and pat dry. Sprinkle the greens with salt and pepper, the basil, and the drained onion.

4. At the table, toss the salad with enough oil to barely coat the greens, about 2 tablespoons. Toss with vinegar to taste, starting with 1 tablespoon. Taste for balance, making sure the vinegar is assertive but not harsh.

Slightly underripe fruit shines here. Through the summer replace the apple with peaches, nectarines, or plums. In fall and winter do grapes, pears, or cooked quince.

New Moms and
BITTER GREENS

Did you ever wonder why pregnant women have such opinionated palates? Their legendary cravings for odd foods are only part of what is happening to their bodies. One of our favorite guests, poet and naturalist Diane Ackerman, shared a theory with us one day.

She said there is scientific speculation that a pregnant woman's heightened ability to pick out bitter tastes during pregnancy is an evolutionary alarm system. Many poisonous plants and fruits taste bitter, and our taste buds may be designed to kick in at a heightened level when a woman is carrying a child, giving her extra protection during those vital months—an early warning system at its very best.

Another piece of science speculates that this explains infants' innate love of sweet flavors. In nature, sweet is safe.

BUILDING
THE LIBRARY

A NATURAL HISTORY
OF THE SENSES
BY DIANE ACKERMAN
(VINTAGE, 1991)

PROVENÇAL TUNA SALAD

Serves 4 or, more truthfully, 2 | *15 minutes prep time* | *Holds for 2 to 3 days in the refrigerator*

Lazy summers in the south of France—that is what this salad tastes like, and it gets better with time. Chunks of olive, fresh lemon, onion, capers, and tomato all come together to prove that a can of tuna can become a majestic thing.

Dill is the surprise. You'd think this reticent herb from the cold north wouldn't belong here. Perhaps it's Scandinavian stoicism at work, but dill corrals together all these raucous children of the Mediterranean in a way no other herb could. Without it, the salad isn't anywhere near as interesting.

Three 6-ounce cans water-packed albacore **tuna**,
  thoroughly drained
1 cup halved **grape tomatoes**
½ cup whole **Kalamata or Niçoise olives**, preferably pitted
3 heaping tablespoons drained **capers**
¼ cup chopped **red onion**
¼ to ½ light-packed cup chopped fresh **dill leaves**
½ cup **extra-virgin olive oil**
½ cup fresh **lemon juice** (about 1½ large lemons)
Salt and fresh-ground **black pepper**

1. Turn the drained tuna into a large bowl, and break it into chunks with a fork. Fold in the tomatoes, olives, capers, red onion, and fresh dill. Pour in the olive oil and lemon juice. Add salt and pepper to taste; toss to blend.

2. If time allows, let stand at cool room temperature for about an hour. This salad was destined to top thick slices of rugged, grainy bread, and salad greens love it, too.

Variation
MEDITERRANEAN CHICKPEA SALAD

Before adding any of the ingredients, rub a split garlic clove over the inside of your serving bowl. Make the salad as described above, replacing the tuna with 2 cans of chickpeas, drained and rinsed, and replacing the dill with ½ light-packed cup of torn fresh basil leaves. Over the salad grate the zest from one quarter of an organic orange, and blend the ingredients together. (Grating the zest directly over a dish ensures that the fragrant oils from the orange will fully perfume it.)

Variation
RUSTIC MARINATED CHEESE SALAD

As easily as picking up a couple of cans of tuna, you can pick up some cheeses in the supermarket—which will take this salad in another direction. For this salad, combine mild farmer's cheese with something with a bit more personality, like Asiago or a mild feta, cut into ¾-inch cubes. You will need about 2 cups.

Begin the recipe by rubbing the inside of your serving bowl with a split garlic clove. Make the salad as described above, replacing the tuna with the combination of cheeses. Use any fresh green herb—dill, basil, flat-leaf parsley, thyme, or rosemary. Add the herb to taste, as some herbs are stronger than others. The longer you marinate the cheese in the dressing, the more character it takes on.

THE VINEGAR MAN

Leaf through this book and it will be obvious how much we love vinegar—but not as much as one of our most beguiling guests, the Vinegar Man.

Lawrence Diggs is the brains and the inspiration behind Vinegar Connoisseurs International and the International Vinegar Museum on Main Street in that crossroads of a million private lives, Roslyn, South Dakota. Go there to taste vinegars made from all kinds of plants, see paper made from vinegar, and partake in the mother of all vinegar contests.

This may be the most overlooked culinary hot spot in the U.S.A. Admission: adults $2, 18 and under $1, with instant scholarships for those too broke to pay. Tell Lawrence *The Splendid Table* sent you. And if you can't make it to South Dakota, go to www.vinegarman.com.

The Do-It-Yourself
DRESSING KIT

Labels on bottled salad dressing can read like high school chem-
istry projects. Get additives off your plate with one easy foundation dressing that takes
you wherever you want to go. Simply combine good olive oil and vinegar
with salt, pepper, and our "secret" ingredient (see below). Use the
dressing as is or as the foundation for new dressings. With this basic formula and its variations, you can replicate (we think surpass) the entire dressing shelf at the supermarket.

BASIC VINAIGRETTE DRESSING

Makes 2½ to 3 cups dressing
Keeps up to 2 weeks in a cool, dark place

John Willoughby, executive editor of *Gourmet* magazine and a fine cook, gave us
an insight into salad dressing that we now rely on constantly. Believe it or not,
adding a tiny amount of Asian fish sauce to your dressings elevates the flavors as
if by magic. You won't really taste it, but it will bring all the flavors into sharper
focus. Be sure not to tell. Most people associate fish sauce with smelly socks.

We have since learned that this technique is a favorite of chefs and a prime
example of working with *umami*, an element known as "the fifth taste." Umami is
that almost indescribable savoriness you find in some foods. Umami pumps up
flavors; it opens up the character of individual ingredients and somehow melds
them together. Other umami-packed foods include soy sauce, anchovies, red
wine, certain mushrooms, Parmigiano-Reggiano cheese, and tomatoes.

When you think about it, nearly everything tastes better with the ingredients on
that list. So when a dish doesn't quite come together, give it a little umami. Here
is how to do it with salad dressing.

> ¾ cup good-tasting **wine vinegar** (or one-third balsamic and two-thirds
> wine or cider vinegar)
> 1½ to 2 cups good-tasting **extra-virgin olive oil**
> ⅛ to ¼ teaspoon **Asian fish sauce** (*nam pla* or *nuoc nam*)
> **Coarse salt** and fresh-ground **black pepper**

Combine the vinegar, olive oil, and fish sauce in a glass jar. Shake to blend. Taste for vine-
gar/oil balance, and add salt and pepper to taste. Each vinegar and oil will be different, so
trust your judgment in adding what is needed. Shake the dressing before using it.

THE DRESSING
COLLECTION

Make these up as you need them and store any excess in the refrigerator for up to 24 hours, no longer.

Fresh Herb: Blend into ½ cup Basic Vinaigrette Dressing: I minced garlic clove, 6 to 7 torn fresh basil leaves, 6 torn fresh oregano leaves, and about ⅛ cup snipped fresh chives or chopped scallion tops.

Creamy Italian: Make the Fresh Herb Dressing, then add to it a generous ¼ cup of fresh-grated Parmigiano-Reggiano cheese, 2 generous tablespoons mayonnaise, and I generous tablespoon sour cream.

Blue Cheese: Combine ½ cup Basic Vinaigrette Dressing, ¼ cup crumbled blue cheese, and I tablespoon minced onion. If you add a little heavy cream, you have a creamy blue.

French Mustard: Stir together ½ cup Basic Vinaigrette Dressing, 2 tablespoons dark mustard, I large minced shallot, and I packed teaspoon chopped fresh tarragon leaves.

Summer Tomato: In a food processor combine ⅓ cup Basic Vinaigrette Dressing with 6 fresh basil leaves, 4 sprigs fresh coriander, the tip of a fresh jalapeño chile, ⅛ of a sweet onion, and 2 large, good-tasting tomatoes (cored but not peeled). Blend until the mixture is nearly smooth. Let the dressing stand for 20 minutes before using.

Honey Mustard: Stir together ½ cup Basic Vinaigrette Dressing, 3 tablespoons dark spicy mustard, I minced garlic clove, I to 2 tablespoons honey, and 2 tablespoons mayonnaise.

Fresh Ranch: Combine ¼ cup Basic Vinaigrette Dressing, ⅓ cup buttermilk, and ¼ cup mayonnaise with I minced garlic clove and I tight-packed teaspoon *each* of fresh parsley leaves, basil leaves, and scallion tops, all chopped together.

Roasted Almond and Sweet Pepper: Blend in a food processor ½ cup Basic Vinaigrette Dressing, ½ small garlic clove, I tablespoon chopped onion, ½ cup whole salted almonds, ½ cup roasted sweet peppers (jarred peppers work well here), and fresh lemon juice to taste. Finish the dressing with 2 generous tablespoons plain whole-milk yogurt.

Creamy Sweet-Sour Dill: Blend in a food processor ½ cup Basic Vinaigrette Dressing, ¼ cup heavy cream, 2 teaspoons chopped onion, ⅓ tight-packed cup fresh dill leaves, I tablespoon dark spicy mustard, and I to 2 teaspoons sugar. Taste the dressing to balance the sweet-tart flavor with more vinegar, mustard, or sugar.

Moroccan Chermoula: In a food processor combine ½ cup Basic Vinaigrette Dressing, ⅓ tight-packed cup fresh coriander leaves, I large garlic clove, I teaspoon ground cumin, 1½ teaspoons medium-hot paprika or medium-hot pure chile powder, and fresh lemon juice to taste. Process until the herbs are finely chopped. Let it mellow for 20 minutes before using.

BIG TOMATO
SWEET-SOUR SALAD

Serves 4 to 6	*10 minutes prep time; 5 minutes stove time*	*Dressing can be prepared up to a week ahead and refrigerated. Serve the salad immediately after dressing it.*

Straight from nineteenth-century American cookbooks, these big chunks of green tomatoes and ripe beefsteaks bathed in a warm, garlicky sweet-sour dressing can stand on their own, top greens, or make a potato-tomato salad you can't stop eating. Bacon fat was favored in this recipe 150 years ago; olive oil works today.

My pet theory that sweet-and-sour is a universal panacea for any dish proved true when we tested this recipe with so-so red winter tomatoes. Make extra dressing; you will use it up in homemade coleslaw, cooked yams, broccoli, and shrimp or salmon salad.

DRESSING

1 cup **cider vinegar**
½ cup **extra-virgin olive oil** or bacon fat
1 medium **red onion**, thin sliced lengthwise into long strips
Salt and fresh-ground **black pepper**
8 large **garlic cloves**, thin sliced
2 tight-packed tablespoons **brown sugar**

TOMATOES

2 or 3 large, delicious, ripe **tomatoes** (1½ to 2 pounds), cored and cut into 1-inch chunks
3 medium **green tomatoes** (about 1 pound), cored and cut into 1-inch chunks

FINISH

⅓ light-packed cup coarse-chopped fresh **dill leaves**

1. To make the dressing, first pour the vinegar into a small sauce-pan and boil it down to about ½ cup, about 5 minutes. Set aside.

2. In a 10-inch skillet set over medium heat, warm the olive oil or bacon fat. Stir in the onion, sprinkling it with a little salt and a generous amount of pepper. Sauté for a minute, or until the onion is softened but not browned. Stir in the garlic and cook for another 30 seconds to 1 minute. You want to soften the garlic but not brown it. Pull the skillet off the heat and blend in the brown sugar to melt it. (You can set the dressing aside at this point for several hours, or refrigerate it for up to a week.)

3. Put the tomatoes into a large serving bowl. When you are ready to serve, warm up the onion mixture if needed—it should be warm, not hot. Pull the pan off the heat, and stir in the boiled-down vinegar and any liquid from the tomatoes. Carefully (the dressing could be quite hot) taste for seasoning and sweet-tart balance. Pour it over the tomatoes, folding in the dill.

4. If you made the salad with olive oil dressing, serve it warm or at room temperature. If bacon fat was used in the dressing, it's best to eat it warm.

The dressing can be prepared a week ahead, up to the point of adding the vinegar. The oil should be warm, but not hot, when the vinegar goes in; that way you won't get spattered, nor will you burn your tongue when you taste it for seasoning.

The smell of an onion from the mouth of the lovely is sweeter than that of a rose in the hands of the ugly.

—Sa'di of Persia

RIPE TOMATO STACK WITH PINE NUTS AND MOZZARELLA

Serves 4 as a main dish;
6 to 8 as a starter | 20 minutes prep time | Salad can be assembled
30 minutes ahead

Garlic and pine nuts, currants and onion, take the ubiquitous tomato-mozzarella salad into new territory. Adapted from my second book, this salad might be *The Splendid Table*'s website's most popular download. We had to include it here.

For me, this dish is all Sicily, but not in the way you might think. It speaks of Sicily's location ninety miles off the coast of North Africa and of the island's Arab occupation from the ninth to twelfth century. That era brought Arab cooks—along with scholars, artists, and politicians—to the island. So today this salad tastes more medieval and Arab than anything like modern Italy. This is pure Sicily, as typical as a view of Mount Etna.

DRESSING

3 tablespoons fresh **lemon juice**

1 large **garlic clove**, minced

⅛ teaspoon fresh-ground **black pepper**

Generous pinch of **red pepper flakes**

⅓ medium **red onion**, cut into ¼-inch dice

3 tablespoons **dried currants**

Salt

2 tight-packed tablespoons fresh **basil leaves**, torn

⅔ cup **pine nuts**, toasted

SALAD

6 medium ripe **tomatoes**

1 pound fresh **mozzarella** packed in liquid, sliced ½ inch thick

About 3 tablespoons **extra-virgin olive oil**

(recipe continues)

1. To make the dressing, in a small bowl, combine the lemon juice, garlic, black pepper, red pepper flakes, onion, currants, and salt to taste. Let the mixture stand for 20 to 30 minutes. Just before assembling the dish, stir in the basil and all but ¼ cup of the pine nuts.

2. Core the tomatoes. Check that each is stable when placed cored side down on a plate. (The idea behind this dish is that each tomato will be sliced horizontally and layered with cheese and seasonings so that it looks whole again on the plate. Keep each tomato's slices in order for easy assembly.)

3. Cut each tomato horizontally into ½-inch-thick slices. Place the bottom slice of each tomato on a serving platter. Season them with a little salt, then top each with a slice of cheese. Season the cheese with a teaspoon or so of the onion mixture. Continue the layers until all the tomatoes are reassembled.

4. To finish the dish, sprinkle the tomatoes with the reserved pine nuts, the olive oil, and any leftover onion mixture. Serve at room temperature.

TAMING THE ONION

My mother served salad every night. Every evening that salad contained raw onion, and not until I reached my teens did I learn that my late-night agony had a name: heartburn. Despite years of this, my love of raw onions has endured.

The trick with raw onions is get to them before they get to you. Cancel out their bite with these tricks:

- **Ice bath:** Bury sliced raw onion in ice water for 20 to 30 minutes.
- **Acid treatment:** Toss slices with vinegar or citrus, and let stand for 20 to 30 minutes. The onion will wilt, but it will also turn sweet.
- **Microwave** the onions in a little vinegar for 3½ minutes at high power. For an unusual salad ingredient we call Melting Paprika Onions, toss the onions with the vinegar and some sweet paprika. Microwave for 3½ minutes, cool, and add to a salad.

No More Soggy Greens
BAGGING YOUR OWN SALAD

Few events beat the "ugh" factor of finding disintegrating lettuce at the bottom of your crisper. Food scientist Shirley Corriher gave us a cure. While talking kitchen science on the show, she explained a technique for keeping washed-and-ready salad greens in prime condition for ten days.

Air and water are the enemies of most vegetables. If you eliminate the oxygen and moisture from your greens, you can have salad ready to go every night. Wash and thoroughly spin-dry your greens as soon as you buy them, keeping the pieces whole. (The more tears in a leaf, the more likely it is to brown.) Place the leaves in a heavy-duty resealable plastic bag with a piece of paper towel to wick up extra moisture. Squeeze out all the air, seal shut, and refrigerate. You'll have bagged salad for half the price.

BUILDING THE LIBRARY

COOKWISE: THE SECRETS OF COOKING REVEALED
BY SHIRLEY CORRIHER (MORROW COOKBOOKS, 1997)

How to Orchestrate
Summer Tomatoes

For me, the tomato obsession began early on. I've been known to give over an entire one-hour broadcast to the subject and still rail about how we couldn't cover enough material.

I think I eye tomatoes the way a conductor scans an orchestra. Each tomato is definitely a player. The exceptional ones fall into one of several distinct flavor groups; orchestrating them together opens up a whole new way of reveling in the fruit. But you can play this game only in high summer, when the greats are in their prime. Below is my own idiosyncratic guide to tomato flavor groups and ideas for how to bring them together.

Next to your own garden, the best and cheapest way to get a tomato that will make you smile is from the farmer who grows it. Never have so many of us been able to get our hands on such a variety of fruit—heirlooms, new strains, and old ones from seeds originally sprouted in places we never looked at before, like Russia, Siberia, Ukraine, and Alaska.

One important thing to remember: Never buy a large quantity of tomatoes for canning or freezing without tasting them first.

Mellow

The suave Strauss waltz of a tomato that is packed with big round flavor and a smooth balance between sweet and acid. **Examples:** Brandywine, beefsteak, Best Boy, Big Boy, Early Girl, German Pink, German Stripe, Purple Calabash, Rutgers, Emerald, and Green Zebra.

These are the heart of tomato salads, sauces, and salsas. Accent the two extreme qualities of mellow tomatoes with small amounts of punchy and gentle varieties.

Punchy Sweet/Tart

These are the bipolars of the tomato world, the accent fruit. They pack extreme highs and lows. It is like having Beethoven's Fifth on your plate. **Examples:** Grape, Early Cascade, Sweet 100, Red Currant, Green Grape, Sweet Baby Girl, and Principe Borghese.

Excellent on their own raw, these are splendid sauce tomatoes and are great sautéed or slow-roasted with lots of olive oil. Their drama holds up with cooking and in freezing.

Sweet and Gentle

Called low-acids, for my taste, these are the wimps of the group: too sweet, too nice—in short, boring. Use them only as a foil for the sweet-tart fruit. **Examples:** red and yellow pear, Taxi, Golden Sunray, White Wonder, and Simpson.

Heat these tomatoes and they dull down to pap; but raw, especially with the punchy tart family, they are good. Don't overlook playing to their sweet side by sugaring the tomatoes and giving them a shot of lemon. Top them with sweetened sour cream, and you have dessert.

Rich and Savory

Perhaps the most opulent and complex tomatoes I've tasted to date, the Blacks from Russia and Eastern Europe remind me of smoke-grilled steak, rich and browned with big velvety red-wine flavors. **Examples:** Black Krim, Chris Ukrainian, Gipsy Black, and Black Russian.

Plum and Paste Tomatoes

The eunuch of the tomato world is the Roma. Tasteless at its best, it was bred to be shipped, not eaten. But there are some plum and paste tomatoes that do pack the flavor. Unlike plum tomatoes, paste tomatoes are usually heart-shaped. Their flesh is dense, with less moisture than other types of tomatoes. **Examples:** Amish Paste, Long Tom, Polish Paste, Oxheart, and Cornucopia.

Yes, the plum and paste tomatoes work in sauces and canning, but it's a shame not to enjoy them raw while you can.

Tomatoes are lusty enough, yet there runs through them an undercurrent of frivolity.

—Tom Robbins

SPRING GRILL OF ASPARAGUS AND SCALLION SALAD

Serves 4 to 6

10 minutes prep time; 8 minutes oven time

We rarely think of scallions as vegetables, yet they are as flexible as carrots. There's an Asian oneness about pairing these two like-shaped vegetables of spring.

In this salad the long stalks are fast-roasted, then finished under the broiler for a touch of char. That char sets off the cool cream of the balsamic vinegar and shallot dressing.

DRESSING

1 medium **shallot**, minced
½ tablespoon **balsamic vinegar**
½ tablespoon **red or white wine vinegar** or cider vinegar
Salt and fresh-ground **black pepper**
2 teaspoons coarse dark **mustard**
5 tablespoons **heavy whipping cream**

SALAD

1 bunch pencil-slim **asparagus** (1 pound), trimmed of tough
   ends
3 bunches **scallions** (20 or so), trimmed of roots and of
   1 inch of their green tops
1 to 2 tablespoons **extra-virgin olive oil**
Coarse **salt** and fresh-ground **black pepper**

FINISH

2 tablespoons minced fresh **chives** or scallion tops

(recipe continues)

1. To make the dressing, in a medium bowl, blend the shallot and vinegars with salt and pepper to taste. Mix in the mustard and heavy cream. Taste for seasoning, and set aside.

2. Set an oven rack about 5 inches from the broiler. Preheat the oven to 450°F. Cover a large baking sheet with foil. Spread the asparagus and scallions over the sheet, leaving enough room so they do not touch. Sprinkle them with the olive oil and a little salt and pepper. Roll the vegetables gently to coat them with the seasonings.

3. Roast for 6 to 8 minutes, or until the asparagus is barely tender when pierced with a knife (you should hear them sizzling). Turn on the broiler and broil for about 2 minutes. The scallions should have some browned leaves and the asparagus should pick up color. If some of the pieces are browning faster, feel free to pull them out and set them aside to wait for the other pieces to finish.

4. Pile the vegetables on a platter, and zigzag the dressing over them. Sprinkle with the chives, and serve.

THE ASPARAGUS EFFECT

CALLER: This is a little personal, but I really want to know why my urine smells after I've eaten asparagus. My wife says hers doesn't. —Jude from Long Island

LYNNE: You have a fabulous nose. Scientifically, a single sulphur-containing compound, called asparagusic acid, is the smelly culprit. We all produce the scent but only a select few of us can pick it up, and therein lies the mystery for scientists. We feel special—don't you?

The ½-tablespoon measure might be new to you—it equals 1½ teaspoons. Our reasoning is that for most savory dishes the difference between being absolutely exact by fiddling with both a 1-teaspoon and a ½-teaspoon measure is not going to make a significant difference in the final dish. Trust your eye and half-fill a tablespoon measure—it will be close enough.

Baking is another story; there be exact as possible.

Measuring
in the Palm
of Your Hand

An easy way of bettering your lot in the kitchen is to skip the measuring spoons and train yourself to do it by sight. It's simple. Every time a recipe calls for 1 teaspoon of anything, measure it into a measuring spoon, then plop it into the palm of your hand. We promise, a couple of recipes in, you will know quarters, halves, and wholes by sight. Think how you will impress your friends and family! **Caveat:** Stick with the measuring spoons when baking. The difference between ½ teaspoon baking powder and ¾ teaspoon can be disaster.

CRISP CUCUMBER SHRIMP IN RETRO GODDESS DRESSING

Serves 2 as a main dish; 4 as a first course

15 minutes prep time

Dressing holds for 2 days in the refrigerator. Once the salad is put together, serve it up.

Every food snob worth his Japanese sushi knife pokes fun at iceberg lettuce, but never underestimate the power of crisp and absolute neutrality.

This salad, with its Green Goddess dressing, is a throwback to the 1950s. Instead of the usual anchovy in the dressing, we have gone for the liquid gold, which embodies the flavor discovery of the new millennium: *umami.* In this recipe Asian fish sauce supplies the umami. It's always in our kitchens, while anchovies are only occasional visitors.

DRESSING

2 tight-packed tablespoons fresh **tarragon leaves**

3 large whole **scallions**

1 tight-packed tablespoon fresh **parsley leaves**

2 tablespoons **extra-virgin olive oil**

1 teaspoon **Asian fish sauce** (*nam pla* or *nuoc nam*)

1 teaspoon dark spicy **mustard**

1 tablespoon **white wine or cider vinegar**

1 ripe **Hass avocado**

¼ cup **mayonnaise**

⅛ teaspoon fresh-ground **black pepper**, or to taste

Salt

SALAD

8 ounces cooked **shrimp**, cut into 1-inch pieces (see Giving Flavor to Frozen Shrimp, page 35)

1 medium **cucumber**, peeled, seeded, and cut into 1-inch pieces

½ medium head **iceberg lettuce**, cut into 1-inch squares
(don't separate into individual leaves; you want intact
chunks or stacks of leaves)
1 to 2 tight-packed tablespoons **celery leaves** (from the top
of the stalks) or additional parsley leaves

1. In a food processor, combine all the dressing ingredients
and puree. Taste it for salt and perhaps more vinegar.

2. In a medium bowl, combine the shrimp, cucumber, and
lettuce with half of the dressing. Toss them together and taste
for seasoning. Serve the salad in soup bowls, drizzled with the
remaining dressing and scattered with the celery or parsley
leaves.

Giving Flavor to
FROZEN SHRIMP

Most frozen shrimp is close to tasteless, which is especially annoying when you consider its price. Chef and Mexican food expert Rick Bayless taught us how to defrost and flavor frozen uncooked shrimp in one step. Even if your shrimp is frozen in a block, this technique separates and cooks them perfectly.

For 1 pound of medium to large frozen shrimp, squeeze the juice of 1 lime into a medium saucepan. Add the squeezed rinds and 1 quart of water. Cover and simmer over medium-low heat for 10 minutes. Raise the heat to high, add the shrimp (no need to separate them), cover, and return to a boil. Immediately remove the pan from the heat. Drain the water off the shrimp but keep

RICK BAYLESS'S
MEXICAN KITCHEN
BY RICK BAYLESS (SCRIBNER, 1996)

them in the pan, off the heat, partially covered, for 15 minutes. Now you have fully cooked shrimp that are worth eating.

AVOCADO SEAFOOD COCKTAIL WITH BITTERSWEET CHIPOTLE DRESSING

Serves 4; doubles easily | *15 minutes prep time* | *Dressing keeps for 4 days in the refrigerator*

Chocolate in a salad dressing? Consider this: Is there anything more sumptuous than a Mexican mole sauce? You can create a fast and decent stand-in for mole (which is one of those marathon dishes, demanding a lot of kitchen time) by crushing bittersweet chocolate into *chipotle en adobo*, the canned mix of smoky chipotle chiles in a tomato-vinegar sauce. You will also have the foundation of a dressing for nearly any food you like.

Avocado and seafood are naturals here. Use whatever seafood appeals most, but cut it all into the same size pieces. Serve them in a stemmed glass and feel terribly elegant.

BITTERSWEET CHIPOTLE DRESSING

1 ounce **bittersweet chocolate**, coarse chopped
1 whole **chipotle chile *en adobo*** with about 2 teaspoons of
  its sauce
½ cup sweet-tasting **grape tomatoes**
2 heaping tablespoons whole **salted almonds**
2 tablespoons **cider vinegar**
¼ cup **mayonnaise**
2 tablespoons **water**, or as needed

SALAD

2 ripe **Hass avocados**, cut into 1-inch chunks
8 to 9 ounces cooked **seafood** (shrimp, scallops, crab,
  salmon, tilapia, or any firm fish), cut to the same size
Salt and fresh-ground **black pepper** to taste
4 small **Bibb lettuce leaves**

FINISH

1 large **lime**, cut in half

1. To make the dressing, have the food processor running as you drop in the chocolate and chop it fine. Scrape down the sides of the bowl. Add the chipotle, its sauce, and the tomatoes, almonds, and vinegar. Process almost to a puree. Blend in the mayonnaise and enough water to make the dressing as thick as heavy cream. Use the dressing right away, or let it mellow in the refrigerator for up to 4 days.

2. To finish the salad, in a medium bowl gently combine the avocado and the seafood with half of the dressing. Season to taste with salt and pepper.

3. Place a lettuce leaf in each of four wine or martini glasses. Pile in the salad. Top with spoonfuls of the extra dressing. Squeeze fresh lime juice over each cocktail just before serving.

Variation
CHEATER'S MOLE SAUCE

Prepare the dressing as described above, but leave out the mayonnaise and water.

In a medium skillet over medium-high heat, sauté a chopped medium onion in olive oil until softened, about 5 minutes.

Add the dressing and bite-sized pieces of raw chicken or seafood. Bring the dressing to a very gentle bubble (adding water or broth if necessary to keep the dressing from scorching), cover, and cook until the chicken or fish is firm (2 to 4 minutes for seafood; 10 to 15 minutes for the chicken).

Finish the mole by tasting the sauce for deep, rich character. If it seems weak, lift the fish or chicken out of the pan with a slotted spoon and boil down the mole sauce until it's enriched.

Rice is a good foil for the mole.

COOK *to* **Cook**

Find canned *chipotle en adobo* in the Southwestern foods section of your supermarket, in specialty stores, and of course in Latino and Mexican groceries. Check the label's ingredients; if sugar is mentioned at all, it should be at the end of the list.

Grape tomatoes have surpassed the sturdy old cherry tomato as the one red tomato that can be good all year. If you can, sneak a taste of one before committing to the entire container.

Hass avocados have dark, pebbly skins.

ASIAN-STYLE CHOPPED SALAD ON LETTUCE SPEARS

Serves 4 to 6 | *20 minutes prep time* | *Dressing keeps for 2 weeks in the refrigerator and doubles as a dip or marinade*

Cabbage never dies. It's the last man standing in the vegetable bin—even the napa cabbage we use here. And talk about democratic: cabbage throws its arms around nearly every ingredient you introduce it to.

A Thai sausage salad with mint and chile led us down this path. Sweet, hot, and tart with the toothiness of cellophane noodles, the crunch of apple, and the meatiness of spicy-hot sausage, this improvisation turned into a full-fledged supper dish.

DRESSING

- 1 large **garlic clove**
- ½ teaspoon crushed **red pepper flakes**, or to taste
- 5 tablespoons **Asian fish sauce** (*nam pla* or *nuoc nam*)
- ¾ cup **water**
- ½ cup **rice or cider vinegar**
- 4 to 6 tablespoons **sugar**
- 1 medium **sweet onion**, such as Walla Walla Sweet, Vidalia, or Maui
- 8 red **radishes**

SALAD

- 4 ounces cellophane (bean thread) or thin **rice noodles**, soaked 10 minutes in hot water (or until softened), rinsed, and drained
- 20 medium inner leaves **napa cabbage**, washed, thoroughly dried, and sliced into thin slivers
- 10 ounces **Asian sausage** or cooked chorizo, or other spicy ready-to-eat sausage, sliced into thin ¼- to ½-inch squares

⅓ light-packed cup fresh Thai or regular **basil leaves**

⅓ light-packed cup fresh **coriander leaves** (optional)

⅔ tight-packed cup fresh **spearmint leaves**

2 **apples** (Honeycrisp, Haralson, Braeburn, Fuji, or Pink Lady), cored but not peeled, cut into ¼- to ½-inch pieces; *or* 1 fresh pineapple cut the same size

1 cup salted **peanuts** (almonds can be substituted), lightly crushed

FINISH

16 **romaine leaves**; *or* 1 head iceberg lettuce, cut into 4 wedges

2 **limes**, quartered

1. To make the dressing, combine the garlic, red pepper flakes, fish sauce, water, vinegar, and sugar in a food processor and blend. Taste for sweet-tart-hot balance; adjust the seasonings as necessary. Switch the blade to a thin slicing blade, and slice the onion and radishes into the dressing. Let them marinate while you pull together the rest of the recipe.

2. In a large salad bowl, toss together the drained noodles, the cabbage, and the sausage. Coarse-chop the green herbs together and add them to the bowl. (This mixture can wait for about 30 minutes at room temperature.)

3. When you are ready to serve, add the apples or pineapple to the noodles and cabbage. Add the dressing, with the onion and radishes, and the nuts. Toss to blend. If necessary, season with salt and pepper. Make a ring of the romaine or separated iceberg lettuce leaves on a platter. Pile the salad in the center. Tuck in the lime wedges.

4. To eat the salad, pile some onto an individual lettuce leaf, moisten it with a squeeze of fresh lime juice, roll it up, and eat it out of hand.

COOK *to* Cook

We're so Eurocentric that we tend to ignore the Asian sausage tradition that has been going on for millennia. Look for the dry-cured sausages made in the Chinese or Southeast Asian style; they are sold in Asian markets. You will need to steam them for 15 minutes to soften them up. When Asian sausage isn't in the house, fully cooked chorizo fills in nicely, if not authentically.

Babes and the Perennial
Sweet Tooth

You will never want to admit this to your kids, but their love of the candy bar and the jug of soda may be the leftovers of a questionable gift from Mother Nature.

According to Julie Mennella of Monell Chemical Senses Center in Philadelphia (www.monell.org) who holds a Ph.D. in biopsychology, babies are clearly living within their own sensory world. They are sweet connoisseurs and can distinguish between different intensities of sweetness. This sensitivity lasts until adolescence. Their taste for salt does not begin to develop until they are four months old.

Julie goes on to say, "Flavor experiences in utero influence a child's taste preferences. A wide variety of flavors are transmitted through amniotic fluid and into mother's milk." Those tastes actually reflect the culture into which the child is born, so an East Indian baby, for example, becomes accustomed to the flavors of its culture before birth.

Julie thinks of human milk as "a flavor bridge from the experiences in the womb to the experiences when a child starts eating the foods of the table." She also speculates that this is one of the first ways a baby learns which foods are safe.

Just as with pregnant women (see New Moms and Bitter Greens, page 17), sweet is safe.

THAI CANTALOUPE SALAD WITH CHILE

Serves 8 | *10 minutes prep time* | *Have everything cut and ready, but combine just before serving*

I love how this salad raises eyebrows. A cantaloupe salad with basil? With chile? On the dinner plate? Oh, yes, a thousand times yes. If ever there was a salad meant for summer grills, this is it. On page 85, you'll see how to transform this salad into a cool summer soup.

When it comes to picking melons, trust your nose. A sweet whiff of ripeness should waft out through its stem end. No fragrance means no taste.

1 medium to large ripe, fragrant **cantaloupe**, peeled, seeded, and cut into bite-sized chunks
1 tablespoon fine-diced seeded green **jalapeño**
⅓ cup stacked and thin-sliced fresh Thai, Cinnamon, Spicy Globe, or regular **basil leaves**
3 to 4 tablespoons fresh **lime juice**
2 drops **Asian fish sauce** (*nam pla* or *nuoc nam*)
Generous pinch of **sugar**
Salt and fresh-ground **black pepper**

In a mixing bowl, gently combine the melon, jalapeño, and basil. One at a time, add the remaining ingredients, tasting as you add each one. Set out in a bowl with long bamboo skewers so diners can spear chunks of melon to eat.

CABBAGE SLAW WITH ORANGE–PUMPKIN SEED DRESSING

Serves 2 as a main dish; 4 as a side

10 minutes prep time

The slaw can be made a day ahead. Serve at room temperature.

Turn on the food processor, and this salad is done. Roasted pumpkin seeds are the main event here. We beefed them up with citrus and the scents of India. Though smoky tempeh, tofu, or meats are optional, they bring a lot to the party.

DRESSING

¼ cup **extra-virgin olive oil**
1 small **garlic clove**, crushed
½ teaspoon **ground cumin**
½ teaspoon **ground coriander**
Shredded zest of ⅛ large **orange**
½ cup roasted, salted **pumpkin seeds**
¼ cup fresh **orange juice**
1 tablespoon **white wine or cider vinegar**
Salt and fresh-ground **black pepper** to taste

SLAW

½ small head **napa cabbage**, bruised outer leaves
   discarded, remainder cut into quarters
1 small **carrot**, halved
⅓ cup diced smoked or savory **tempeh** or tofu, ham,
   smoked turkey, or cooked bacon (optional)

1. In a food processor fitted with the steel blade, combine the dressing ingredients and puree. Remove the blade, leaving the dressing in the processor. Insert the slicing disk.

2. Using the slicing disk, slice the cabbage and carrot into the dressing. Turn the salad into a serving bowl and toss. Sprinkle with the smoked tempeh or other protein of choice, or with nothing at all.

Cabbage, *n.* A familiar kitchen-garden vegetable about as large and wise as a man's head.

–Ambrose Bierce

Soups

FEATURING

CHEATER'S HOMEMADE BROTH

Soup of Fresh Greens and Alphabets

SIMPLE GARDEN-IN-A-POT SOUP

Vietnamese Rice Noodle Soup with Beef
and Fresh Herbs (Pho)

CORN CHOWDER

South of France Tomato Soup with Young Chèvre

CURRIED CAULIFLOWER CREAM SOUP

Coriander-Orange-Scented Red Lentil Soup

SMOKY AND SPICED DUTCH SPLIT PEA SOUP

Cuban Black Bean Stew

ICED CANTALOUPE SOUP WITH
JALAPEÑO AND BASIL

Only the pure of heart can make a good soup.

—Ludwig van Beethoven

Just say the word
"soup," and something about those vowels and the way your mouth shapes them calls up the classic corny image:

the big pot perpetually simmering on the back of the stove in the cozy kitchen where your lovingly functional family thrives.

As you might imagine, a can of chicken noodle just doesn't do it for us. In this chapter we hope to give you a soup vocabulary and enough information to make outstanding soups in a short time. Soup doesn't have to be a long-suffering affair on the back of the stove. It adapts remarkably well to quick cooking, and no other dish is as forgiving.

You will find a lexicon of soups here—the brothy, the beany, the soup thick with vegetables, the creamed as well as the iced. There is logic behind these choices. Many of the recipes have variations, so you can use the same techniques and produce a brand-new dish.

Nearly anything can become soup, and included here is a guide to improvising that shows you how to make that idea a reality. Creating soup like this can become second nature; may it become yours.

CHEATER'S HOMEMADE BROTH

| *Makes about 4 cups; doubles and triples easily* | *5 minutes prep time; 30 minutes stove time* | *The broth keeps for 4 days refrigerated and 6 months frozen* |

Let's face it: I can extol the glories of homemade chicken and vegetable broths until Hades freezes over. In reality, the only people still making their own broth are me and an eighty-year-old woman in Siberia. The can of "low-sodium" broth is winning.

How about meeting me halfway? Take that can, add a few ingredients, give them 30 minutes on the stove, and you will have a broth you can build a reputation on. You can prepare this recipe with either vegetable or chicken broth.

Every flavor-boosting trick we know goes into this recipe. There is garlic, there are aromatic vegetables and herbs, and most important of all, there are wine and tomatoes, two umami superstars. (Umami is a chemical component that heightens flavors and makes the whole greater than the sum of its parts; see page 20 for more on umami.)

½ cup **dry white wine**

2 large **garlic cloves**, crushed (leave unpeeled if organic)

2 whole **cloves**

1 canned **tomato**

1 **bay leaf**, broken

½ teaspoon **dried basil**, crumbled

Three 14-ounce cans **chicken or vegetable broth**
   (see Tasting Canned Broth, page 52)

1 medium to large **onion**, coarse chopped (if organic, trim
   away root but leave skin)

½ large **celery stalk** with leaves, coarse chopped

½ medium **carrot**, coarse chopped (leave unpeeled if
   organic)

1. In a 4-quart pot, combine all the ingredients. Bring to a simmer, partially cover, and cook for 30 minutes.

2. Strain the broth into a bowl or a storage container. Either use it right away, refrigerate it, or freeze it.

Variation

CLASSIC CHICKEN NOODLE SOUP

Bring to a simmer 1 recipe Cheater's Homemade Broth prepared with chicken broth. Drop in a handful of dried egg noodles, ½ cup *each* fine-cut carrot (or parsnip) and onion, a little fresh parsley, and 2 sprigs fresh thyme or 1 tablespoon chopped fresh dill.

Bring the soup back to a simmer and cook for 5 minutes, or until the noodles are tender. Stir in 1 to 2 cups of leftover cooked chicken. Heat through and serve.

Variation

FARMER'S TORTELLINI IN WINE BROTH

A glass of red wine, a bowl of tortellini in broth, and a spoonful of Parmigiano—a typical supper in farmhouses across the northern part of Italy's Emilia-Romagna region. But the wine is not solely for sipping; it is used to create what old-timers call the farmer's supper in a bowl. This is how to do it:

Bring to a simmer 1 recipe Cheater's Homemade Broth (either chicken or vegetable broth). Add 2 cups frozen tortellini and boil, covered, until the tortellini are tender. Ladle the soup into bowls. At the table pour 2 to 4 tablespoons red wine into each serving, and sprinkle them with generous spoonfuls of fresh-grated Parmigiano-Reggiano cheese.

(variations follow)

{ **COOK** *to* Cook }

One of the over-looked bonuses of cooking with organic vegetables is that you get to use the whole vegetable, peels and all, without worrying about questionable elements.

For instance, an onion's skin is literally and culinarily pure gold. A good example is this soup, where the organic onion is simply rinsed, the root trimmed away, and the rest put in the pot. That skin turns the broth tawny gold and lends an edge of flavor.

Variation

SWEET PEA AND GREEN HERB POTAGE

This is France in spring, when herbs are in their first leaf and the peas are new and sweet.

Bring to a simmer 1 recipe Cheater's Homemade Broth (either chicken or vegetable broth). Combine 1 tight-packed tablespoon *each* of fresh tarragon, chives, basil, and parsley leaves, and chop fine. Just before serving the broth, drop in peas, either shelled from 1 pound of fresh peas in the pod or a 10-ounce package of frozen tiny sweet peas, and the herbs. Cook for 1 minute. Quickly season the soup to taste with a little grated nutmeg and 2 to 3 tablespoons heavy cream, sour cream, or plain whole-milk yogurt. Serve the soup while the herbs are still bright.

Variation

TUSCAN SOUP BOWL

Tuscans can't resist a stale slice of coarse, chewy bread. In fact, they prefer their bread that way, and almost no soup gets to the table without a hunk of bread in the bottom of the bowl. Use Cheater's Homemade Broth (either chicken or vegetable broth) for the simplest expression of this tradition.

For each serving, toast a ½-inch-thick slice of coarse whole-grain bread. Rub it with garlic, place the slice in the soup bowl, and drizzle it with a little olive oil. Ladle in the hot broth. Some people love Parmigiano-Reggiano on this; others say, "It is a sacrilege—only black pepper is needed." You decide.

OLD BREAD

Tossed out in America, revered elsewhere; we need to look at that stale loaf as an opportunity.

- Put a crouton in anything, and it's guaranteed a kid will eat it. Consider old bread a windfall. Make croutons by tossing chunks with olive oil, salt, pepper, and garlic and toasting them in a 350°F oven. Add them to a salad, top a soup, dot them on cooked spinach, or pop them directly into your mouth.
- Line the bottoms of soup or stew bowls with a slice of toasted and garlic-rubbed bread. Now you have *crostini*. Very fancy.
- Whirl slices of stale bread in the processor for better bread crumbs than you will ever get from a can. Toast them in a dry skillet if you have time. Either way, they keep in the refrigerator for months. Top beans, mac 'n' cheese, baked fruits, and casseroles of all sorts.
- Create a bread salad, called *panzanella* in Italy and by so many other names all over the Mediterranean: Moisten stale chunks of chewy bread in vinegar and water. Squeeze them almost dry and blend with tomatoes, olives, raw vegetables, capers, and olive oil. Add more vinegar if you'd like. A simpler version is a mix of celery, anchovy, onion, and garlic.
- Italian kebabs (a.k.a. *spiedini*) are skewered chunks of bread and firm cheese, brushed with olive oil and grilled. Try using rosemary branches as skewers.
- Make a main-dish bread pudding: In a baking dish, soak chunks of bread in beaten eggs and milk that you have seasoned with salt, pepper, and possibly nutmeg and herbs or spices. Top with cheeses and leftover vegetables. Cover with foil and chill for several hours or overnight. Bring the pudding to room temperature and bake, covered, at 350°F for about 1 hour, or until a knife inserted 2 inches from the edge comes out clean.
- Sweeten up this idea for a bread-and-butter pudding: Spread stale slices with butter and jam, line a baking dish with the pieces, and pour in sweetened eggs and milk. Let soak for several hours in the refrigerator, and bake as above.

TASTING CANNED BROTH
The Chicken and the Vegetable

We get calls every week about what kind of canned broth we prefer. What's available can range from canned to boxed, from low-fat to high-sodium, and from good, to bad, to downright ugly.

We collected every broth we could find in our area and did a side-by-side tasting. Surprisingly, organic broths did not stand up well.

These are the chicken broths that stood out for us, followed by the ones that did not make the cut.

1. **College Inn Chicken Broth,** boxed or canned, tasted of real chicken, had a richness to it, and was not overly salty.
2. **Swanson's Chicken Broth All Natural, 99% Fat Free,** in a box. A very close second with sound chicken flavor, but with some of that "canned" broth taste creeping in.
3. **Kitchen Basics Natural Chicken Cooking Stock,** in a box. More "canned" taste, but with a more subtle chicken flavor.

Those that did not make the cut: Campbell's, Low Sodium; Cub Foods, 99% Fat Free; Emeril's All Natural; Health Valley Low Fat; Health Valley Fat Free; Imagine Free Range; Knorr; Manischewitz Clear, Condensed; Pacific Organic Free Range; Pacific Organic Free Range, Low Sodium; Shelton's All Natural with Salt and Spices; Shelton's All Natural, Fat Free, Low Sodium; Shelton's Organic; Shelton's Organic, Fat Free, Low Sodium; Swanson, All Natural, 100% Fat Free, Less Sodium; Swanson Certified Organic Free Range.

Here are our top-rated vegetable broths, followed by the broths that didn't make the cut. Unlike chicken broths, vegetable broths were all over the map; none were totally neutral. You need to pick the vegetable you want to feature, then select the broth.

1. **College Inn Garden Vegetable Broth** is actually cloudy with tomatoes; it tastes of delicate tomato broth. A decent broth, if tomatoes are what you are after.
2. **Pacific Organic Mushroom Broth,** in a box. True mushroom flavor that would be good for making Cheater's Homemade Broth (page 48). This is the only organic broth that stood out.

Vegetable broths that did not make the cut: Emeril's All Natural Organic; Imagine Organic; Kitchen Basics Natural; Pacific Organic; Swanson Vegetarian; and Swanson Certified Organic Vegetarian.

SOUP OF FRESH GREENS AND ALPHABETS

Serves 6 to 8 as a first course; 4 to 6 as a light main dish | *15 minutes prep time; 35 minutes stove time* | *You could cook the soup a day ahead, up to adding the pasta*

For some people the gutsiness of escarole and curly endive can be hard to take in a salad, but cook them into a soup like this one and those same folks will fall in love. Those greens simmered in good broth with a little wine, tomato, pasta, and chickpeas is pure Italian home food.

This was how my Italian grandmother got me to eat the greens I detested. They say I was a bright child, but I didn't catch on to what she was doing until I was well into my teens.

8 cups (double recipe) **Cheater's Homemade Broth**
(page 48) or canned chicken broth
½ cup **dry white wine**
1 cup canned whole **tomatoes**, crushed with your hands
(do not use canned crushed tomatoes)
2 large **garlic cloves**, minced
1 medium to large **onion**, minced
One 15-ounce can **chickpeas**, rinsed and drained
2 large handfuls **escarole** or curly endive leaves, fine
chopped (2½ to 3 cups)
⅓ tight-packed cup fresh **basil leaves**, fine chopped
½ cup tiny **pasta** (alphabets, orzo, or stars)
Salt and fresh-ground **black pepper**
1 cup or more fresh-grated **Parmigiano-Reggiano cheese**

1. In a 6-quart pot combine the broth, wine, and tomatoes. Simmer, uncovered, for 5 minutes. Add the garlic, onion, chickpeas, greens, and basil. Simmer, partially covered, for 20 minutes.

2. Stir in the pasta and simmer, partially covered, for 6 minutes or until the pasta is tender. Taste the soup for seasoning, adding salt and pepper as needed. Serve hot, passing the cheese at the table.

Dorie Greenspan
ON STOCKPOTS

Splendid Table contributor and cookbook author Dorie Greenspan cannot resist kitchen equipment. She's always "test-driving" something new.

Dorie says every kitchen needs a stockpot. Before you buy one, she warns, "Spend a little time considering how you cook. **It's like adopting a pet: will it fit with your life?**" Things to think about before buying a stockpot:

SIZE

- A stockpot must be *at least* as tall as it is wide.
- Consider the size of your stove. Will it fit on the burners and under the hood or microwave?
- Consider how tall *you* are. You want to be able to comfortably stir and lift the pot when it's full.
- Do you have room to store it?
- Given all those considerations, Dorie believes you should always buy a larger pot than you think you need. An 8- to 12-quart pot covers your present, your future, and your everyday cooking. It will handle soup for three, pasta for twelve, and curry for a party. When it isn't on the stove, use it to store sacks of beans, grains, and pastas—or even the dog food.

CONSTRUCTION

- A stockpot must have sturdy handles that flare out and are easy to grasp. Dorie instructs us to look for "elephant ears" that are literally riveted through the pot's sides.
- Avoid pots with a thick disc of heat-conduction metal solely at the base. You want that thick metal, which gives an even heat spread when you cook, to continue up the side of the pot. When you brown in pots with heavy discs only on their bases, you end up with a ring of scorched food.

MATERIALS

- Copper: According to Dorie, this is the sexiest pot you can buy. It's also the most expensive, the heaviest, and the hardest to maintain. If you splurge, you want copper lined with stainless steel, with iron handles (they stay cooler than brass).
- Stainless steel: This is Dorie's first choice. Stainless does not react with any foods, but it is a terrible conductor of heat. So buy a pot with a thick heat-conducting outer layer of aluminum or copper that covers the bottom and comes up the sides. The heavy bottom and sides give you the even heat conduction you need for sautéing and browning without scorching.

  From where we sit, stainless steel has another charm. Since it doesn't react with foods, you can take the broth, chili, or soup from the stove straight to the refrigerator, then back to the stove.
- Aluminum: Aluminum pots are lightweight, inexpensive, and good heat conductors, but they are not versatile because they react with dairy, eggs, tomatoes, and other acids.
- Nonstick coating: Nonstick eventually scratches and/or wears off into your food. This is not the pot for the long haul.

BUILDING THE LIBRARY

BAKING: FROM MY HOME TO YOURS
BY DORIE GREENSPAN (HOUGHTON MIFFLIN, 2006)

SIMPLE GARDEN-IN-A-POT SOUP

Serves 4 as a main dish; 6 to 8 as a first course | *15 minutes prep time; 45 minutes stove time* | *The soup will hold for 4 days in the refrigerator and up to 3 months in the freezer*

A sip of this soup is like a tight three-part harmony; no single flavor stands out. The idea of slow-cooking vegetables and seasonings until they practically melt together is very simple but often overlooked. Each step of this soup softens, mellows, and marries. Give the vegetables time to give up everything they've got. You can't overcook the soup, but you can undercook it.

As Sally says every time she makes it, "This is about the bottom of the crisper drawer and those vegetables that last forever." I think of it as a supermarket soup—no trips to special shops are needed.

Good-tasting **extra-virgin olive oil**

2 medium **onions**, thin sliced

2 medium **carrots**, thin sliced

Top third of 2 **celery stalks** with their leaves, thin sliced

6 large **garlic cloves**, thin sliced

Salt and fresh-ground **black pepper**

2 tablespoons **tomato paste**

2 generous teaspoons **dried basil**

2 generous teaspoons **sweet paprika**

2 small **zucchini**, thin sliced

A handful of fresh **spinach leaves**, chopped

1 **portobello mushroom**, washed and rough chopped

¼ large head **green cabbage**, chopped (thin-slice the core, too)

6 to 8 cups **Cheater's Homemade Broth** (page 48), *or* canned chicken broth or vegetable broth

1½ cups (6 ounces) shredded **Asiago**, Fontinella, or sharp cheddar cheese (optional)

(recipe continues)

1. Film the bottom of a heavy 6-quart pot with olive oil. Add the onions, carrots, celery, and garlic. Season with salt and pepper. Cover and cook over medium-low heat for 15 minutes, or until the vegetables are wilted and aromatic. Stir often, and don't let anything burn.

2. Uncover, raise the heat to medium high, and stir in the tomato paste, basil, and paprika. Cook for 3 minutes, stirring often. Then add the zucchini, spinach, mushrooms, cabbage, and broth. Bring the soup to a simmer, partially cover the pot, and cook for 30 minutes, or until the vegetables are very tender and the soup tastes of deep, satisfying flavors. If it tastes weak, uncover the pot and simmer for 5 minutes or more to boil off some of the liquid and concentrate the soup's character.

3. Serve the soup in deep bowls. If you'd like, sprinkle each portion with some of the cheese.

Variation
FARMHOUSE MINESTRONE

Follow the recipe as written, adding 2 large stalks of Swiss chard, chopped (stems and all), to the vegetables in Step 2.

When the broth is stirred into the soup, also add a can of rinsed and drained cannellini or pinto beans, and a 28-ounce can of whole tomatoes, crushed.

Give the soup its final seasoning at the table, either with a swirl of olive oil and a generous grinding of black pepper or with some fresh-grated Parmigiano-Reggiano cheese.

Slice everything in the food processor. Each time you reheat the soup, you can transform it into something new by adding yet another ingredient—pasta, a teaspoon of India's garam masala blend of spices, hot sauce, or a can of black beans, chickpeas, or pintos.

TUSCAN BAKED MINESTRONE WITH GARLIC BREAD (*RIBOLLITA*)

In Lucca, my family's home base in Tuscany, there was a trattoria that was always jammed at lunch with locals and a few lucky tourists. While we Americans go out to eat what we don't cook at home, Italians go out to eat the very food they *do* cook at home. Heaven help the place that doesn't get it right.

This place did. They took the standard Tuscan dish of leftover minestrone mixed with stale coarse bread and olive oil, called *ribollita,* a step beyond. This is a sterling meatless one-dish supper or Sunday lunch. You serve it in the kind of dish you would use for lasagne. This version of *ribollita* shows how a soup can become a casserole.

Start with the Farmhouse Minestrone variation opposite. Then rub chunks of stale coarse whole-grain bread with garlic. Tear it into bite-sized pieces, scatter them in a large, shallow baking dish (about 2-quart capacity), drizzle with a bold-flavored olive oil, and ladle on the minestrone. The minestrone should nearly cover the bread; you want 1 part bread to about 3 parts soup.

Tuck big spoonfuls of grated Parmigiano-Reggiano or other cheese amid the bread pieces. Cover the casserole and refrigerate it overnight.

To serve, bring the casserole to room temperature. Then sprinkle it with more olive oil, salt, pepper, and cheese. Cover the dish with foil and bake at 375°F until hot and bubbling, about 40 minutes. Uncover for another 5 minutes to lightly color the top.

Salad is the traditional partner to *ribollita.*

VIETNAMESE RICE NOODLE SOUP WITH BEEF AND FRESH HERBS (PHO)

Serves 2, and doubles easily | *10 minutes prep; 30 minutes stove time* | *The broth can be made ahead and frozen. Assemble the soup just before serving.*

Hot steaming broth with wafts of ginger, anise, and clove, slick rice noodles, slices of rare beef, and flanking the bowl a plate of what is called "table salad" (*sa lach dia* in Vietnamese), a heaping platter of additions like fresh herbs, bean sprouts, greens, lime, and chiles—this is the essence of North Vietnam's *pho* (pronounced "fuh") soup. Entire restaurants are built on this one dish and all its variations.

Making quick work of long-cooked pho was tricky. I owe a great debt to the work of Vietnamese chef and cookbook author Mai Pham, who gave me the missing link to a fast broth: toasting the onions and spices before they go into the stock.

You make this soup your own with what you choose to add to it from the table salad. Try a little of everything. No two spoonfuls need be the same.

CHEATER'S ASIAN BROTH

1 medium **onion**, thin sliced
4 large **garlic cloves**, thin sliced
One 2- to 3-inch piece fresh **ginger**, peeled and thin sliced
6 whole **cloves**
1 whole **star anise**, bruised; or ½ teaspoon **anise seeds**
Fresh-ground **black pepper**
Four 14-ounce cans **chicken broth**
2 tablespoons **sugar**
2 teaspoons **Asian fish sauce** (*nam pla* or *nuoc nam*)

SOUP

6 to 8 ounces linguine-style **rice noodles**
6 to 8 ounces top round **steak** (chicken breast can be substituted),
  sliced extremely thin (see Cook to Cook)

TABLE SALAD

10 sprigs fresh **coriander**
6 to 8 sprigs Thai or other fresh **basil**
2 serrano **chiles** or jalapeños, thin sliced
Generous handful **bean sprouts**
1 large **lime**, cut into wedges

SAUCES

Hoisin sauce
Hot sauce

1. Position an oven rack 4 to 6 inches from the broiler, and preheat. Double a very large piece of heavy foil. Scatter the onion, garlic, ginger, cloves, anise, and 5 grinds of pepper on the foil. Broil for 5 minutes, turning the pieces once. You want the onion to have some toasted edges, and the spices should be fragrant. Scrape everything into a 6-quart pot. Be sure to get all the anise seed if that's what you used.

2. Add the broth, sugar, and fish sauce, and bring to a gentle bubble. Cover tightly, and simmer for 20 minutes.

3. Meanwhile, put the rice noodles in a large bowl, and cover them with very hot tap water. (To keep them hot, cover the bowl with a plate.) Soak the noodles for 10 to 15 minutes, or until they are tender but with a little more firmness than you want. Stir a few times. When they are ready, drain and rinse well with cold water. Divide the noodles between two large soup bowls.

4. While the broth is simmering and the noodles are soaking, arrange the table salad on a platter and set out the sauces.

5. To serve, divide the beef between the soup bowls. Ladle the bubbling broth into the bowls. Top each serving with selections from the table salad.

(variation follows)

Notice that the thin-sliced beef goes into the bowl raw. The beef cooks in seconds under ladles of simmering broth. To slice meat extremely thin, freeze it for 20 to 30 minutes first. If fresh Asian herbs like perilla (a.k.a. shiso) and water mint are available, add them to the table salad.

CAMBODIAN NOODLE SOUP WITH PINEAPPLE AND TOMATO

Our neighborhood Cambodian restaurant serves this soup as one of their own special dishes.

Combine all the ingredients for the Cheater's Asian Broth as described, adding 1 to 1½ cups peeled butternut squash cut into ¼-inch dice, and half of a seeded jalapeño chile, thinly sliced. Cover tightly and simmer for 20 minutes, or until the squash is tender.

Prepare the rice noodles and table salad as described.

Replace the beef with the same quantity of diced firm tofu or thin-sliced raw chicken breast.

Just before ladling the broth into the bowls, stir in 1 cup unsweetened pineapple pieces, a handful of halved grape tomatoes, and the juice of 1 lime. Serve the soup with the table salad.

How CHEFS *Think*

For all the chef books that come out each year, not many focus on how to build tastes. I am not talking about scientific treatises; I'm talking about a gifted cook thinking on the page about how he or she builds his dishes. It's the thought process I am after because that helps we home cooks.

As of this writing the works of three chefs stand out: *Cooking by Hand* by Paul Bertolli, *The French Laundry Cookbook* by Thomas Keller, and Gray Kunz's book, *The Elements of Taste.* We've talked to each of them on the show; their approaches are telling.

PAUL BERTOLLI makes no bones about the fact that he stands on the shoulders of Italy's great *salume* artisans and the country's deeply traditional cooks. The logic of taste in his dishes is inseparable from understanding the heritage behind them.

For THOMAS KELLER, starting at ground zero is how he works. He accepts nothing as it stands and begins with examining every dimension of an ingredient. His chapter on foie gras may seem light years away from what you will ever attempt in your kitchen, but it is a valuable template for those who want to know how to truly grasp what is possible with any ingredient.

GRAY KUNZ sees tastes in terms of what they do in a dish. He divides them into categories. He envisions tastes that push, like salt and sweet; ones that pull by urging out underlying flavors, like those of wine; the punctuations of sharp and bitter; and taste platforms like meaty and oceanic.

Perhaps the lesson here is that talent is only the beginning of craft.

CORN CHOWDER

Serves 4

20 minutes prep time; 15 minutes stove time

The soup can be made several days ahead up to the point of adding the corn. Refrigerate, then rewarm before adding corn.

Nothing is more beguiling nor more satisfying than a big bowl of chowder. This recipe has been streamlined to get you pretty close to an authentic bowl in a minimal amount of time. Absolutely make it with fresh corn when you get the chance.

The recipe begs for variations. For instance, skip the corn and add a can of clams.

> People have tried and they have tried, but sex is not better than sweet corn.
>
> —*Garrison Keillor*

4 slices **bacon**, sliced into ⅛-inch-wide pieces
2 tablespoons good-tasting **extra-virgin olive oil**
1 medium to large **onion**, chopped into ½-inch dice
2 **bay leaves**, broken
4 to 5 sprigs fresh **thyme**
¼ teaspoon **salt**, or to taste
⅛ teaspoon fresh-ground **black pepper**, or to taste
1 medium (7 ounces) **red-skin potato**, peeled and cut
   into ¼-inch dice
4 large **garlic cloves**, coarse chopped
1 recipe **Cheater's Homemade Broth** (page 48);
   or two 14-ounce cans chicken or vegetable broth
1 pound (3⅓ cups) Niblets frozen **corn** with no sauce; *or*
   kernels from 8 ears fresh corn
2 cups **milk** or cream, or a blend of both
⅛ to ¼ teaspoon **Tabasco sauce**
2 tablespoons minced fresh **flat-leaf parsley leaves**

1. Put the bacon, olive oil, onion, bay leaves, thyme sprigs, salt, and pepper in a 6-quart pot. Sauté over medium-high heat, stirring occasionally, until the onion begins to color, about 5 minutes. Stir in the potato, garlic, and broth. Cover the pot tightly and simmer the soup over medium to medium-low heat for 10 minutes, or until the potato is tender.

2. Stir in the corn, milk or cream, and Tabasco. Remove from the heat. Pull out the thyme sprigs and bay leaves. With a slotted spoon, transfer about one-third of the solids to a food processor or blender. Blend for a few seconds to crush the corn. Return the mix to the pot.

3. Heat the chowder to a bubble, and taste it for seasoning. Serve immediately (so the corn doesn't overcook), topped with the parsley.

Variation
SEAFOOD CHOWDER

Prepare the recipe as written up to Step 2. Instead of the corn, substitute 1½ pounds seafood cut into bite-sized pieces (it could be frozen). You could do a mix of fish and shellfish, like firm fillets with mussels, shrimp, clams, and scallops, or you could focus on a single fish, as in salmon chowder with both smoked and fresh fish.

Remember that clams take the longest to open, followed by mussels. Fillets, shrimp, and scallops cook in a minute or two. Finish the soup as directed in the original recipe.

Variation
THREE-POTATO CHOWDER

This is the recipe for when you come home from the farmer's market with one too many bags of potatoes.

Follow the recipe as written, substituting potatoes for the corn. You could do a mix of waxy, sweet-tasting newbies, like Yellow Finns, Red Bliss, Desiree, or fingerlings, combined with yams and starchy baking potatoes like russets and Idahos.

COOK *to* **Cook**

After testing many brands of unsauced frozen corn, Niblets brand corn came out in front of the pack. Avoid supersweet corn here; it overwhelms the soup. For a chunkier soup, you could skip the blender step.

Building a Soup
HOW TO IMPROVISE YOUR OWN

The Three Opportunities: You can dictate the character of your soup by how you begin cooking it.

- **Bold and sturdy flavors** come from starting the soup by fast-browning the onions and some of the vegetables in good-tasting oil or butter over medium-high heat.

- **Mellow flavors** are achieved with slow-stewing onions and key ingredients, like herbs, in a little oil or butter in a covered pot over low heat.

- **Clear, true flavors** come from simmering everything in liquid with no pre-sautés.

A BASIC FORMULA

2 parts **onion**
½ part **garlic**
2 parts members of **cabbage** family (cabbage, cauliflower, broccoli, etc.)
½ part **carrot**
¼ part **celery** with leaves
½ part **root vegetables** (celery root, rutabaga, turnips, etc.)
1 part **leafy vegetables** (salad greens, chard, kale, turnip greens, mizuna, dandelion, escarole, endive, collards, etc.)
1 part **dry white or red wine**
Water as needed

Note: Wine is a powerful flavor booster because alcohol opens up flavors that neither fats nor water release. Also, red wine is high in umami, a chemical component of some foods which heightens flavors. So be generous with the wine. Use white wine in pale soups, red in dark ones, and anticipate ½ cup for every 8 cups of liquid. Contrary to rumor, all the alcohol in wine and other spirits does not cook off.

More Opportunities

- **Asian fish sauce** is another taste-building soldier because of its umami content. Half a teaspoon in a soup for four or six lifts flavors.
- Consider **pan juices** from roasts, sautés, and stews to be gifts. Ridiculous amounts are charged for little pots of their commercial equivalents, and you can have them for nothing.

  Whenever you brown something and there are brown bits on the bottom of the pan, add a little water and scrape them up over heat. (This is where a flat-bottomed wooden spatula is indispensable.)

  Pour the liquid into the individual sections of ice cube trays. Once they are frozen, turn the cubes into labeled freezer bags. When you need to boost the character of a pan sauce, a soup, or a stew, pull out 1 or 2 cubes and cook them into the dish. Each cube equals about 2 tablespoons.
- Most **tomato sauces** make good soup. Dilute them with broth or water, enrich them with cream, puree them for a smooth soup, or leave them chunky, served with crusty croutons and fresh herbs.

- Finish soups with a squeeze of **fresh lemon** or a small spoonful of a **favorite vinegar**. It is like placing an exclamation point at the end of a sentence—the soup's flavors brighten up.
- A spoonful of **plain whole-milk yogurt or sour cream** has saved many a dull bowl.
- A spoonful of grated **Parmigiano-Reggiano** cheese in a bowl of soup saves the blandest recipe. It does even more for a good one. (See Save the Cheese Rind, page 81.)
- **Fresh herbs,** torn and scattered over a serving of soup, brighten and refresh it.
- The unexpected combination of **olive oil and fresh-ground black pepper** works with any Mediterranean-style soup, especially the bean and lentil varieties.
- Mediterranean-style soups take on whole new personalities with a last-minute seasoning called **gremolata**. It is a lot like pesto in the way it complements so many things.

  In a food processor mince together the shredded zest of 1 lemon, $\frac{1}{2}$ tight-packed cup flat-leaf parsley leaves, and 3 or 4 large garlic cloves. Moisten the mix with a little olive oil, and season with salt and pepper. Spoon a little into each serving of soup.

THICKENING WITH FLAVOR

Cream soups were traditionally thickened with flour as well as cream. For a modern, lighter take, thicken with flavor instead of starches or fats.

For bean soups, crush a cup of the beans and return them to the pot. With vegetable soups, stews, and meat braises like pot roast, puree a few of the vegetables that have been cooked in the pan liquid, then stir them back into the pot. In many cream soups you can do what Sally did in her Curried Cauliflower Cream Soup (page 71): skip the cream and instead use a good-tasting potato for more substance.

SOUTH OF FRANCE TOMATO SOUP WITH YOUNG CHÈVRE

Serves 3 to 4

10 minutes prep time; 25 minutes stove time

The soup holds for 5 days in the refrigerator and is good hot or at room temperature

This soup tastes as if it comes from Provence's culinary central casting. All the usual (and lovable) characters are here: the tomatoes, the garlic, the goat cheese, and those herbs that actually do scent the air the way hyperventilating travel writers say.

Generous ½ teaspoon **dried basil**
Generous ½ teaspoon **fennel seeds**
Generous ½ teaspoon **dried oregano**
Generous ½ teaspoon **dried thyme**
Good-tasting **extra-virgin olive oil**
3 medium **onions**, fine chopped
Salt and fresh-ground **black pepper**
3 large **garlic cloves**, minced
Generous ¼ cup **tomato paste**
⅓ cup **dry vermouth**
2 pounds good-tasting fresh **tomatoes** (do not use Romas;
　　see page 28), peeled, seeded, and chopped; *or* one
　　28-ounce can whole tomatoes with their liquid, crushed
1 recipe **Cheater's Homemade Broth** (page 48); *or* two
　　14-ounce cans chicken or vegetable broth and
　　⅔ cup water
Generous ¼ teaspoon **ground cinnamon**, or to taste
4 ounces fresh **goat cheese**, crumbled

(recipe continues)

1. Combine the dried herbs in a small cup. Crush them lightly until they become fragrant. Set aside.

2. Film the bottom of a 6-quart pot with olive oil. Heat over medium-high heat. Stir in the onions, season with salt and pepper, and cook until the onions are golden brown, 5 to 8 minutes, stirring often. Add the reserved herbs and the garlic. Continue cooking until their aromas open up, about 30 seconds.

3. Blend in the tomato paste until there are no lumps; then add the vermouth and tomatoes. Boil for 2 minutes. Pour in the broth, stir, adjust the heat to a light bubble, and cover the pot tightly. Cook for 20 minutes. Then blend in the cinnamon, and taste the soup for seasoning.

4. Ladle the soup into bowls, and top each serving with crumbles of goat cheese.

Variation

OLD-TIME SUMMER TOMATO SOUP

Prepare the recipe as written, substituting ½ tight-packed cup torn fresh basil leaves for all the dried herbs.

Sauté the onions as directed, adding the garlic and fresh basil once the onions are golden. Omit the tomato paste and vermouth. Increase the 2 pounds of fresh tomatoes to 3 pounds (do not use Romas). Leave skin and seeds intact; they add flavor.

Stir in the broth and bring the soup to a lively bubble. Cover and cook for 5 to 10 minutes. You want to keep the bright fresh tomato flavor, so it is better to undercook. Check the seasonings. Cool for 10 minutes, and then lightly puree the soup. Serve it hot or cold.

{ **COOK** *to* Cook }

Resist substituting fresh herbs for the dried ones called for here. They should be dried (but never powdered), just as they are in Provence's famous blend, herbes de Provence. The ready-made blend is often stale. Here you will be making your own.

STOCKHOLM CREAM OF TOMATO SOUP WITH DILL

Make the summer variation above, replacing the basil with 1 teaspoon ground allspice and 2 tablespoons chopped fresh dill.

Add 1 cup of the broth and 2 tablespoons vinegar to the cooked onions, and boil until reduced by half. Stir in the remaining broth with 2 to 3 pounds chopped fresh, delicious tomatoes (do not use Romas). Leave the skin and seeds intact; they add flavor. Alternatively, you could use two 28-ounce cans of whole tomatoes.

Bring the soup to a lively bubble, cover, and cook for no more than 5 to 10 minutes. The tomatoes' bright, fresh flavor is essential. Check the seasonings, and add water to the soup if it needs thinning. Stir in 1 cup heavy cream. Serve the soup hot or cool, topping each serving with a tablespoon of chopped fresh dill.

Real tomatoes are an article of faith, a rallying point for the morally serious, a grail.

—*Raymond Sokolov*

The Canned Tomato
CONTROVERSY

By now we know that unless tomatoes are in season, canned are better than fresh. But which canned tomatoes?

A decade ago, when I started doing canned tomato tastings in my travels around the country, I was surprised to find that American brands surpassed many of the imports. With imports, "San Marzano" is supposedly the pinnacle. Well, if all the tomatoes in those cans labeled "San Marzano" actually came from that tiny area south of Naples with its special volcanic soil, that piece of geography would have to cover half of Italy.

This is what I have learned so far in my samplings. Not all of these brands are available across the country. Try the ones you find in your area to augment these picks.

These are our preferred canned whole tomatoes:

1. Muir Glen Organic Whole Peeled Tomatoes—Rich, bright, and balanced, with full-blown ripe tomato flavors, packed in juice with salt.

2. Hunt's 100% Natural Whole Tomatoes— In a close second place, these are full-bodied, nicely colored, and firm, with bright tomato flavor, packed in juice with salt.

3. Bella Terra from Racconto, Organic San Marzano Italian Whole Peeled Tomatoes—The only Italian tomato worth considering, these are sweet, meaty, and rich, with a nice acid balance.

Canned whole tomatoes that did not make the cut: Bionature Organic; Cento Italian; Cub Foods; Cucina Viva Italian; Dei Fratelli; Delallo; Eden Organic; Hunt's Organic; La Valle; Monte Pollino; Red Gold; Rega Marca; Vine Ripe.

Diced tomatoes are underripe fruit, so expect more acid to contrast with their sweetness. **These are the diced tomatoes we preferred:**

1. Contadina Diced Roma Style Tomatoes—Meaty, bright tomato taste, packed with juice and salt.

2. Hunt's Diced Tomatoes—Not as ripe as Contadina, but good flavor, packed with juice and salt.

3. Muir Glen Organic Diced Tomatoes— Solid tomato flavor.

Canned diced tomatoes that did not make the cut: Bionature Organic; Cub Foods; Delallo; Del Monte; Hunt's Organic; Pacific Organic; Red Gold; Roundy's Organic; Vine Ripe.

CURRIED CAULIFLOWER CREAM SOUP

Serves 4 to 6 as a main dish; 8 as a first course | *10 minutes prep time; 35 minutes cooking and finishing* | *The soup will hold in the refrigerator for up to 4 days*

A "virtual" cream soup, this is a creamy soup made without the cream, and it is one of Sally's moments of brilliance. We don't want to oversell, but this soup comes together in a blink and proves that simple really can fly. The essential finale is fresh lemon and generous spoonfuls of whole-milk yogurt.

Good-tasting **extra-virgin olive oil**

1 medium to large **onion**, chopped

5 large **garlic cloves**, coarse chopped

3 tablespoons **curry powder** (yes, the cheapest market brand will do)

1 large head **cauliflower**, trimmed of greens, washed, cored, and cut into chunks

3 medium **red-skin or Yukon Gold potatoes** (about 1 to 1¼ pounds), peeled and cut into 1-inch chunks

1 recipe **Cheater's Homemade Broth** (page 48); *or* two 14-ounce cans chicken or vegetable broth

Water

Salt

2 large **lemons**, cut into wedges

1½ cups **plain whole-milk yogurt**

1. Film the bottom of a 6-quart pot with olive oil, and heat over medium heat. Stir in the onion, garlic, and curry powder. Reduce the heat to medium low, and sauté for 3 to 5 minutes, taking care not to let the onion color. The onion and garlic should be softened a little, but the point is to let the curry's aroma blossom without burning it.

(recipe continues)

2. Add the cauliflower, potatoes, broth, and enough water to barely cover the vegetables. Bring the soup to a boil, partially cover the pot, and cook for 15 minutes, or until the vegetables are fork-tender. Cool for 15 minutes. Then puree with a hand-held blender (for less cleanup) or *in small batches* in a regular blender. Taste the soup for seasoning.

3. Ladle out the soup, then finish each bowl with a squeeze of lemon and a generous dollop of yogurt.

Variation

CARROT-LEEK CREAM SOUP WITH NUTMEG

Prepare the recipe as written, but replace the onion with the white part of 3 large leeks (slit them, rinse out any sand, and then chop). Sauté them as the recipe describes, but substitute ¼ teaspoon fresh-grated nutmeg for the curry powder.

Substitute 1 pound peeled, thin-sliced carrots (use the food processor to slice them) and 1 peeled and chopped medium-sized potato for the cauliflower.

Cook as directed in the original recipe. Season the finished soup with salt, pepper, and fresh-grated nutmeg to taste.

Be careful! If using a blender, be sure to puree in small batches, or you stand a good chance of being burned when the heat from a large batch causes the lid to fly off.

CAULIFLOWER

The garden's pale brain,
it knows the secret
lives of all the vegetables,
holds their fantasies,
their green libidos
in its fleshy lobes.

—Lorna Crozier, from The Blue Hour of the Day
(McClelland & Stewart Ltd., 2007)

CORIANDER-ORANGE-SCENTED RED LENTIL SOUP

Serves 2 to 3 as a main dish; 4 to 5 as a first course

10 minutes prep time; 25 minutes stove time

The soup can be made up to Step 4 three days ahead and refrigerated; it also freezes well

This is not your grandmother's lentil soup. Light and fragrant with two kinds of coriander (ground and fresh), this soup's citrus finish is a modern take on a very old idea. True to tradition, there is no meat. The inspiration here is pure East India.

India glorifies dried peas and lentils like no other place on Earth, and Indian meals often include a souplike dish called *dal*. Cooks there marry lentils and spices in a unique way with a technique you'll find yourself using in other dishes.

Since legumes are notorious for smothering flavors, Indian cooks sauté the seasonings separately, adding them toward the end of the cooking time to create bright, true tastes.

1 small bunch (1-inch-diameter bouquet at stems) fresh **coriander**
Extra-virgin olive oil
3 medium **onions**, chopped into ¼-inch dice
Salt and fresh-ground **black pepper**
4 large **garlic cloves**, fine chopped
One ½-inch piece fresh **ginger**, peeled and fine chopped
2 teaspoons **ground coriander seed**
Zest and juice of 1 medium **orange**
One 14-ounce can **vegetable or chicken broth**
2½ cups **water**
¾ cup **red lentils**, rinsed and sorted
Juice of ½ to 1 **lemon**
⅔ to 1 cup additional fresh **orange juice**

1. Wash and dry the bunch of coriander. Cut off the bottom 2 to 3 inches of the stems and chop them fine. Set them aside. Coarse-chop half of the remaining coriander leaves, refrigerating the rest for another dish.

2. Generously film the bottom of a 4-quart saucepan with olive oil and heat it over high heat. Stir in two-thirds of the onions, and season with salt and pepper. Sauté until the onions begin to brown. Blend in the coriander stems, garlic, ginger, ground coriander seed, and the orange zest. Sauté for about 20 seconds over high heat, or until fragrant. Scrape into a bowl and set aside.

3. Pour the broth, water, lentils, and remaining onions into the same saucepan. Bring to a gentle bubble, partially cover, and simmer for 7 to 10 minutes, or until the lentils are nearly tender. Add the sautéed seasonings and additional salt and pepper to taste. Cover the pot tightly and simmer for another 15 minutes to blend the flavors. (At this point the soup could be refrigerated for up to 3 days, or frozen, and reheated.)

4. Just before serving, stir in the juice from half a lemon, the juice of the zested orange, and the additional orange juice to taste, starting with ⅔ cup. You will probably want almost the entire cup of additional orange juice, but trust your own taste. Then sample the soup for salt, pepper, and lemon juice, and adjust them as needed.

5. Scatter the coriander tops over the soup, and ladle it into deep bowls.

COOK *to* Cook

If you use only one organic ingredient for this recipe, let it be the orange, since the peel is cooked into the dish.

SMOKY AND SPICED DUTCH SPLIT PEA SOUP

Serves 3 to 4 as a main dish; 5 to 6 as a first course

20 minutes prep time; 30 minutes stove time, or more (see Cook to Cook)

The soup holds for 3 to 4 days in the refrigerator and freezes well. Add the final swirl of butter and allspice just before serving.

My very own Dutch Auntie Mame, Cecile Van Lanschott, gifted me with a Dutch cookbook from the 1600s. Hand-bound in vellum and filled with handwritten recipes, the book traces one family's food through two centuries. More than a culinary chronicle, the book is a personal portrait of the Netherlands' changing fortunes and tastes. Our pea soup comes straight from its pages.

What chicken soup is to us, pea soup is to the Dutch—an everlasting standby and cure-all. But as this recipe proves, it was far sexier in the 1600s. Spices are the tipping point of the dish. Holland reigned as one of Europe's prime spice traders in the seventeenth century, and this recipe was no doubt a family show-off piece, proving they could afford its ginger, allspice, and cloves. Don't hesitate to cook it a day or two ahead.

1 large **leek**

4 tablespoons **butter**

1 large **carrot**, fine chopped

3 medium **onions**, chopped into ¼-inch dice

Meat cut from 2 large smoked **ham hocks** (2 to 2½ pounds)

Salt and fresh-ground **black pepper**

3 medium **red-skin potatoes**, peeled and cut into ¼-inch dice

1½ cups **dried split peas** (yellow ones are preferred in Holland)

3 whole **cloves**

1 teaspoon **ground allspice**

1 teaspoon **ground ginger**
¾ teaspoon **dried thyme**
1 large **garlic clove**, minced
Two 14-ounce cans **vegetable or chicken broth**
3 to 4 cups **water**

FINISH

2 tablespoons **butter**
¼ teaspoon **ground allspice**

1. Prepare the leek by cutting away the green top and the root. You'll use only the white portion. Slice the white stalk down its length and rinse it under cold running water to wash away any sand. Pat the leek dry with paper towels and slice it thin.

2. In a 6-quart pot, melt the 4 tablespoons butter over medium-high heat. Stir in the leeks, carrots, onions, meat, and salt and pepper to taste. Sauté until the onions begin to brown. Then stir in the potatoes, split peas, cloves, 1 teaspoon allspice, the ginger, thyme, garlic, broth, and water. There should be enough liquid to cover the peas and vegetables by an inch. Add more water if necessary.

3. Simmer the soup, partially covered, for 30 minutes, or until the split peas are almost dissolved and the potatoes are tender. Taste the soup for seasoning, and just before serving it, swirl in the 2 tablespoons butter. Finish the soup by stirring in the last ¼ teaspoon allspice.

Split peas' cooking time can range from 30 minutes to an hour, depending on their age. If you buy them where there is a fast turnover, the soup should cook up quickly.

CUBAN BLACK BEAN STEW

Serves 4 as a main dish; 8 as a
first course

15 minutes prep time; 30 minutes
stove time

The soup holds for 4 days in the
refrigerator and freezes for up to
3 months

Cuban black bean soup ranks with France's *steak frites* and Italy's spaghetti with red
sauce as a national obsession. It is a touchstone dish of the Caribbean. Usually made with
dried beans (and definitely worth the extra time when you have it), the dish can nonethe-
less be adapted to a streamlined model with canned beans.

One way to make up for the lack of long simmering is to blend the beans and some
liquid into a highly flavored sauté and give everything a short time on the stove.

The soup blossoms with a rest off the heat, and an overnight stay in the refrigerator
gives it even fuller flavor.

This soup demands a finish of onion and lime juice or vinegar (sherry vinegar is
our pick).

1 or 2 meaty smoked **ham hocks** (about 1½ pounds)
Good-tasting **extra-virgin olive oil**
3 whole **cloves**
2 medium to large **onions**, chopped into ½-inch dice
1 small to medium **green bell pepper**, cut into ½-inch
   pieces
1 small to medium **red bell pepper**, cut into ½-inch pieces
2 teaspoons **kosher salt**
2 14-ounce cans **chicken or vegetable broth**
6 large **garlic cloves**, coarse chopped
3 **bay leaves**, broken
2 teaspoons **ground cumin**
1½ teaspoons **dried oregano**
¾ to 1 teaspoon fresh-ground **black pepper**
3 generous tablespoons **tomato paste**

(recipe continues)

Three 15-ounce cans **black beans**, drained and rinsed
3 **limes**, halved *or* about ½ cup sherry, wine, cider,
    or palm vinegar

GARNISHES

1 cup chopped mild **onion**
½ cup chopped fresh **coriander leaves**
Hot sauce

1. Trim the meat away from the ham hock bone, cutting it into small pieces. Don't be too fussy; leaving some on the bone is fine. Film the bottom of a 10-quart stockpot with olive oil and heat over medium-high heat. Stir in the meat, bone, cloves, onions, bell peppers, and salt. Sauté for 8 minutes, stirring occasionally, or until the vegetables are sizzling and there's a brown glaze on the bottom of the pan (the vegetables need not brown, and take care not to let that glaze blacken).

2. Add a little of the broth along with the garlic, bay leaves, cumin, oregano, black pepper, and tomato paste. With a wooden spatula, scrape up the glaze as you simmer the mix on medium-high heat for 3 minutes. Then add the beans and the remaining broth. Adjust the heat so the soup bubbles gently. Cover the pot tightly, and cook for 20 minutes.

3. Stir in the juice from 2½ limes or ⅓ cup of the vinegar. Taste the soup for seasoning. Adjust salt, pepper, and lime juice or vinegar to taste.

4. Ladle the soup into bowls, topping each serving with a heaping tablespoon of chopped onion and a little fresh coriander. Have the hot sauce on the table. In Cuban style, you could ladle the stew over Dumbed-Down Rice (page 297).

We use a 10-quart pot because its size provides a broader cooking surface. Cooking that all-important sauté on the larger surface discourages steaming and helps build up a flavor-packed brown glaze on the bottom of the pot. That glaze is a key to the soup's success.

Don't worry if the vegetables don't brown—the glaze is the thing. This, and the pork, creates the heart of the soup. If you have only a 6-quart pot, do Step 1 in a big sauté pan, then combine the sauté with the beans and broth in the 6-quart pot.

SOUTH OF FRANCE BEAN POTAGE

This is a liberal and meatless takeoff on Provence's great *pistou* soup.

Prepare the recipe as written, but eliminate the pork, bell peppers, cumin, oregano, tomato paste, black beans, limes, and garnishes.

Sauté the onions with chopped carrots, the cloves, garlic, and the bay leaves. Add a handful of green beans and a chopped stalk of celery. Stir in the broth, a 14-ounce can of diced tomatoes, 1 medium potato cut into thin slices, and a 15-ounce can *each* of rinsed and drained chickpeas and Great Northern beans. Add a 10-ounce package of frozen limas.

Partially cover the pot and simmer the soup for 20 minutes, or until the potato is very tender. Just before serving, stir a big spoonful of fresh or jarred pesto and a generous cup of fresh-grated Parmigiano-Reggiano or Gruyère cheese into the soup. Black olive tapenade is good here, too.

SAVE THE CHEESE RIND

Never throw away the rind from Parmigiano-Reggiano cheese. Even if the cheese were not premium-priced, you would want to use it all. This could be one of our oldest flavor boosters.

Use the rind the way Italians do: simmer it into stews, braises, and every kind of soup. Frugal cooks even cook the rind into the soup, pull it out, dry it, and use it again (and again). At Parmigiano-Reggiano prices, it's good to know this cheese never dies.

Those cooks have known all along what scientists uncovered only recently: Parmigiano lifts, amplifies, and melds the flavors of other ingredients. Research shows that the cheese is loaded with what is called the "fifth taste," or *umami,* which acts as a catalyst to enhance other flavors. So tightly wrap those pieces of rind and store them in the refrigerator or freezer until the opportune moment arises.

Beans
THE PLAIN TRUTH

- To soak or not to soak: **Food scientist Harold McGee** explained to us on the show that the fastest way to cook beans is to soak them in hot water. As the water temperature goes up, the cooking time shortens. Simply cover the dried beans in boiling water and let them soak as long as is convenient. If you are leaving the beans for more than a couple of hours, refrigerate them.

  Discard the soaking water and add fresh water to cover by about 2 inches. (Cooking the beans in fresh water will decrease their aftereffects, but it will also leach out most of the water-soluble vitamins and minerals. It comes down to pay now or pay later; it is your choice.) Gently simmer the beans until they are tender. If the beans are heavily patterned, as with Christmas beans and Appaloosas, you can keep the patterns intact by not stirring the beans often.

BUILDING THE LIBRARY

ON FOOD AND COOKING: THE SCIENCE AND LORE OF THE KITCHEN
BY HAROLD McGEE (SCRIBNER, 2004)

- To salt or not to salt: Salting beans at the first bubble slightly shortens the cooking time but turns their interiors mealy rather than creamy. Salting at the end of cooking is ideal.
- Flavor the cooking liquid with anything but acids or wine, which slow down cooking. Salt and sweet things speed it up.
- Store cooked beans in the refrigerator for up to 4 days. They are like money in the bank when time is short.

Probably nothing
in the world arouses
more false hopes
than the first four
hours of a diet.

—Samuel Beckett, playwright, novelist, and poet

ICED CANTALOUPE SOUP WITH JALAPEÑO AND BASIL

Serves 2 to 4 as a first course | *10 minutes prep time; no stove time* | *Make this a day ahead and keep it chilled*

What's not to love when with an effortless twist, a dish becomes something brand-new? Puree the Thai Cantaloupe Salad with Chile (page 41) with an adjustment or two, and you will have a soup that is heaven in a bowl at the end of a steamy summer commute home.

Icy and gorgeously orange, this puree is flecked with the bright green of fresh-grated lime zest. When you get down to eating the soup, you pile in extras of red onion, green chile, and fresh basil. It's an uncommon mix that always delights.

Track down a truly sweet cantaloupe for the soup. The commitment will pay back tenfold. A melon's fragrance tells you everything you need to know: if it smells sweet, almost perfumed, you have a good one. If a melon has no scent, it will have no flavor.

One 2½-pound intensely sweet-smelling ripe **cantaloupe**
2 cups **ice cubes**
Generous pinch of **salt**
4 or 5 grinds of **black pepper**
2 tablespoons **sugar**
Juice of 2 large **limes** (about ½ cup)
Grated zest of ½ large **lime**

FINISH

1 or 2 **jalapeños**, seeded and cut into fine dice
10 to 12 fresh **basil leaves**, coarse chopped
½ medium **red onion**, cut into ⅛-inch dice (optional)

(recipe continues)

1. Cut the melon into quarters. Scoop out its seeds and trim away the rind. Slice it into chunks and put them into a food processor. Add the ice, salt, pepper, sugar, and lime juice, and puree. Stir in the grated zest.

2. Place the jalapeños, basil, and onion in separate small serving bowls. Pour the puree into individual soup bowls or into a pitcher for further chilling.

3. To serve, pour the soup into bowls and pass the condiments. The basil and jalapeño are the essential finishes for the soup, while the onion is an attractive option.

Variation
CANTALOUPE-JALAPEÑO COOLER

When colleague Judy Graham gave this soup recipe a run-through, she went into overdrive and came up with this drink, perfect for brunch.

Prepare the soup as described up to the point where it has been pureed. Before adding the lime zest, strain the soup. Then blend in the lime zest and 1 seeded and minced jalapeño.

Divide the blend among 4 to 6 tall glasses filled with ice. Add a splash of vodka to each one, and stir. Serve garnished with wedges of lime or a sprig of basil.

Queen Anne's
POCKET MELON

Sally is the gardener in this duo. She loves planting stuff that comes with a story, and this is her next summer project.

Gardening expert Jack Staub told us the story of a kind of melon we didn't know existed—a petite "hand" melon.

Seventeenth-century gardeners developed tiny melons to nestle in ladies' pockets. Like the scented pomanders so popular then, this especially sweet-smelling fruit counteracted the effects of the resistance to bathing so fashionable at court in those days.

Jack's pick is a pocket melon striated with orange and green stripes. Supposedly a favorite of England's Queen Anne, the melon took her name. You can grow your own:

BUILDING THE LIBRARY

75 EXCITING VEGETABLES FOR YOUR GARDEN BY JACK STAUB (GIBBS SMITH, 2005)

seeds are available at Seed Savers Exchange, www.seedsavers.org (see page 171).

There are three things which cannot support mediocrity—poetry, wine and melons.

—Anonymous French poet

E
Eggs and
SMALL PLATES

FEATURING

PAN-CRISPED DEVILED EGGS
ON FRENCH LETTUCES

Green Apple, Cheese, and Chard Oven Omelet

SCANDINAVIAN FLOWER EGGS WITH
SWEET-TART MUSTARD DILL SAUCE

Jane and Michael Stern's Broccoli Casserole

CRISPY TORTILLA EGGS WITH
AVOCADO AND LIME

Luxury Scrambled Eggs

MIDNIGHT ASPARAGUS WITH CREAMY EGGS

Almond Chutney Chicken in Lettuce Roll-Ups

WARM WHITE BEAN SALAD WITH
FRAGRANT GARLIC AND ROSEMARY

Belgian Beer Bar Tartine

One of the most private things in the world is an egg until broken.

—M.F.K. Fisher

We all have nights

when we hit the kitchen at 8 p.m. On those days, these are the dishes we reach for. Scoops of cheesy baked eggs, lettuce roll-ups of take-out chicken dressed with chutney, Belgian tartines, warmed garlicky beans, and broccoli casserole done Southern soul-food style. These are light, fast, *real* suppers with a twist.

Eggs are the saviors of parents, lovers, and the ravenous everywhere. You can take them anywhere, from the very French Pan-Crisped Deviled Eggs on French Lettuces (page 93), to showy Scandinavian Flower Eggs (page 100), to Green Apple, Cheese, and Chard Oven Omelet (page 97), to Midnight Asparagus with Creamy Eggs (page 110).

A simple slice of bread is a powerful ally to the hungry, something we nearly lost when years ago bread was banished from the center of the plate. The idea of the quintessential Belgian pub lunch of bread with fresh cheese and radishes is worth revisiting, as is the South's bread casserole and Italy's bruschetta.

There are culinary lessons here as well. For instance, how coddling a can of beans can turn them into glamour queens; how an essential tool may be waiting for you in the dirt; and how earlobes make your brown eggs brown.

PAN-CRISPED DEVILED EGGS ON FRENCH LETTUCES

Serves 4 as a main dish; 6 as a first course

15 minutes prep time; 5 minutes stove time

The eggs could be stuffed a day ahead and refrigerated until you are ready to sauté them

Who would imagine browning deviled eggs to caramelize their edges and crisp their fillings? What a sensual turn with a hard-cooked egg.

We owe the idea to Jacques Pépin and his memoir, *The Apprentice: My Life in the Kitchen* (Houghton Mifflin, 2003). The inspiration comes from war-torn France and a recipe born of scarcity that Jacques' mother created during World War II, though you'd never know it when you pick up your fork.

This is the kind of double-edged story that we love to find in the things we eat.

> # Put all your eggs in one basket and—watch that basket.
>
> *—Mark Twain*

EGGS

8 large **eggs**, hard-cooked and peeled
1 scant teaspoon **Dijon mustard**
2 medium **garlic cloves**, minced
2½ teaspoons minced **onion**
2½ tight-packed tablespoons fresh **flat-leaf parsley leaves**, coarse chopped
2 to 3 tablespoons **milk**
2½ teaspoons **mayonnaise**
1½ teaspoons **white wine vinegar**
Salt and fresh-ground **black pepper**
2 to 3 tablespoons good-tasting **extra-virgin olive oil**

(recipe continues)

The leftover **egg stuffing**
3 tablespoons good-tasting **extra-virgin olive oil**
1 generous teaspoon **Dijon mustard**
2½ tablespoons **milk**
2½ teaspoons **white wine vinegar**
Salt and fresh-ground **black pepper**

SALAD

4 generous handfuls **mixed greens**, such as Bibb lettuce,
  mâche, and dandelion greens or frisée, washed and dried

1. Cut the hard-cooked eggs in half lengthwise. Gently remove
the yolks (fingers work best), and place them in a medium bowl.
Reserve the whites.

2. Add the mustard, garlic, onion, parsley, milk, mayonnaise,
and vinegar to the yolks. With a fork, crush everything together
into a thick paste. Add salt and pepper to taste.

3. Pack the mixture back into the hollows of the egg whites, so
the filling is even with the surface of the egg, not mounded. You
will have leftover stuffing (this becomes the salad dressing).

4. In a large nonstick skillet, heat the oil over medium heat.
Gently place the eggs in the pan, stuffed side down. Cook until
the eggs are beautifully browned, 3 to 5 minutes. Sprinkle them
with salt and pepper as they cook.

5. As the eggs sauté, combine in a large bowl the leftover egg
stuffing with all the dressing ingredients. Add the salad greens to
the bowl, and toss. Heap them on a serving platter.

6. Gently lift the eggs from the pan, turn them filling side up,
set them on the greens, and serve.

**Since the eggs are
the main event here,
go for organic.**

THE SARDINIAN WAY WITH HARD-COOKED EGGS

In an old Sardinian recipe, hard-cooked eggs aren't stuffed; instead they are halved lengthwise and sautéed in oil and vinegar (essentially a salad dressing), then finished with parsley, garlic, and toasted bread crumbs.

This concept was recorded by Italy's culinary iconoclast, Ada Boni. In the 1950s, when Italian cookbook writers were slaves to the French way with food, Boni dug deep into Italy's regions, reviving old dishes, working with home cooks, and never giving an inch to *la haute cuisine française.*

Her books are still in print, often on the remainder stacks, and always worth picking up if you have an interest in Italian food.

BUILDING THE LIBRARY

ITALIAN REGIONAL COOKING (BONANZA BOOKS, 1959) AND THE TALISMAN ITALIAN COOKBOOK (CROWN, 1950), BOTH BY ADA BONI

To make the golden eggs of Sardinia, halve 8 hard-cooked eggs. Film a large nonstick skillet lightly with olive oil, then add about ¼ cup white wine vinegar. Heat until the vinegar is bubbling. Sprinkle the pan with salt and pepper and add the eggs, cut side down. Cook the eggs over medium heat, turning them gently a few times, until the vinegar has evaporated and they are golden.

Transfer the eggs to a platter, arranging them yolk side up. Add a minced clove of garlic to the skillet, along with several tablespoons chopped fresh parsley leaves and ½ cup fresh bread crumbs. Sauté until the bread crumbs are golden, taking care not to burn the garlic. Scrape the crumb mixture over the eggs, and serve.

GREEN APPLE, CHEESE, AND CHARD OVEN OMELET

Serves 3 to 4 | *15 minutes prep time; 45 minutes oven time* | *Excellent hot or at room temperature. Reheats well.*

Whether you call them frittatas or oven omelets, baking eggs with a sauté or filling is much easier than fussing with a traditional omelet. Instead of the gymnastics involved in cooking and rolling a perfect folded omelet out of the pan, you put everything together, put it in the oven, and set a timer.

With its cheesy greens and garlic, this oven omelet comes off more like a pizza than an omelet. The shards of tart green apple are totally unexpected and a great accent. This is portable food—good for potlucks, boat rides, and office lunches.

1 bunch (5 stalks) **Swiss chard**, stems and leaves separated
Good-tasting **extra-virgin olive oil**
2 medium **onions**, cut into 1-inch dice
Salt and fresh-ground **black pepper**
1 large **garlic clove**, minced
¼ cup **water**
½ large **Granny Smith apple**, peeled, cored, and cut into
    ½-inch dice
5 large **eggs**
¾ cup **milk**
⅛ teaspoon fresh-grated **nutmeg**
⅛ teaspoon **salt**
⅛ teaspoon fresh-ground **black pepper**
1 cup fresh-grated **Parmigiano-Reggiano**, Asiago, or
    Fontinella cheese
1 cup shredded **Muenster or Monterey Jack** cheese

(recipe continues)

1. Preheat the oven to 350°F. Chop the chard stems into 1-inch pieces, then chop the leaves the same way. Film a 10-inch skillet (with an ovenproof handle) with oil, and heat over medium-high heat. Add the onions, chard stems, and a little salt and pepper. Sauté until the vegetables are golden brown.

2. Stir in the garlic and chard leaves in two batches. (As the first batch wilts, add the second.) Add the water, and stir over medium-high heat until the leaves look like cooked spinach and the liquid has evaporated. Then stir in the apple and remove the skillet from the heat.

3. In a bowl, beat together the eggs, milk, nutmeg, salt, pepper, and ⅔ cup of *each* of the cheeses. Pour the mixture over the cooked greens. Sprinkle with the remaining cheeses, cover with foil, and bake for 30 minutes. Uncover and bake for 10 to 15 minutes more, or until a knife inserted in the center comes out with only a few bits of creamy egg and cheese clinging to it.

4. Let the omelet stand for 5 to 10 minutes before cutting it into wedges.

Use a skillet with an ovenproof handle, and be careful when setting it out: the handle will be hot.

Variation

SPANISH PAPRIKA–POTATO OVEN OMELET

Substitute for the chard 1 medium to large red-skin potato, sliced as thin as potato chips; and use only 1 medium onion, sliced into thin rings. Add them to the oiled skillet as described, sprinkle with salt and pepper, and sauté until the potatoes are tender. Remove from the heat.

Sprinkle the potatoes with 1 tablespoon mild Spanish paprika. As directed above, blend together the eggs, milk, and cheeses, omitting the nutmeg. Pour the mix into the skillet, lifting the potatoes so the custard covers the bottom of the pan. Sprinkle with the remaining cheeses, cover with foil, and bake as described above.

The poets have been mysteriously silent on the subject of cheese.

—G. K. Chesterton

CHEESE *and* DREAMS

When we heard about a British Cheese Board study on how cheese affects your sleep, we called to interview board secretary **Nigel White**.

The Cheese Board set out to disprove an old wives' tale, common in England, that eating cheese before bed affects one's sleep. Two hundred volunteers took part in the weeklong study. They were divided into five groups—one group for each of five different types of cheese. The volunteers had to eat one ounce of cheese before bed each night. While all the survey participants slept well, an unexpected result turned up: it seems different cheeses brought on different dreams.

• **The Stilton eaters** had vivid, but not necessarily disturbing, dreams—as in a vegetarian crocodile who was upset because it couldn't eat children, talking cuddly toys, dinner party guests being traded for camels, and soldiers fighting with kittens instead of guns.

• **The cheddar-eating group** dreamed of celebrities, footballers, and characters from British soaps; and one lucky girl helped build a human pyramid under the supervision of Johnny Depp.

• **British Brie** gave dreams of TV chef Jamie Oliver cooking dinner for the dreamer and vacations on a sunny beach.

The natural tryptophan in cheese probably accounts for the good sleep, but the dreams are another issue. Secretary Nigel White would not commit as to whether there would be a follow-up study.

SCANDINAVIAN FLOWER EGGS WITH SWEET-TART MUSTARD DILL SAUCE

| Serves 4 to 5 | 15 minutes prep time; 5 minutes assembly | The potatoes and eggs could be cooked a day ahead and refrigerated. The sauce holds for 3 days in the refrigerator. |

Wedges of hard-cooked egg tucked into chopped salad greens mimic tightly clustered chrysanthemum petals—a great presentation.

What no one knows until they dig into the salad is that hidden under the greens are slices of potato. Slathering the platter first with mayonnaise ensures that the salad is flavored from the bottom up as well as the top down.

Given some hard-cooked eggs and boiled potatoes, you can make this fancy-looking dish in a few minutes. Zigzag the mustard sauce over the eggs, and you are done.

POTATOES

1 pound (7 to 8) small **red-skin potatoes**

MUSTARD DILL SAUCE

1 small **garlic clove**, minced
3 tablespoons minced **onion**
¼ cup **plain distilled vinegar** or cider vinegar
2 tablespoons **sugar**, or more to taste
3 tablespoons cold-pressed **canola or safflower oil**
Generous ½ cup dark grainy **mustard**
⅓ to ½ cup chopped fresh **dill leaves**
Salt and fresh-ground **black pepper**

2 generous tablespoons **mayonnaise**
Salt and fresh-ground **black pepper**
1 small head **Bibb lettuce**, leaves stacked and sliced into thin
   strips
8 large hard-cooked **eggs**, peeled and cut into 4 wedges each
2 tablespoons chopped fresh **dill leaves**
¼ cup chopped **sweet onion** (Vidalia, Maui, Walla Walla, etc.)

1. In a 6-quart pot, simmer the potatoes in water to cover for 15 minutes, or until they offer a little resistance when pierced with a knife. Drain, and rinse them with cold water to cool. Peel and slice them about ¼ inch thick.

2. While the potatoes are cooking, make the sauce: In a medium bowl, blend together the garlic, onion, and vinegar. Let stand for 10 minutes to mellow. Then whisk in the 2 tablespoons sugar, the oil, the mustard, and ⅓ cup of the dill. Add salt and pepper to taste. Taste for sweet-sour balance, adding sugar or vinegar as needed. Add more dill if you like.

3. On a large platter, spread the mayonnaise to form a 9- or 10-inch round. Top with the potatoes, overlapping the slices. Sprinkle them with salt and pepper, then pile the lettuce on the potatoes. Top with the egg wedges, tucking them into a tight sunburst pattern (like flower petals). Season them with salt and pepper.

4. Before serving, zigzag streaks of the mustard dill sauce over the eggs and greens. Scatter the chopped dill and sweet onion over the eggs, and serve with additional sauce at the table.

Variation
FLOWER EGGS WITH BLUE CHEESE DRESSING

Substitute blue cheese dressing (page 21) for the mustard sauce. Instead of dill, use fresh basil.

I don't know how long I like my egg boiled, but it's exactly right by the time I finish my hair.

—Betty Furness

Over the past several years THE $65°$ EGG has become a new frontier for French chefs.

It is like nothing you have ever tasted. The white is custardy and the yolk is soft and yielding, basically melting in your mouth. Put it next to a salad or a bundle of asparagus, or eat it all by itself. **You will be enchanted.**

BUILDING THE LIBRARY

MOLECULAR GASTRONOMY: EXPLORING THE SCIENCE OF FLAVOR
BY HERVÉ THIS (COLUMBIA UNIVERSITY PRESS, 2005)

The 65° egg, as in 65° Celsius (149° Fahrenheit), is the creation of one of our more captivating guests, chemist and self-proclaimed molecular gastronomist Hervé This. He wanted to find out why hard-boiled eggs could be tough and have that green ring. His experiments led him down the path of unraveling egg proteins and the effects of heat.

His "aha!" moment came when he recalled a traditional Jewish dish, an egg baked for hours in dying embers. Remarkably, that egg was silky and tender despite the long cooking time. He duplicated those eggs by using a low-temperature oven instead of a dying fire.

Hervé This cooks his 65° eggs with French schoolchildren, while chefs all over the country charge their parents outrageous amounts for this transcendental *oeuf*.

Here is how you do a 65° egg at home:

- Put a thermometer in the oven. Set the oven at just below 150°F—ideally 149°F, but not lower. Wait 20 minutes.
- Put your eggs on the oven rack, and forget about them for a couple of hours. (If your oven goes 5 or 10 degrees higher, your eggs will survive and still be remarkable, but they will be less custard-like. And don't worry about salmonella; it meets its demise at 140°F.)
- After a few hours, take out the egg. Gently crack the shell and ease out the egg, taking care not to puncture it. It will quiver like a gelled cream. Sprinkle some salt over it, and dip in your spoon.

JANE AND MICHAEL STERN'S BROCCOLI CASSEROLE

Serves 2 as a main dish; 4 to 6 as a side dish | *10 minutes prep time; 35 minutes oven time*

Ever brainy, irreverent, and lovable, Jane and Michael Stern have become our radio family. It's been suggested that they be given their own room in the Smithsonian. Obviously we agree, because we talk to them every single week. We've even assigned them their own theme song, "Two for the Road."

All these years later they still make us hungry and envious. Only Jane and Michael can turn up week after week those local places we all hunt for but rarely find. They call their kind of eating "sleeves-up dining."

In this recipe they pay homage to the late Mama Lo Alexander and her soul-food restaurant in Gainesville, Florida, where she was a local folk hero.

They write: "Her broccoli casserole magically transformed the dour stalks of green into something rich, sweet, and satisfying by combining them with a luxurious and ultra-soulful mélange of eggs, cheese, sugar, and cushiony white bread. We make a batch to split (with a tiny bit left over for the next day) whenever we are in desperate need of culinary comfort, southern-style."

5 or 6 slices soft **white bread**, torn into bite-sized pieces
3 large **eggs**
¼ cup **milk**
4 tablespoons **butter**, melted
1 cup grated **cheddar cheese**
1 teaspoon **salt**
3 tablespoons **sugar**
1 small bunch **broccoli**, florets only (1½ to 2 cups), fine chopped

1. Preheat the oven to 350°F. Butter an 8-inch square Pyrex baking dish. Cover the bottom of the dish generously with the torn bread.

2. Combine the eggs, milk, melted butter, cheese, salt, and sugar in a bowl. Mix until combined. Stir in the broccoli, and pour the mixture over the bread.

3. Cover with aluminum foil, and bake for 35 minutes. For a chewier top, remove the foil during the last 10 to 12 minutes of baking. If you want a crisper crust, run the casserole under the broiler.

The Egg: *A Secret Life*

A confession: When life is dull, some people turn on the TV, others try hang-gliding, and we go to the American Egg Board website (www.aeb.org). It has become a beloved resource for the trivia challenge portion of *The Splendid Table* radio show. Some favorites:

- Of course, everyone knows that egg color is dictated by earlobes and feathers. (Who knew chickens had earlobes!) Breeds with white feathers and white earlobes lay snowy white eggs, and breeds with red feathers and red earlobes lay brown ones.
- The size of the egg is dictated by the age of the hen. Young hens lay peewees, middle-aged ladies give us large eggs, and the grandes dames lay the jumbos.
- Talk about being barefoot and pregnant: It takes a hen about 24 hours to develop and lay a single egg. She gets only about 15 minutes respite before a new egg starts growing.
- Just as women are born with a set number of eggs, hens are born with a set amount of shell material. As they age, their eggshells get thinner.
- Shell color is only a coating; you can rub it off.

CRISPY TORTILLA EGGS WITH AVOCADO AND LIME

| Serves 4 | 5 minutes prep time; 5 minutes stove time | Stale tortillas are a must; fresh won't crisp as well |

Blindfolded, you'd know Sally's house because of the aroma of cumin. She's bewitched by Mexican cuisine. Good-quality corn tortillas are a staple in her house, as are books by Diana Kennedy and Rick Bayless.

The recipe for this dish, at its most primal, begs for variations, so follow your heart: add shrimp, roasted chiles, olives, fresh herbs—you get the idea.

BUILDING THE LIBRARY

THE CUISINES OF MEXICO
(HARPER AND ROW, 1986) AND
FROM MY MEXICAN KITCHEN
(CLARKSON POTTER, 2003), BOTH BY DIANA KENNEDY

3 tablespoons good-tasting **extra-virgin olive oil**, or more as needed

4 stale **corn tortillas**, cut into long narrow strips

2 tablespoons chopped mild **onion**

Salt and fresh-ground **black pepper**

6 **eggs**, beaten

⅓ cup good-quality **salsa**

⅓ cup crumbled **mild cheese**, such as Monterey Jack or Brick

1 **avocado**, sliced

1 **lime**, halved

¼ cup **Mexican** *crema*, sour cream, or plain whole-milk yogurt (optional)

1. Film a large sauté pan with the olive oil, and heat over medium-high heat until the oil looks wavy. Add the tortilla strips and fry until they are beginning to crisp, about 1 minute. Don't move them around too much; let them crisp on one side and then turn them.

2. Add the chopped onion and continue frying until the tortilla strips are crispy and nicely browned. Season with salt and pepper. Remove from the heat and spoon off any extra fat, reserving 1 tablespoon in the pan.

3. Return the pan to the burner, reducing the heat to medium. Move the majority of the strips to the edge of the pan, leaving about 3 inches clear in the center. Pour the eggs in the center and partially over the strips. Allow the eggs to set, and then gently pull them apart, letting the uncooked egg reach the surface of the pan. Once the eggs are firmly set, turn them in large pieces to finish cooking.

4. Serve with the salsa, cheese, slices of avocado, a squeeze of lime, and if you wish, the *crema* or sour cream.

Look for organic sprouted-corn tortillas in your supermarket freezer case. They are toothy and rustic and very delicious. We like the Food For Life brand out of Corona, CA (www.foodforlife.com).

A nonstick pan works well here. If you are using a conventional pan, be generous with the oil.

LUXURY SCRAMBLED EGGS

Serves 2 generously; multiplies easily

5 minutes prep time; 6 to 8 minutes stove time

Serve hot, with a salad of tart greens and orange sections for contrast

Leave it to our listeners and readers to lead us down unexpected paths and sometimes turn the show into an advice column for the romantically challenged. This was sent to our "Ask The Splendid Table" newspaper column:

DEAR LYNNE: I need an alluring breakfast dish for a new woman in my life. She's dynamite, and she loves to eat. —Luring a Lover in Raleigh

DEAR LURING: You are fortunate. My single friends say the eating side of romance has taken a turn for the worse. People's fear of food has wiped out all the fun.

This dish is bliss on a fork. I think of it as quiet cooking. The easy, slow stirring of the eggs over low, low heat protects their tenderness. The cream cheese lends the luxurious touch.

6 large **eggs**

2 tablespoons **heavy whipping cream**

3 ounces **cream cheese**, cut into about ¾-inch pieces

1 large whole **scallion**, thin sliced

½ tight-packed tablespoon fresh curly **parsley leaves**, chopped

½ tight-packed tablespoon fresh **basil *or* tarragon leaves**, chopped

Salt and fresh-ground **black pepper**

2 tablespoons **butter**

1. In a medium bowl, use a fork to loosely blend the eggs and cream. Stir in the cream cheese, scallions, parsley, basil, and a little salt and pepper. Don't beat—just blend them until combined.

2. In a 10-inch heavy nonstick skillet, melt the butter over medium heat. Add the eggs, and stir them with a heatproof plastic spatula for a few seconds.

3. Lower the heat to medium low and keep stirring, scraping up any egg sticking to the pan, for 3 minutes, or until large curds form. The eggs can be served almost wet; moist yet approaching firm (my preference); or quite firm.

Variation

LATIN SKILLET SCRAMBLED EGGS

Film the bottom of the 10-inch skillet with olive oil, and sauté 1 medium onion, 1 red bell pepper, and 1 yellow bell pepper, all cut into ¼-inch dice. As the peppers soften, blend in 1 teaspoon fresh oregano leaves, 1 minced garlic clove, and 2 chopped fresh tomatoes (or 3 well-drained canned ones). Sauté for 3 minutes.

Blend the eggs with water instead of the cream, and stir in the cream cheese, scallions, parsley, and basil as described above. Add the eggs to the skillet, and cook as directed above.

Variation

SCRAMBLED EGGS WITH SPRING "GREENS"

Follow the basic recipe, substituting ⅓ cup snipped fresh chives for the scallions and ⅓ cup thin-sliced sugar snap peas (in their pods) for the parsley. Use the tarragon rather than the basil.

MIDNIGHT ASPARAGUS WITH CREAMY EGGS

Serves 2 to 3 | *10 minutes prep time; 4 minutes cooking time*

You've worked late or celebrated late. You are hungry. You could manage washing asparagus and slicing an onion, but not much more. Sultry, slightly seductive, with the egg becoming a cream for the stalks, this is what to eat when the clock's ticked over to a new day. Have some ragged chunks of bread to sop it all up.

1¼ to 1½ pounds slender **asparagus** (⅓ to ½ inch thick), trimmed of tough stems
Good-tasting **extra-virgin olive oil**
¼ medium to large **onion**, fine chopped
About ½ teaspoon **kosher or coarse salt**
About ¼ teaspoon fresh-ground **black pepper**
4 large **eggs**
Juice of ½ **lemon**
4 or 5 slices chewy **bread**

> Love and eggs are best when they are fresh.
>
> —*Russian proverb*

1. Cut the asparagus into 1½-inch pieces.
2. Put the oven rack in the center of the oven, about 5 inches below the heat source, and preheat the broiler.
3. Film the bottom of a straight-sided 12-inch sauté pan (with ovenproof handle) with olive oil. Set the empty pan beneath the broiler to heat for 2 minutes.
4. Pull the oven rack out. Then, taking care not to touch the hot handle, turn the asparagus, onion, salt, and pepper into the pan. With a wooden spatula, turn the asparagus to coat it with the oil (adding more oil if necessary), and spread the pieces out. Let them cook under the broiler for 3 minutes, stirring them once. You want them to brown slightly but not become mushy.

5. Again, being careful not to touch the pan's handle, use the spatula to push the asparagus to the edges of the pan, leaving the center empty. Carefully break the eggs into that space, so they look like a four-leaf clover. Broil for 1 more minute. Immediately, and carefully, remove the pan from the oven.

6. Squeeze the lemon juice over everything. Give the pan another sprinkle of salt. You could eat right from the pan, or divide the dish onto dinner plates. As you fork the asparagus, dip them in the egg yolk—it is part of the "sauce" of the dish. Sop up the juices with the bread.

Sally's
NEW YEAR'S RESOLUTION

Rather than work on a, shall we say, "private area of improvement," **I prefer a more gently positive approach to the New Year's resolution.** I pick a cookbook, and cook my way through it all year. It is an incredibly simple way to learn a cuisine. Be choosy. I started with Diana Kennedy's *The Cuisines of Mexico,* moved on to Lynne's *The Splendid Table* (before we had met), dug into Madhur Jaffrey's *Flavors of India,* and have not looked back since. I could not have had better teachers. Once you have made the commitment to a cuisine and have built your pantry, you are off and running.

ALMOND CHUTNEY CHICKEN IN LETTUCE ROLL-UPS

Serves 4

15 minutes prep time; 20 minutes resting time

The chicken salad is better if made a day ahead, but don't add the celery and nuts until serving time

Vietnamese restaurants taught us to love the fresh roll-up—a cup of lettuce, some cunningly spiced meat, raw vegetables, and leaves of basil and fresh coriander. What a way to eat, especially in summer. You can stretch a little bit of this and that into a generous, lovely little feast of Asian-style finger food.

Here, the feast centers on the take-out chicken. With chutney, lemon, herbs, and almonds, the plebeian bird emerges as the classiest of chicken salads. Add the Vietnamese elements, and there's no need to turn on the stove.

CHICKEN SALAD

One 3-pound **roasted chicken**

1 medium **red onion**, cut into ¼-inch dice

Grated zest of 1 large **lemon**

Juice of 3 large **lemons**, or more to taste

2 **jalapeños**, seeded and minced; *or*
    hot sauce to taste

One 9-ounce jar **Major Grey Chutney**, cut into bite-sized
    pieces if necessary

½ cup **mayonnaise**

Salt and fresh-ground **black pepper**

3 large **celery stalks**, cut into ¼-inch dice

1 cup whole **salted almonds**, coarse chopped

LETTUCE CUPS AND HERBS

1 large head **Bibb lettuce**, leaves separated, washed,
    and dried

(recipe continues)

1 large bunch fresh **basil**, washed and dried

1 large bunch fresh **coriander**, washed and dried

8 **radishes**, thin sliced

1 large **cucumber**, peeled and sliced into thin rounds or 2-inch sticks

1. Pull the meat from the chicken carcass, discarding the skin and bones. Cut it into bite-sized pieces.

2. In a large bowl combine the onions, lemon zest and juice, jalapeños, chutney, mayonnaise, and salt and pepper. Fold in the chicken. Taste the mix for lemon, mayonnaise, and herbs, adding more as needed. Let it stand for 20 minutes to blend the flavors, or cover and refrigerate overnight.

3. To serve, blend the celery and nuts into the chicken mixture. Mound the salad at one side of a big platter. Pile up the lettuce leaves at the other side, and cluster the sprigs of herbs in the center. Tuck the radishes and cucumbers next to the herbs.

4. Put a few herb leaves in the bottom of a lettuce "cup," top them with a spoonful of the salad, add a slice each of radish and cucumber, and roll up.

BUILDING THE LIBRARY

PLEASURES OF THE VIETNAMESE TABLE BY MAI PHAM (HARPERCOLLINS, 2001)

Variation
IMPROVISING SPRING ROLLS

Vietnamese chef Mai Pham does home-style spring rolls with the remnants of a good meal. A little goes a long way with this approach.

She softens rounds of rice paper in warm water, piles on fresh mint or basil with the leftovers, and rolls them into neat burrito-style packages.

Vietnam's classic spring roll dipping sauce, *nuoc cham,* is worth making and keeping in the refrigerator: Blend to taste Asian fish sauce (*nam pla* or *nuoc nam*), lime juice, sugar, water, minced garlic, and chopped fresh chiles.

Imagine dipping into this with a spring roll filled with leftover baked yams, fresh mint, and fresh coriander. Get the idea?

FAST FOOD, FAST WINE
A PAIRING GUIDE FROM
Joshua Wesson

When you find someone who knows the wine world from the inside out, who believes in good sipping for modest money, and who has an irreverent streak a mile wide, this is the person you want to guide you through the confusion of the wine shop. An agnostic in the world of wine worship, Joshua Wesson has been advising us on wine every month since nearly the show's inception.

Josh's first piece for *The Splendid Table* laid out the fundamentals of pairing food with wine. Tongue-in-cheek aside, the tastes we deal with every day are captured in this quartet of fast food.

Josh's premise is that "wine and foods can only fall in love based on their similarities or their contrasts. When matching wines, go for style and flavor—think sweet, tart, fruity, fizzy, soft, bold, luscious, juicy, or big."

The Big Mac. "You need to deconstruct the two-all-beef-patties-special-sauce-lettuce-cheese-pickles-onions-on-a-sesame-seed-bun.

"The special sauce trumps all. We know it is Russian dressing, a nice combo of sweet and tart. You need to match that sauce. Go for a slightly sweet or off-dry wine. Think rosés, Gewürztraminer, and Chenin Blanc."

Taco Bell Spicy Burritos. "There is a reason why everyone drinks beer with spicy foods. Carbonation and tartness balance off the spiciness.

"To find the right wine, go for beer's stunt doubles. Try sparkling wine—not champagne, but something cheaper. You want crisp and clean qualities to cool the palate. Look for non-vintage sparklers from California, Spanish Cavas, Italian Prosecco, and Crémant d'Alsace from the Alsace region of France."

Chinese Takeout. "The all-time favorite sweet-and-sour pork gives us the answer in its title. Look for sweet-sour wines to go with that sweet-sour sauce. Think Rieslings from cool-weather climates where the grapes do not get intensely sun-ripe—Germany, Washington State, and New Zealand."

BUILDING THE LIBRARY

RED WINE WITH FISH: THE NEW ART OF MATCHING WINE WITH FOOD
BY DAVID ROSENGARTEN AND JOSHUA WESSON
(SIMON & SCHUSTER, 1989)

The Twinkie. My last question to Josh that day was a tease: what to drink with Twinkies. Not missing a beat, he came back with "You need to match that creamy, gloppy center. A palate cleanser is essential. Asti Spumante is the answer."

WARM WHITE BEAN SALAD WITH FRAGRANT GARLIC AND ROSEMARY

| *Serves 3 to 4* | *15 minutes prep time; 10 minutes stove time* | *Holds for 2 days in the refrigerator. Serve warm or at room temperature.* |

Sally relates to beans like no one else I know. I am convinced that her last wish will be for a bowl of beans. She's somehow even trained her kids to crave them. She declares this recipe her midweek savior. Even the kids scarf it directly from the pan.

"I see it as training wheels, a lesson in understanding how the shape and wholeness of a bean can make the dish. I learned this technique for the slow braising of garlic in oil from Lynne. You must be careful not to brown it, but the results are so silky and fragrant, it's well worth the babysitting. I always have a can of good-quality organic white beans in the cupboard. Organic beans simply taste better."

TOPPING

½ slice coarse **whole-grain bread**, coarse ground in a food processor (2 generous tablespoons crumbs)
3 tablespoons fresh-grated **Parmigiano-Reggiano cheese**
Generous ¼ teaspoon fresh-ground **black pepper**

SALAD

5 large **garlic cloves** crushed with ½ teaspoon **salt** and coarse chopped
¼ cup good-tasting **extra-virgin olive oil**
½ tight-packed tablespoon fresh **rosemary leaves**, coarse chopped
Two 15-ounce cans organic **white beans** (cannellini or Great Northern), drained and rinsed

1 large handful mixed **salad greens** (frisée and romaine, spring mix, or a blend of baby greens)
Additional **salt** and fresh-ground **black pepper**

1. In a 12-inch skillet or sauté pan over medium heat, toast the bread crumbs until lightly browned, stirring often. Transfer the crumbs to a small bowl to cool. When cooled, stir in the Parmigiano and pepper. Set aside.

2. In the same pan, slowly warm the garlic in the olive oil over low heat for 30 seconds to 1 minute. Stir in the rosemary, blending for another minute or so, taking care not to burn the garlic. It should be very fragrant and just beginning to soften.

3. Immediately add the beans and fold them in *very gently*. Turn the heat to medium. Heat the beans through, about 3 minutes, occasionally lifting and turning them as they heat, as stirring will turn them to mush. Add the greens and gently move them around in the pan until they are slightly wilted, 30 seconds to 1 minute. Turn into a serving bowl, top with the bread-crumb mixture, and season with salt and pepper.

Handle these beans as gently as you would eggs in their shells; you want to keep them as whole as possible. I use a rubber spatula to fold them together with the other ingredients instead of stirring. Don't be tempted to use a tougher bean like pinto or kidney; their thicker skins keep the beans from drawing in all the flavors.

Sally's GARLIC ROCK

Years ago I discovered I really wasn't comfortable smashing garlic cloves with the side of a chef's knife. I worried about that sharp edge. So I found a rock. It fits snugly in the palm of my hand, it's easy to grasp, and it has a nice flat side that crushes my garlic to smithereens.

I simply throw it in the dishwasher, and I always get a comment from the galley crew about **"Where does the rock go?"**

BREAD
at the Center of the Plate

We Americans are in the minority. Two-thirds of the world looks down at its collective supper to see, not a hunk of meat as the heart of the meal, but rather a bowl of rice, a mound of fou-fou, a mash of yucca, a pile of tortillas, or a slice of bread. Meat, if it's there, is a condiment.

In today's world I wonder if modern wealth is defined as bread showing up only occasionally at our table. We don't need to live on bread anymore. But it's worth reconsidering its old role.

If you pulled up a stool to a banquet table in medieval Europe, bread was the dinner plate. You would have eaten off a thick square called a trencher. Even though it soaked up the best part of the meal, you couldn't take your plate home; trenchers were servants' plunder, often sold off to the poor who hung around the kitchen door. You have to wonder if referring to money as "bread" didn't come from that time.

For long before and long after, that "staff of life" business was true. People lived on bread. It was a way of life and of cooking— they cooked simple things to go with it. The word "accompaniment" comes from the Latin, literally meaning "to go with bread."

The immortal bruschetta—and all its kin from other countries (including Britain's beloved baked beans on toast)—wasn't always a snack; frequently it was supper. Warm bread, with or without its garlic and olive oil, was covered with salads, or cheese and cooked spinach, or spreads, or heated-up leftovers. Today those toppings could come from a jar or from the hands of the cook.

THESE ARE SOME THOUGHTS FOR SUPPER ON A SLICE OF BREAD:

- Olive or herb bread toasted and spread with fresh cheese, topped with chopped dried apricots and salted pistachio nuts.
- Toasted whole-grain bread seasoned with olive oil and garlic, sprinkled with Crossover Spice Blend (page 128), spread with feta cheese, and finished with cucumber slices and chopped scallions.
- Challah toasted and topped with a salad of apples, nuts, and greens.
- Nut-and-grain bread covered with roasted peppers, pitted olives, and frisée leaves.
- Toasted country bread bathed in olive oil and covered with a salad of tart greens, onion, and shaved cheese.
- Ciabatta slices rubbed with garlic and spread with ricotta, topped with chopped onion, tomato slices, fresh basil, and generous olive oil.
- Nut-and-fruit bread toasted and heaped with scrambled eggs.
- Baguette heated, moistened with olive oil, spread with tapenade, and garnished with either thin-sliced preserved lemons or a little fresh lemon juice.

BELGIAN BEER BAR TARTINE

Serves 1, and multiplies easily | *5 minutes prep time*

Some nights you want truly simple—a supper you can carry on a napkin to that chair in front of the TV. Inspiration is found in Belgium, where brew pubs are a way of life and their lunches are an answer to the napkin supper.

If I could take you to my favorite Brussels pub, this is the typical lunch we'd have, along with a big glass of Brussels's own Mort Subite (which translates as Sudden Death), a bitingly tart Gueuze-style beer. The *tartine* is an open-faced sandwich, usually made with coarse grainy bread that is spread with fresh cheese (*fromage frais*) and topped with piquant vegetables or herbs.

To get it to taste as it does in Brussels, use sturdy country-style bread. Instead of looking for a fresh European cheese, track down the new fresh cheeses from American artisans.

You want a cheese that tastes clean and creamy, yet tangy. A few to look for are Zingerman's Sharon Hollow fresh cheeses from Michigan, New York State's Old Chatham Sheepherders' ricotta, and the fresh goat cheeses from Capriole Farm in Indiana. That said, well-seasoned cream cheese would do in a pinch.

1 large slice **multigrain country bread**, cut about ½ inch
  thick
2 to 3 ounces fresh **cheese**
1 or 2 whole **scallions**, thin sliced
3 **radishes**, thin sliced
Coarse salt

1. Spread the bread with the cheese. Press the scallion slices into the cheese, then fan the radishes over them. Sprinkle with coarse salt.

2. Serve the *tartine* on a large plate, and eat American-style with your fingers or Belgian-style with a knife and fork.

Steve Jenkins's
SPRING CHEESES—
TASTING THE SEASON

Our opinionated cheesemonger, Steve Jenkins, is a cheese activist. Long before the word "artisanal" came to America, Steve was hunting down hand-made cheeses and using his cheese counter as a pulpit to preach the importance of raw milk and traditional production. He has been giving our listeners memorable advice for over a decade, and he's taught us to think of cheese as a seasonal food.

Steve declares, **"Spring is the cheesemonger's glory period.** There is a romantic image of cows, sheep, and goats in the spring pastures, grazing amid buttercups and succulent new grass. But the truth is those poor animals have been shut up in barns for months, eating musty old silage, and are dying to get outside. Those pastures are filled with sweet grass, wild onions, and garlic, which ramp up mammolactation and give a milk that is remarkable for cheese making."

Steve names names: Cheeses to Eat in Spring

FRESH GOAT CHEESES UNITED STATES—*Cheeses from Coach Farm (NY), Cypress Grove (CA), Capriole Farm (IN), Fromagerie Belle Chèvre's fresh chèvres and fromage blanc (AL)* CANADA—*Quebec's Fromagerie Tournevent.* FRANCE—*Selles-sur Cher, Valençay, Pouligny-Saint-Pierre, Crottin de Chavignol, and Le Chevrot.*

FRESH SHEEP CHEESES ITALY—*Marzolino, ricotta fresca, Robiola, and fresh sheep's milk ricotta.* CORSICA, FRANCE— *Brindamour or Fleur du Maquis.* SPAIN—*Can Pujol "Nevat" (Catalonia).*

FRESH COW CHEESES ITALY—*Any Robiola cheeses.* FRANCE— *Brie-region's triple-crèmes Gratte-Paille, Pierre Robert, Jean Grogne; also Brie de Meaux (not factory Brie); and double-crème Chaource (Champagne).*

BUILDING
THE LIBRARY

STEVEN JENKINS
CHEESE PRIMER
(WORKMAN, 1996) AND
THE FOOD LIFE
BY STEVEN JENKINS
(ECCO/HARPERCOLLINS, 2008)

Never commit yourself to a cheese without first examining it.

—T. S. Eliot

V

Vegetable
MAIN EVENTS

FEATURING

MOROCCAN GREEN BEAN TAGINE

Supper Tart of Red Onions, Greens, and Grapes

REFRIED BEANS WITH CINNAMON AND CLOVE

Edamame and Smoked Tofu Succotash

PEPPER AND ONION ROAST
WITH SOFT INDIAN SPICES

Spring Vegetables and White Beans Scented
with Fresh Bay

THE QUINTESSENTIAL PESTO WITH RISOTTO

Let my words, like vegetables,
be tender and sweet, for tomorrow
I may have to eat them.

—Anonymous

Not to be name-droppers, but we remember interviewing Nell Newman, who regaled us with tales of the things she would do

to avoid the dreaded soybean loaf served by her mother (Joanne Woodward). For those of you too youthful to remember, soybean loaf was the vegetarian embodiment of political correctness and deep self-awareness during the 1970s.

These days, no matter what our philosophy, our politics, or the state of our psyche, we're all eating at the low end of the food chain at least some of the time. This focus begs for shopping with an eye toward how an ingredient is raised and where it comes from.

The dishes in this chapter borrow shamelessly from the most extraordinary culinary traditions of the world. The rest of the globe has been eating this way for eons; we Americans are just beginning to catch up.

When you start looking at other cultures for inspiration, the ethnic market becomes a new recreational opportunity. In this chapter we give you a primer on navigating an Indian market, one of our favorite haunts. It's the next best thing to getting on a plane, and always a graceful initiation into world citizenship.

MOROCCAN GREEN BEAN TAGINE

| Serves 6 | 15 minutes prep time; 30 to 40 minutes stove time | The tagine keeps for 5 days in the refrigerator and is excellent at room temperature |

Tagines, the stews of North Africa, marry the soft and piquant tastes of spices with foods that are cooked to near-to-melting tenderness. Here is a riff on that concept with a new blend of Moroccan-inspired spices and green beans. But it's the method behind the stew we want to share as well.

Most vegetable stews, no matter what their origin, follow the same five steps. First, you sauté the vegetables. Second, you spice them generously. Third, you add some good-tasting liquid. Fourth, you simmer the stew until everything is tender. The fifth and final step makes or breaks the dish: you boil down the liquid to a rich glaze that cloaks the vegetables. This recipe walks you through the process.

Do this dish once as written; then substitute vegetables singly or in combinations, and change the spices, herbs, and liquids to your heart's content.

THE SAUTÉ

2 to 3 tablespoons good-tasting **extra-virgin olive oil**

2 to 2¼ pounds **green beans**, trimmed

2 medium to large **onions**, coarse chopped

¼ teaspoon **salt**, or to taste

¼ teaspoon fresh-ground **black pepper**, or to taste

5 large **garlic cloves**, minced

SPICE BLEND

½ teaspoon **ground allspice**

¼ teaspoon **pure chile powder**, or to taste

2 teaspoons **Crossover Spice Blend** (page 128) or garam masala

2 teaspoons **dried basil**

2 generous tablespoons **sweet paprika**

LIQUIDS

⅓ cup **red wine or cider vinegar**
⅓ cup **dry red or white wine**
One 28-ounce can whole **tomatoes**
Water as needed

1. In a straight-sided 12-inch sauté pan, heat the oil over medium-high heat. Add the green beans and onions. Sprinkle them with the salt and pepper, and sauté for 10 minutes, or until the vegetables are browning. (Browning deepens flavors and opens up new character.) Stir in the garlic and all the ingredients in the spice blend. Cook until the spices are fragrant, no more than 1 minute.

2. Pour in the vinegar and wine, and boil them down as you scrape up any brown glaze on the bottom of the pan. When there is no moisture left, stir in the tomatoes and their juices, crushing them with your hands as they go into the pan. The vegetables should be barely covered with liquid. Add a little water if necessary.

3. Bring the liquid to a gentle simmer, cover the pan, and cook for 10 minutes (check for sticking), or until the beans are tender. Uncover the pan and turn up the heat so the liquid is at a fast bubble. Cook off the excess liquid, stirring the stew often to protect the beans and spices from burning. You want the sauce to be thick and rich-tasting. Don't worry about overcooking the green beans; they will not cook much further.

4. Season the stew to taste. Serve it hot, at room temperature, or reheated.

COOK *to* Cook

This is a good way to use vegetables at the end of their respective ropes. If you want to serve something with the stew, make No-Cook Whole-Wheat Couscous (page 296), Dumbed-Down Rice (page 297), or Working Mother's Barley (page 294).

We know we've said it so many times, but we like to use organic vegetables for flavor and politics.

Crossover SPICE

There is a trio of spices that easily crosses borders from North Africa to the Middle East, to India, to Mexico: cumin, coriander, and pepper. Make up this foundation blend, then alter where needed as you take it from cuisine to cuisine. For instance, Morocco might demand the addition of sweet paprika, while an Indian recipe could call for more coriander and black pepper, and Mexico more cumin and the addition of ground chiles.

Rub or sprinkle the blend over vegetables and meats when roasting, sauté it into stews and soups, and use it as a finishing spice on salads and grains. Try mixing the blend with an equal amount of brown sugar and rubbing it into meats before placing them on the grill. That same mix offers a new take on grilled fresh pineapple.

CROSSOVER SPICE BLEND

Makes about ¾ cup
Keeps for 3 to 4 months in a dark, cool cupboard

> ¼ cup **ground cumin**
> ½ cup **ground coriander**
> ⅛ cup (2 tablespoons) fresh-ground **black pepper**

Blend the spices together in a jar, and seal. Store away from heat and light.

 **You can tease even more flavor from Crossover Spice Blend by fresh-grinding whole cumin and coriander seeds.**

Surfing the Indian Grocery

Those of us with culinary pretensions turn up our noses at the way folks head for the packaged-food aisles of the supermarket. But turn us loose in an ethnic grocery, and guess what ends up in our carts.

In self-defense we have to point out that ethnic markets are gold mines for high-quality, ready-to-go shortcuts and meal boosters at sensible prices. Remember, the idea isn't that you will serve nothing but Indian or Thai or Mexican food; the magic is in the mix. Who says tandoori spice doesn't work on a piece of salmon—or over cheesecake?

The only time to buy these products is when their labels read like homemade food. If they don't, leave them on the shelf.

LOOK FOR:
Breads for the freezer
Consider these as snacks, for dipping and wrapping, and for hors d'oeuvres: chapati (plain and spiced), roti, paratha, and nan.

Sauces, curry pastes, and chutneys
These are pantry staples. Use them for marinating, saucing, sautéing, and for dressing. Patek and Deep are two sound brands.

Tamarind concentrate
Tamcon brand's intense fruit flavor and mahogany color make it the first choice. The opened concentrate keeps for a year in the refrigerator. Once opened, it will become your constant companion. Stir it into yogurt for breakfast, spread it over onions for grilling, and simmer it into soups and stews.

Spices and aromatics
Spice blends are to Indian groceries what breakfast cereals are to American supermarkets: there are more than you can tally. Try chaat masala, garam masala, chana masala, biryani blends, kofta mixes, tikka masala. Their labels will give you ideas for how to use them, and their ingredient lists will give you a preview of their flavors. Remember, the first ingredients are the strongest ones.

And don't miss fresh seasonings like curry leaves and kaffir lime leaves, which you can store in the freezer for months.

Snacks
Cheetos, Doritos, and potato chips have serious opponents in the Indian snack aisle. Chakali, from Vijaya Foods, are crunchy deep-fried rings of hot-spiced lentil and chickpea batter. Cassava chips, from the potato of the tropics, are crackly, salty-sweet, and good with salsa.

BUILDING THE LIBRARY

THE INDIAN GROCERY STORE DEMYSTIFIED
BY LINDA BLADHOLM
(RENAISSANCE BOOKS, 2000)

SUPPER TART OF RED ONIONS, GREENS, AND GRAPES

Serves 3 to 4 with a salad

10 to 15 minutes prep time; 20 minutes stove time

Although best eaten the day it's made, this tart does reheat well in a pinch

Our wine-making pal, Nan Bailly, is the local Tom Sawyer. At harvest time at her Alexis Bailly Vineyard we are all invited to lunch, but first we have to pick. Kids and bees are everywhere, and appetites build to farmhand stature by noon.

Being lazy by nature, we bribe our way into the party with this harvest tart rather than with sweat equity. The idea is borrowed from France, but it gets more applause here in the Midwest. Garlic, greens, and onions are spread on puff pastry and gilded with cheese and cream—but the grapes make it harvest food for us.

1 light-packed cup mixed **salad greens** (spring mix or baby romaine)

Generous ½ cup good-tasting **seedless grapes**

1 medium **red onion**, sliced into ¼-inch-thick slivers

Shredded zest of ½ large **lemon**

1 large **garlic clove**, fine chopped

Leaves from 5 fresh **thyme sprigs**

1 tablespoon good-tasting **extra-virgin olive oil**

Generous ¼ teaspoon **salt**

⅛ teaspoon fresh-ground **black pepper**

2 sheets frozen **puff pastry**, defrosted (one 17.3-ounce package)

¼ cup **heavy cream**

1 cup shredded **Asiago cheese**

(recipe continues)

1. Set one oven rack as low as possible. Preheat the oven to 500°F. Tear the greens into bite-sized pieces as you add them to a large bowl. Toss them with the grapes, onion, lemon zest, garlic, thyme, olive oil, salt, and pepper.

2. On a large ungreased cookie sheet, lay out the pastry sheets side by side so they overlap by ¼ inch. Press the overlapping edges together to seal. Create a rim by folding the pastry edges up and over on themselves and pinching them together. You'll end up with a rectangle that is about 7½ x 17 inches.

3. Fill the center of the tart with the vegetable-grape mixture, spreading it out so there is space between the pieces. Slip it onto the bottom rack of the oven, and bake for 15 minutes. As the tart bakes, blend the cream and the cheese in a small bowl.

4. Remove the cookie sheet from the oven. Spoon the cheese mixture over the tart, spreading it out. Slip it back into the oven and bake for another 6 minutes, or until the cheese is melted and barely picking up color. Pull the tart from the oven. Let it stand for a few minutes, and then cut it into 8 squares. Serve it right away or at room temperature.

Puff pastry is surprisingly sturdy— it bakes fast, doesn't sog out, and handles reheating like an old pro. And no other pastry comes off with such élan.

Variation
SUMMER TOMATO TART

Follow the recipe as described above, substituting for the greens and grapes 1 or 2 ripe tomatoes, sliced ¼ inch thick, and 8 fresh basil leaves torn into small pieces. Do not blend them in a bowl; just have them ready, along with the sliced onion, lemon zest, and thyme called for in the original recipe.

Lay out the puff pastry as described above. Spread the tomatoes and onions on the tart. Scatter them with the garlic, the herbs, salt, pepper, and 1 to 2 tablespoons olive oil. Zigzag 3 tablespoons heavy cream in ribbons over the tart.

Bake the tart as directed above. Instead of using Asiago, finish it with thin slices of soft-style mozzarella or fresh goat cheese (about 2 ounces) during the last few minutes of baking. If you'd like, snipped chives could garnish the tart.

WINTER TART OF ROAST VEGETABLES AND ENDIVE

Prepare the original recipe, substituting for the greens 1 or 2 thin-sliced Belgian endives, and 1½ cups roasted winter vegetables (rutabaga, carrots, turnip, yams, cauliflower, cabbage, etc.) that have been cut into small bite-sized pieces. Substitute 1 cut-up Granny Smith or other tart apple for the grapes.

Continue the recipe as written.

A man who drinks only water has a secret to hide from his fellow men.

—*Charles Baudelaire*

Vegetarian Cookbooks and References
The Classics

A total absence of meat is not a requirement for an outstanding vegetarian book; you want excellent recipes with imaginative and skillful twists. Not all of these volumes are new, but all are worth considering. This is a gathering of prime teaching tools created by masters. **Build a library around these books.**

Vegetables from Amaranth to Zucchini by ELIZABETH SCHNEIDER. Perhaps the most thorough and thoughtful reference book on the subject produced so far. Schneider explains origins, describes tastes, tells what to look for when shopping, and gives simple recipes.

DEBORAH MADISON's name on a cookbook is a stamp of excellence. *The Savory Way* and *The Greens Cookbook* broke new ground, proving that sophisticated food worthy of a top restaurant didn't need meat. *Local Flavors: Cooking and Eating from America's Farmers' Markets* is Deborah's tribute to farmers markets and the answer to what to do with what we find there. Her *Vegetarian Cooking for Everyone* ranks with *The Joy of Cooking* as an all-purpose guide.

Madhur Jaffrey's World Vegetarian: More Than 650 Meatless Recipes from Around the World by MADHUR JAFFREY. Jaffrey's work never disappoints. She and Julie Sahni, author of *Classic Indian Cooking,* are the two people who first introduced authentic Indian cooking to the United States. All of their works on the foods of India include vegetarian recipes—

this is a country that embraces some of the oldest and most evolved vegetarian foodways.

From My Mexican Kitchen: Techniques and Ingredients by DIANA KENNEDY. A foreigner who took on Mexico back in the 1970s, a time when American cooks were immersed in France, Kennedy is the queen of authentic Mexican flavors. The core of Kennedy's writing is about making the food taste as it does in Mexico. Use this book as your doorway into a kind of Mexican eating you've never experienced.

Passionate Vegetarian by CRESCENT DRAGONWAGON. Stylish, committed, and opinionated, this is the book for soy foods, for imagination, and for the vegetarian lifestyle.

Vegetable Love by BARBARA KAFKA. This book was inspired not by a philosophy of meatless eating but solely by a love of vegetables. It's a modern eating guide, written by one of the most brilliantly informed food professionals on the American food scene. Barbara writes for the family cook. The recipes are short and to the point.

REFRIED BEANS WITH CINNAMON AND CLOVE

| *Serves 4 to 6* | *5 minutes prep time; 18 minutes stove time* | *The beans hold in the refrigerator for 5 days; add liquid as needed when reheating* |

You'd never guess you can create such lushness from opening three cans. Cinnamon and cloves with beans make an uncommon blend—one that turns the beans sweet and fragrant.

This was Sally's first grown-up recipe, the remains of her obligatory vegetarian phase in college. These beans are what she craves when she's tired, what she makes when she comes home from a trip and the cupboard is bare, and what she relies on when she suddenly has seven children for dinner instead of two.

The beans make a sublime burrito. Dip tortilla chips or stovetop-grilled whole-wheat tortillas into them, and be sure to pass hot sauce and grated cheese at the table.

Good-tasting **extra-virgin olive oil**
1 large **onion**, chopped into ¼-inch dice
Salt and fresh-ground **black pepper**
4 **garlic cloves**, fine chopped
1 fresh **jalapeño**, seeded and fine chopped
2 teaspoons **ground cinnamon**
½ teaspoon **ground cloves**
One 14-ounce can whole **tomatoes**, drained
Two 15-ounce cans **red kidney beans**, rinsed and drained
1½ cups **water**
2 tablespoons **butter**

(recipe continues)

1. Generously film the bottom of a 10-inch skillet with olive oil, and heat over medium-high heat. Sauté the onions with salt and pepper to taste until they begin to soften, about 3 minutes. You want to hear a sizzle as they cook.

2. Add the garlic, jalapeño, cinnamon, and cloves, and cook the mix until it is fragrant, about 1 minute, taking care not to burn the spices. Add the tomatoes, crushing them as they go into the pan. Sauté for another minute.

3. Stir in the beans and water. Bring to a fast simmer, crushing the beans with a potato masher (or the back of a large spoon) as they cook, and scraping the bottom of the pan as the beans begin to thicken. Simmer until the beans are thick, about 10 minutes. Blend in the butter, and taste for seasoning just before serving.

Melting in a small amount of butter after mashing the beans brings this dish together. Don't skip this step.

Measuring Fresh Herbs
GETTING IT RIGHT
THE FIRST TIME

It's the little stuff that can get to you in night-to-night cooking, like measuring things that nature didn't intend to fit neatly into tablespoons and teaspoons. I am talking about the leaves of fresh herbs.

Long ago I got fed up reading "1 tablespoon chopped parsley" in a recipe, chopping what looked like the right amount, then measuring it and seeing that I had maybe a ½ tablespoon. Back to the cutting board for double the work. Finally, I realized this was more a question of physics than of cooking—quantity is quantity, no matter how it is sliced.

My solution was deceptively easy: Pack uncut herb leaves firmly into the measure called for. When you can't tamp in any more, and the herbs are level with the top of the measure, chop, mince, or tear. The measurement will be accurate.

POLAR EXPLORER
ANN BANCROFT
and the *Mystery of the Lost Expedition*

Although *The Splendid Table* radio show focuses on the pleasures of food, sometimes interviews spin out in directions we can't anticipate.

On a snowy day in 2000, the phone rang in the control room. It was Arctic explorers Ann Bancroft and Liv Arneson calling in from their tent 80 miles from the South Pole. They were in the process of skiing 1,700 miles across the continent of Antarctica. The temperatures jockeyed around 30 degrees below zero, they were skiing against 100-mph winds, and each one was pulling a 250-pound sled of supplies. The Pole was only partway on their trek.

Ann and Liv talked about how important their meals were, as fuel for the body and also as a respite and a way to feed their morale. They'd been eating chocolate, soup, and instant oatmeal with spoonfuls of oil added, and when asked what they yearned for, a chunk of cheese was the answer. When we spoke that day, they were quickly running out of food. They each needed to eat a minimum of 5,000 calories a day to maintain their weight and strength. If they were too fatigued to rendezvous with the supply plane scheduled to meet them at the South Pole, their entire quest would be in danger as winter closed in. To add to the pressure, children's science classes around the world were tracking the trip.

Happily Ann and Liv reached their goal, and became the first women to ski across Antarctica. Months later, Ann joined us in the studio to talk food technology and the history of polar exploration. As Ann explained, every bit of the latest in food technology and nutritional discoveries goes into equipping expeditions. The party needs to be well fed, but not only with enough calories for survival. As Ann reiterated, "If morale breaks down, it doesn't matter how many calories you eat."

Ann recounted the confounding mystery of Sir John Franklin's 1845 expedition to find a northwest passage from Europe to Asia. His was the best-equipped expedition in history, with enough food for three years, much of it preserved by the latest technology—canning. He also made sure there was plenty of lemon juice; its vitamin C would protect the crew from scurvy.

Within twelve months the expedition had disappeared—no one survived. Over the next 150 years, puzzling evidence of the crew was found. For instance, much of their food was intact, yet groups of men had trekked off without provisions, carrying instead books, pictures, and bric-a-brac.

In 1982 forensic anthropologist Owen Beattie discovered the reason for the deranged behavior: it was lead poisoning. But botulism and scurvy were the final blows to the expedition. Franklin took the lowest bid for his canned supplies; the vendor sealed the expedition's cans with lead. Unsanitary canning conditions created the botulism, and the scurvy resulted from the nutritionists not knowing that over time the vitamin C in that lemon juice would lose its potency.

Ann concluded: "They had the latest technology, and it killed them."

EDAMAME AND SMOKED TOFU SUCCOTASH

Serves 2 to 3 as a main dish; 4 to 5 as a first course | *10 minutes prep time; 12 minutes stove time* | *This is good warm and cool and keeps in the refrigerator for a day or two*

This recipe's inspiration was Chinese chef Susanna Foo of Philadelphia. When we interviewed Susanna, we were struck by her lack of rigid culinary rules. She interprets the traditional Chinese palate with modern Western ingredients, boldly mixing balsamic vinegar with soy sauce, or rosemary with dried yellow soybeans. Surprises fill her books. For instance, did you know that fresh corn is used often in the northern regions of China?

1½ tablespoons **soy sauce**

1 teaspoon **balsamic vinegar**

2 tablespoons **chicken or vegetable broth** (preferably Cheater's Homemade Broth, page 48)

Good-tasting **extra-virgin olive oil**

1 small **red onion**, cut into 1-inch chunks

2 **garlic cloves**, minced

One 6- to 8-ounce block of "smoked" or "savory flavored" **tofu**, cut into ½-inch dice

1½ cups fresh-cut **corn** kernels; *or* one 9-ounce box frozen corn kernels, defrosted

1 cup cooked shelled **edamame** or cooked lima beans (both available frozen)

1 large **tomato**, diced

3 whole **scallions**, diced

Red pepper flakes

Salt and fresh-ground **black pepper**

(recipe continues)

1. Mix the soy sauce, vinegar, and broth together in a small bowl.

2. Lightly film the bottom of a large skillet with olive oil and heat it over medium-high heat. Add the onion and cook until slightly softened, about 3 minutes. Reduce the heat to medium and add the garlic, tofu, and soy sauce mixture. Sauté for about 3 minutes more. Be careful not to fully reduce the cooking liquid. If you run out, simply add a bit more broth to the pan to keep things moist.

3. Turn the heat to low and stir in the corn, edamame, tomatoes, and scallions. Sauté, stirring gently, for 5 minutes. Turn the heat up to medium and cook for a few more moments, until there is a slight golden glaze in the bottom of the skillet and the flavors are rich and concentrated.

4. Season to taste with red pepper flakes, salt, and black pepper. Serve in a shallow bowl.

While frozen corn works here, fresh is best. In addition to plain, you can find both smoked tofu and tofu labeled "savory flavored."

Variation
BUTTER-STEAMED LIMAS WITH PINK LADIES

Apply this same approach to a different set of ingredients for another unexpected take on the vegetable sauté: Using 3 tablespoons of butter instead of the olive oil, sauté the onion and garlic, adding 3 cups fresh or frozen lima beans with ¼ cup of the broth. Cook, covered, over medium heat until the beans are tender. Season them to taste with salt, black pepper, and red pepper flakes. Stir in 2 chopped (skin on) Pink Lady apples, and serve. (Fujis or Braeburns could be used as well.)

CHARLIE TROTTER
on the Food of the Future?

The spins on the nutritional advantages of vegetarianism and veganism are legion. The raw food movement of recent years challenges the cook's imagination in new ways and opens up intriguing possibilities. By raw food standards, nothing can be warmed beyond 188°F. What does this mean?

In an interview, chef Charlie Trotter said, "The raw food movement is about taking apart what we eat and putting it together in brand-new ways." By way of an example, he walked us through a mushroom pavé.

"Simply take thin-sliced raw mushrooms, and macerate them in soy, sesame oil, garlic, ginger, and scallions. Stack and layer them into a rectangle resembling a deck of cards. Put them into a pan with a weight on them and compress in the refrigerator for a couple of hours. The mushrooms become very complex, with the texture of meat. Slice, and dress the pavé with the remaining marinade."

BUILDING
THE **LIBRARY**

RAW
BY CHARLIE TROTTER AND
ROXANNE KLEIN
(TEN SPEED PRESS, 2007)

As Charlie pointed out, the process of "cooking" raw opens up roads much less traveled in the world of cooking. Sometimes making foods edible is more about mental gymnastics than about the act of cooking.

The disparity between the restaurant's price and the food quality rises in direct proportion to the size of the peppermill.

—Bryan Miller, former restaurant critic for the New York Times

ROASTING VEGETABLES
HOW TO COOK BY INSTINCT

All cooking breaks down into a series of logical steps, and all seasonings come down to what tastes right to you. Once you know which collection of steps gives you a particular dish or taste, you can cook anything. **It's all about sharpening your instincts;** roasting vegetables is a great way to begin. With vegetables the steps are always the same—only the seasonings and mix of produce change. Here is a quick reference to get you started:

- Turn the oven to 450°F, and slip in a big shallow pan to heat up with the oven. Your pan should be large enough so the vegetables can be spread out. The gold standard of shallow roasting pans is the heavy-duty half-sheet pan.
- Mix your vegetables by balancing earthy with sweet (e.g., cauliflower and turnips with carrots, tart greens with parsnips, Brussels sprouts with yams). A generous amount of onion is essential. For even quicker cooking, thin-slice the harder root vegetables.
- Toss the vegetables with good-tasting oil and seasonings.

  Determine how spices and/or herbs will taste when mixed together by putting them on the tip of your tongue. If you don't like the mix, try something else.

  Some dependable combinations are sage, rosemary, and lemon zest; allspice, cumin, coriander, and chile powder; minced fresh ginger, soy sauce, and rice vinegar. For more seasoning ideas, look at the combinations in our recipes.

- Allow 30 to 40 minutes of roasting time for soft vegetables like zucchini, peppers, onions, tomatoes, and fruits. Root vegetables may need another 20 to 30 minutes.
- Turn the vegetables two or three times during cooking. Use a wooden spatula to scrape up the brown glaze that collects on the bottom of the pan. This is pure flavor, so keep blending it back into the mix.

Caveats

- Garlic burns in longer-cooking roasts, so add it in the last half hour.
- Sweet sauces like barbecue blends burn within minutes, so it is best to add them during the last 15 minutes.
- Vinegar, citrus, and other acids slow down browning. When you use them as seasonings, you may need to brown the vegetables at the end of cooking by slipping them under the broiler for a few minutes.

PEPPER AND ONION ROAST WITH SOFT INDIAN SPICES

Serves 3 to 4

10 minutes prep time; 40 minutes oven time

Serve hot, at room temperature, or reheated. The roast keeps for 2 days in the refrigerator.

This is the subtle side of Indian spicing. Along with the sweetness of peppers and onions you'll taste the hint of orange that ground coriander always brings, the funkiness of cumin, and the sweet nutlike quality of roasted chickpeas.

Piled in a soup bowl with a finish of tamarind and plain whole-milk yogurt, the roast is a full supper. That touch of tamarind brings up all the other flavors.

3 large **garlic cloves**

2 tight-packed tablespoons fresh **coriander leaves**

One 1-inch piece fresh **ginger**, peeled and sliced thin

1 large **red bell pepper**, cut into ½-inch pieces

2 large **yellow bell peppers**, cut into ½-inch pieces

1 large or 2 medium **red onions**, cut into ¼-inch-wide wedges

1 tight-packed cup **arugula**, curly endive, or spring mix, torn into bite-sized pieces

One 15-ounce can **chickpeas**, rinsed and drained

1 teaspoon **Crossover Spice Blend** (page 128) or a blend of ground coriander, ground cumin, and fresh-ground black pepper

1 tablespoon **tamarind** concentrate; or 2 teaspoons lime juice with a little grated zest and a generous pinch of sugar

¼ to ½ teaspoon **kosher or sea salt**

3 tablespoons cold-pressed **vegetable oil** or good-tasting extra-virgin olive oil

FINISH

1 to 2 tablespoons **tamarind concentrate** (optional)

¼ cup fresh **coriander leaves**

1 cup **plain whole-milk yogurt** (optional)

(recipe continues)

1. Heat the oven to 450°F, and put a large shallow pan on the middle rack (a half-sheet pan is ideal because you don't want to crowd the vegetables).

2. In a food processor, combine the garlic, fresh coriander leaves, and ginger. Process until chopped fine—don't puree them.

3. Turn the mix into a large bowl. Add all the other ingredients except the finishing seasonings. Toss to blend. Carefully turn the mixture out onto the hot pan, spreading the pieces to cover the entire pan. Roast for 40 minutes, turning often and scraping up the brown glaze from the pan's bottom. Once the peppers are tender, the greens browned, and the chickpeas crisp, the roast is done.

4. Taste the roast for seasoning, and turn into a serving bowl. If using the tamarind, blend it in. Drop the coriander leaves over the vegetables, and pass the yogurt separately.

Tamarind tastes of dense, sour dried fruit with a strong sense of citrus and a lingering sweetness. You must try it. You can find tamarind concentrate in Asian, Hispanic, and Mediterranean groceries, and in some supermarkets. The brand we like is Tamcon. Once opened, it keeps for a year in the refrigerator. Tamarind drizzled in whole-milk yogurt is the stuff of dreams.

Mario Batali
on the Spice Cupboard

In an interview on the show, Mario had this advice for home cooks: "Go directly to your spice cabinet and throw all of your spices away. Because the last time you made Bengali curry was five years ago, and there is no curry left in that curry."

I am not a vegetarian because I love animals, I am a vegetarian because I hate plants.

—*A. Whitney Brown*

SPRING VEGETABLES AND WHITE BEANS SCENTED WITH FRESH BAY

Serves 4

10 minutes prep time; 15 minutes stove time

Easily made ahead, this dish is good at room temperature or reheated

This is a bowl brimming with the fresh, clear tastes of spring: sticks of carrots, slivers of garlic, handfuls of baby spinach, all married with the earthy meatiness of white beans and the citrus scent of fresh bay leaves.

2 cups **Cheater's Homemade Vegetable Broth** (page 48) or canned vegetable broth

4 medium **carrots**, sliced into thick 3-inch-long matchsticks

8 **garlic cloves**, thin sliced

2 fresh **bay leaves**, bruised

One 15-ounce can **cannellini** or other white beans, rinsed and drained

3 cups fresh baby **spinach**, washed

Salt and fresh-ground **black pepper**

1 **lemon**, halved

1 to 2 tablespoons good-tasting **extra-virgin olive oil**

¼ cup fresh-grated **Parmigiano-Reggiano cheese**

1. In a 6-quart pot with a tight-fitting cover, combine the broth, carrots, garlic, and bay leaves. Bring to a simmer, cover, reduce the heat, and cook for 8 to 10 minutes, or until the carrots are tender.

2. Add the beans, spinach, and salt and pepper, and stir to wilt the spinach into the stew. Cover and cook for 5 minutes, or until the spinach is wilted and the beans are heated through.

3. Squeeze the juice of the lemon into the pot, remove the bay leaves, and serve the stew with drizzles of olive oil and sprinklings of grated Parmigiano.

The PESTO *Chronicle*

Pesto. I tend to rant on the subject of young basil and the proper pesto. I have tracked pesto to its region of origin, Liguria; to its city of origin, Genoa; and finally to its supposed neighborhood of supreme excellence, Pra'.

And that is where I learned that there is a fleeting moment for basil—about three weeks before it begins to flower. The sweetest, most perfect pesto is made with young basil, ideally when the plant is 6 to 9 inches tall. It should not have even thought of budding. Once flowering begins, that basil becomes bitter and tastes of anise.

If this isn't enough of a pesto briefing, frequent guest and Italian expert Fred Plotkin offers a treatise on pesto in his book, *Recipes from Paradise: Life and Food on the Italian Riviera.*

In the real world, the pesto for this risotto could come from a jar, or, heaven forbid, from over-the-hill basil.

THE QUINTESSENTIAL PESTO WITH RISOTTO

Serves 3 to 4

10 minutes prep time; 20 minutes attended stove time

Risotto is like pasta; it should be eaten as soon as it is done. See variations for what to do with leftover risotto.

Fragrance billows out of this risotto. Risotto might even be a better vehicle for pesto than the usual pasta.

People don't think of risotto as work-night food, but it is. You sauté some onion, then sauté the rice, add broth a little at a time to cook the rice, and finally you season the risotto however you'd like. Total cooking time: 15 to 20 minutes.

Risotto's only rules are to use medium-grain rice (see Risotto Rice, page 153) and never cover the pot.

PESTO

1 large **garlic clove** (remove any green center)
⅛ teaspoon **salt**
⅔ tight-packed cup fresh young **basil leaves**
2 heaping tablespoons **pine nuts**
¼ cup grated **Fiore Sardo sheep cheese** or American Stella Fontinella; *or* 3 tablespoons fresh-grated Locatelli Romano
½ cup fresh-grated **Parmigiano-Reggiano cheese**
4 tablespoons good-tasting **extra-virgin olive oil**

RISOTTO

3 tablespoons **butter** or good-tasting extra-virgin olive oil
1 medium **onion**, minced
Salt and fresh-ground **black pepper**
1 large **garlic clove**, minced

(recipe continues)

1 heaping cup (8 ounces) **Italian Arborio or Carnaroli rice**

¼ cup **dry white wine**

3½ to 4 cups **Cheater's Homemade Vegetable Broth** (page 48)

GARNISH

¼ cup **pine nuts**

1. You can prepare the pesto in a mortar and pestle or in a food processor with the motor running. Start by pureeing the garlic and salt. Gradually add the basil and then the pine nuts, crushing or processing everything into a rough paste. Pour in the cheeses and the oil, and stir to blend. The pesto should be a rough paste. Set it aside.

2. In a heavy 4-quart saucepan, heat the butter or oil over medium heat, adding the onions with a light sprinkling of salt and pepper. Sauté until the onions are soft and clear, about 3 minutes. Blend in the garlic and rice, and cook for 3 minutes, stirring often.

3. Raise the heat to medium high. Stir in the wine, and cook until it's absorbed. Begin adding the broth, 1 cup at a time, simmering and stirring each addition until the liquid is absorbed by the rice before adding the next cup. Never cover the pot. Once you start adding the broth, the cooking time will be about 15 minutes. After cooking in about 2½ cups, start adding the broth in ½-cup portions. Begin tasting the risotto.

4. When it's ready, the rice should be close to tender, with a little more firmness to the bite than you'd like, and it should be nearly soupy (it will finish cooking and absorb a little more broth in the next step). Never cook the rice to a mush.

5. Immediately remove the pot from the heat; let it stand for 3 minutes. Then fold in the pesto, sprinkle with the pine nuts, and serve.

A YEAR OF RISOTTI

Instead of the pesto, try these additions in Step 5:

- **Spring**: 2 cups cooked sweet peas and ½ cup fresh-grated Parmigiano-Reggiano.
- **Summer**: 2 or 3 ripe summer tomatoes, chopped fine, and ½ cup coarse-chopped pitted oil-cured black olives.
- **Fall**: 20 sage leaves that have been fried in hot olive oil for a few seconds until crisp and then salted, plus 1 ripe pear, cored and cut into bite-sized pieces.
- **Winter**: 3 cups roasted diced yam and thin-sliced Brussels sprouts.

Variation
QUINTESSENTIAL PESTO WITH LINGUINE

In Liguria people cook linguine with green beans and thin slices of potatoes for a more substantial meal. Pesto loves these vegetables, especially almost creamy overcooked potatoes.

Prepare the Quintessential Pesto as described above and bring 5 quarts of salted water to a boil.

For 1 pound of linguine, peel and thin slice 1 medium red-skin potato, and cut ½ pound green beans into 1-inch lengths.

Add the linguine and the vegetables to the boiling water and cook until the pasta is tender but still a little firm to the bite. The vegetables should be very soft.

Scoop ½ cup of the pasta water from the pot and set it aside. Quickly drain the pasta and vegetables. Toss with the pesto and the reserved pasta water. Serve hot, with extra Parmigiano if you'd like.

Variation
PAN-CRISPED RISOTTO PATTIES

Maybe the best part of risotto is the leftovers—at least that's how a lot of people in Italy's risotto territories feel. This is the basic concept behind making pan-fried patties, called *risotto al salto*.

Prepare any of the risotti mentioned on page 151. Refrigerate the leftovers for up to 3 days. To make the patties, scoop up ½ to ⅔ cup of the risotto per patty. Wet your hands and shape the rice into burger-sized rounds that are no more than ¾ inch thick.

Beat 2 large eggs in a shallow bowl. Place 2 to 3 cups of fresh bread crumbs or Japanese panko crumbs on a dinner plate.

Generously film a large skillet with good-tasting extra-virgin olive oil. Heat over medium-high heat. Once the oil looks almost wavy, dip the patties into the egg, then roll them in the crumbs.

Carefully slip the patties into the oil. Lower the heat to medium, and cook them to golden on one side. Turn with a spatula, and cook to golden on the second side. Drain on paper towels, and serve hot with a squeeze of lemon.

Cooking Rule . . .
If at first you don't succeed, order pizza.

—Anonymous

Risotto Rice
THE LONG AND THE SHORT

For successful risotto with an undulating creaminess, you need medium-grain rice. **This is not the obsessive Italian purist shaking a finger;** it is actual science. Medium-grain and long-grain rices cook differently.

With the myriad of rices around the globe, it is surprising that all of them break down into just three categories: long-grain, medium-grain, and short-grain. THE LONG-GRAIN has its very own starch called amylose, which makes the grains separate and fluffy. MEDIUM- AND SHORT-GRAIN rices share the same starch, amylopectin. This waxy starch makes the rice sticky or creamy when cooked.

If Italian medium-grain rices, like Carnaroli, Roma, Arborio, Vialone Nano, Baldo, and Corallo, aren't to be had, supermarket medium-grain could be substituted.

P

Pasta

FEATURING

SICILIAN CORKSCREWS WITH WHITE BEANS

Cheese-Gilded Linguine with Smoky Tomatoes

HOLLOW PASTA WITH GREEK
CINNAMON-TOMATO SAUCE

Sweet Roasted Butternut Squash and Greens
over Bow-Tie Pasta

TWO BROCCOLIS WITH CAVATAPPI
AND RAISIN–PINE NUT SAUCE

Summer Zucchini Pasta

PASTA WITH CHOPPING-BOARD
PISTACHIO PESTO

Lynne's Retro Garlic Bread

THE TRUE FETTUCCINE ALFREDO

21st-Century Mac 'n' Cheese

HOISIN CHINA NOODLES WITH FOUR FLAVORS

Ah, yes, cold spaghetti eaten
at midnight, eaten with your fingers,
your body hanging on the open
refrigerator door, your bare feet
squishing around in whatever doesn't
make it to your mouth.

–Maggie Waldron

What is it about

a noodle? Flour, water, maybe egg—nothing exotic here, yet the noodle is irresistible. From toddler to toothless, no age is immune to the yearning for a bowl of noodles.

Pasta has always invited new interpretations. In this chapter you'll find some of the most popular, from a twenty-first-century version of mac 'n' cheese (page 182) to a recipe for The True Fettuccine Alfredo (page 180). A colleague's Greek tomato sauce evolved into Hollow Pasta with Greek Cinnamon-Tomato Sauce (page 166).

You'll encounter a provocative technique from Naples of tossing pasta with the cheese before the sauce in Cheese-Gilded Linguine with Smoky Tomatoes (page 163). There is also a bow to the East with an old favorite from my Chinese cooking days, Hoisin China Noodles with Four Flavors (page 184), that's unlike anything you'll encounter in a restaurant.

Essential pasta information is here as well: which pasta to buy, why salt the water, swapping pasta shapes, how to make a sauce from pasta water, and even the best kitchen sink to drain the pasta in.

IMPORTED ITALIAN PASTA
WHY AND WHAT TO BUY

The best dried pastas cook up light and supple with a little chewiness and a pebbly texture that grips the sauce. They are never gummy or soggy. So far, domestic pastas haven't measured up, but they will, because many American producers have begun emulating Italian models. Besides, much of the flour in Italy's pastas comes from North America.

Four things dictate quality in a dried pasta: the quality of the wheat, how long the dough is worked, the rough textures of the dies through which the pasta is extruded, and how slowly the pasta is dried, which makes for even cooking.

Modest-priced pastas to look for include De Cecco, Delverde, La Molisana, Geraldo & Nola, and Barilla Plus, which is a particularly good-tasting pasta made of dried legumes and whole wheat. (Other Barilla pastas tend to be gummy.) One standout whole-wheat pasta is Bionaturae.

Some higher-priced artisan pastas to seek out are Rusticella, Michele Portoghese, Cav. Giuseppe Cocco, Latini, Settaro, Dallari, Benedetto Cavalieri, and Bigoli Nobili from Pastificio Sgambaro.

Spinosi and Cipriani are the two brands that come closest to tasting like stunningly good homemade, hand-rolled egg pasta, cooking up incredibly light—with equally stunning prices.

Caveat: When deciding whether or not to buy a pasta you've not seen before, check the cooking instructions. If they say to rinse the pasta after cooking, the noodles have been made from inferior wheat. They will be starchy, gummy, and not worth eating.

SICILIAN CORKSCREWS WITH WHITE BEANS

Serves 3 to 4

10 minutes prep time; 15 minutes stove time

Could be served hot or at room temperature, and reheats well with a few tablespoons of water

With squiggly noodles and tomato, this is a gem of a kid's pasta. And it has a sneaky side—they will eat beans without even thinking about it. Whether they're called *rotini*, *fusilli*, or "squiggly," you want a corkscrew-shaped pasta for this recipe so it can hold the bits of sauce and beans.

The optional can of tuna is a standard Mediterranean combination. It is best to use tuna packed in olive oil. The chile vinegar may seem an odd addition, but it's found all over southern Italy, made from homegrown, stingingly hot peppers. Our Tabasco sauce is a respectable stand-in.

5 quarts **salted water** in a 6-quart pot

6 tablespoons good-tasting **extra-virgin olive oil**

½ large red **onion**, sliced into thin half-rounds

Salt and fresh-ground **black pepper**

6 large **garlic cloves**, fine chopped

3 tight-packed tablespoons fresh **flat-leaf parsley leaves**, coarse chopped

1 heaping tablespoon **tomato paste**

½ teaspoon **hot chile vinegar or Tabasco sauce**, or more to taste

⅔ cup **water**

Two 15-ounce cans **cannellini** or Great Northern beans, rinsed and drained

½ pound imported **Italian fusilli** (corkscrew pasta; whole wheat or dried legume style preferred; see Imported Italian Pasta, opposite)

(recipe continues)

½ cup fresh-grated **Parmigiano-Reggiano** or Pecorino Romano cheese

One 6-ounce can **tuna** packed in olive oil, partially drained (optional)

1. Bring the salted water to a boil.

2. Combine the oil and onions in a straight-sided 12-inch sauté pan, and set the pan over medium heat. Sprinkle the onions with salt and a generous amount of pepper. Sauté until the onions are softened. Blend in the garlic, parsley, tomato paste, chile vinegar, and the ⅔ cup water. Stir and simmer until most of the water has evaporated.

3. With a wooden spatula, gently fold in the beans, and simmer for 2 minutes so they absorb the flavors. Taste for seasoning, adjust as necessary, remove the pan from the heat, and cover.

4. Drop the pasta into the boiling water and cook for about 10 minutes, or until it is a little firmer than you like it. Scoop up about 1 cup pasta water and save it; then immediately drain the pasta in a colander.

5. Reheat the sauce, adding the reserved cup of pasta water to the pan. Stir gently, scraping up any glaze on the bottom of the pan. Cook for a minute or so to blend, and to slightly reduce the pasta water. Fold in the pasta, warming it for a few moments. Blend in the cheese, and taste for seasoning. Turn the pasta into a serving bowl, and if you want, fold in the tuna. Serve immediately.

Handle these beans gently, keeping them as whole as possible. Whole-wheat and other whole-grain pastas do well in this recipe.

PASTA WATER: THE HIDDEN SAUCE

To create a sauce where there isn't one, or not enough, use the common Italian technique of adding starchy, salty pasta water to sautés. It could be pan-browned zucchini, shrimp cooked with garlic, or a rough chop of herbs and salami. Pasta water's starch lends body to the mix, and the salt lifts the other flavors.

The moment before you drain the pasta, scoop out a cupful of water. Simmer half of it into the sauté, using the liquid to help scrape up any brown bits on the bottom of the pan. If the pan still looks dry, stir in more pasta water.

WHY SALT THE PASTA WATER?

I have to smile when people tell me about the fabulously flavorful pasta they ate in Europe. True, the pasta might be of better quality, but that's not what they're tasting. It is the salt. If you could step into a restaurant kitchen in Italy, your jaw would drop—*handfuls* of salt are thrown into the pasta water. Salt is the pasta cook's weapon of choice, which makes sense.

People assume you can salt after cooking—not so with pasta. Pasta does not absorb salt once it is cooked, so if the water is not seasoned, the pasta won't be either. Properly salted pasta water should taste like the sea, or at least like a well-seasoned broth. You will end up using less salt in the finished dish if you start out with well-salted pasta water.

CHEESE-GILDED LINGUINE WITH SMOKY TOMATOES

Serves 4 as a main dish | *15 minutes prep time; 20 minutes stove time* | *The sauce can be made 1 hour before serving*

You can buck up the personality of a bowl of pasta by merely switching the order of how grated cheese and tomato sauce are blended with the noodles. Bring in smoky flavors and a snap of chile, and you have a modern improvisation.

This cheese trick comes from Naples, where cooks make simple tomato-sauced pastas more substantial by tossing the pasta first with the grated cheese, then with the sauce.

5 quarts **salted water** in a 6-quart pot
Good-tasting **extra-virgin olive oil**
6 thick slices **bacon**, sliced into ¼-inch-wide sticks
1 medium to large **onion**, chopped into ¼-inch dice
Salt and fresh-ground **black pepper**
¼ teaspoon **red pepper flakes**, or to taste
5 large **garlic cloves**, minced
2½ to 3 pounds delicious ripe **tomatoes**, cored and fine chopped (do not peel or seed); *or* one 28-ounce can whole tomatoes with their liquid, plus one 14-ounce can, drained
1 pound imported **linguine**
1 generous cup fresh-grated **Parmigiano-Reggiano cheese**, plus more for the table

(recipe continues)

1. Bring the salted water to a boil.

2. Lightly film a straight-sided 12-inch sauté pan with oil, add the bacon, and set over medium-high heat. Sauté until the bacon is golden. Remove it with a slotted spoon, setting it on paper towels to drain. Pour off all but about 3 tablespoons of the fat from the pan.

3. Return the pan to the heat, and stir in the onions, salt and pepper, and red pepper flakes. Reduce the heat to medium. Sauté until the onions soften and start to color, 5 to 8 minutes.

4. Blend in the garlic, cooking for 1 minute, and then add the tomatoes. If using canned ones, crush them as they go into the pan. Stir in the cooked bacon. Bring the sauce to a lively bubble and cook until it is thick, 7 to 8 minutes, stirring to keep it from sticking. Remove from the heat, taste for seasoning, and cover the pan. The sauce can wait on the stovetop for up to an hour. Bring it to a bubble before adding it to the pasta.

5. Drop the pasta into the boiling water, and cook until it is tender but still a little firm to the bite. Drain, and turn it into a serving bowl. Toss with the 1 cup cheese until it clings to the noodles, then toss with the sauce. Serve hot, with additional cheese at the table if desired.

Variation
SPAGHETTI ALLA GRICIA

Before the tomato took over the Italian kitchen, this pasta was made in the hills of the Abruzzo and Lazio regions.

Instead of the bacon, use ½ pound *guanciale* (cured pork jowl), pancetta, or, ideally, smoked pancetta. Cook as directed, adding the garlic, salt, a lot of black pepper, and a bit more red pepper flakes. Eliminate the onion and tomatoes.

Just before draining the pasta, scoop out ½ cup of the pasta water and add it to the sauté pan. Drain the noodles, and add them to the sauté pan. Toss over medium-high heat for 30 seconds. Blend in a generous amount of grated Pecorino Romano. The pasta should taste peppery, with a good shot of hot pepper.

The Kitchen Sink
WHAT YOU NEVER CONSIDERED

Odd though it may seem to be mulling kitchen design in a pasta chapter, consider how much time you spend at the sink draining pasta, rinsing mops, piling dishes, washing dogs, rinsing produce—you get the picture.

Our contributor **Deborah Krasner,** a cookbook and design author, is a kitchen designer who cooks (dare we say a rare combination?). She believes that choosing the right sink is one of the most important kitchen design decisions you make.

Sink Thinking from Deborah Krasner:

YOUR PHYSICAL RELATIONSHIP WITH THE SINK Think about your arm reach, your height, and the depth of the sink. Deb believes we need to get back to the farmhouse sinks, the ones that hang off the wall and can be set at any height with a faucet that comes out to meet *you,* instead of you leaning in to meet the faucet. You should be able to stand relaxed, belly to the sink, with no straining when you work. If you're under 5 foot 3, go for a shallow sink with a bottom you can reach easily. If you're tall, you'll be comfortable with a deeper sink.

BUILDING THE LIBRARY

THE NEW OUTDOOR KITCHEN
BY DEBORAH KRASNER
(TAUNTON, 2007)

HOW YOU USE THE SINK Think about the dirty and clean-up functions. You rinse out the dirty mop and you wash your greens in the same place, unless you have two sinks. But Deborah says the combined double sink that most of us live with was invented before dishwashers. Aren't there always clean dishes in one half? Instead, Deborah thinks you should go for two separate sinks in separate parts of the kitchen if you can manage it.

HOLLOW PASTA WITH GREEK CINNAMON-TOMATO SAUCE

Serves 4 as a main dish | 15 minutes prep time; 25 minutes stove time | The sauce can be made several days ahead and kept in the refrigerator

Greek pastas are so seductive, especially the ones done with tomato sauces. I think of them as another world to plunder. Cinnamon always scents the tomatoes, along with garlic, oregano, and wine. This sauce was inspired by the work of Greek culinary authority Aglaia Kremezi.

It began as hers, but over the years of cooking, the mix of seasonings became my own, along with the occasional additions of lamb or chicken; and I have substituted goat cheese for her feta. It turns to cream in the sauce.

5 quarts **salted water** in a 6-quart pot

SAUCE

Good-tasting **extra-virgin olive oil**
1 medium **onion**, chopped
⅓ tight-packed cup fresh **flat-leaf parsley leaves**, coarse chopped
Salt and fresh-ground **black pepper**
1 heaping tablespoon **tomato paste**
6 large **garlic cloves**, minced
1¼ teaspoons **dried oregano** (Greek oregano preferred)
2 teaspoons **ground cinnamon**
1 teaspoon **sugar**
1 teaspoon **ground Aleppo pepper** or other medium-hot chile; or ½ teaspoon red pepper flakes
½ cup **dry white or red wine**
2 pounds ripe summer **tomatoes**; or one 28-ounce can whole tomatoes with their juice

1½ to 2 cups diced cooked **chicken or lamb** (organic if possible; optional)

PASTA

1 pound imported long **hollow pasta** like perciatelle, maccheroncelli, or ziti, broken into more or less 2-inch pieces, or short hollow pasta
1½ cups (6 ounces) fresh **goat cheese**, crumbled

1. Bring the salted water to a boil.

2. Generously film the bottom of a straight-sided 12-inch sauté pan with olive oil and heat it over medium-high heat. Stir in the onions, parsley, and generous sprinklings of salt and pepper. Sauté the onions to golden brown. Then stir in the tomato paste, garlic, oregano, cinnamon, sugar, and Aleppo pepper. Turn the heat down to medium and sauté for 1 minute. Add the wine and cook for 1 minute.

3. If using fresh tomatoes, grate them on a grater over a bowl, and add the pulp with its juices to the pan. For canned tomatoes, crush them as they go into the pot. Raise the heat to medium high and cook the sauce for 8 minutes, or until thick. Taste for seasoning, remove the pan from the heat, and if using the chicken or lamb, stir it in. Cover the pan.

4. Drop the pasta into the boiling water. Boil, stirring often, for 8 minutes, or until the pasta is tender but still has a little bite. As the pasta cooks, reheat the sauce over medium-high heat. Once the pasta is done, drain it in a colander and add it to the sauce. Toss over the heat for a minute or more to help the sauce permeate the noodles. Turn half of it into a serving bowl and dot with half of the cheese. Add the rest of the pasta and top with the remaining cheese.

You will love the unruliness of this hollow pasta. It fights the fork but picks up all the goodness of the sauce.

This recipe is one of the few that call for you to break the pasta before dropping it into the pot.

SWEET ROASTED BUTTERNUT SQUASH AND GREENS OVER BOW-TIE PASTA

Serves 4 to 6

10 minutes prep time; 35 minutes oven time

You could cook this dish ahead through Step 6 and then bake it in a shallow casserole, topping it with extra cheese in the last 5 minutes of baking

An autumn supper in a bowl, this is a "sauce" that you roast in the oven in about 30 minutes: chunks of sweet squash, roasted herbs, and greens. Add half-and-half, toss with hot pasta and cheese, and you have a great sell to the anti-vegetable contingent.

5 quarts **salted water** in a 6-quart pot

ROASTED VEGETABLES

3 to 3½ pounds **butternut squash**, peeled, seeded, and cut into bite-sized chunks (see Cook to Cook, page 170)

1 medium to large **onion**, cut into 1-inch chunks

2 big handfuls **escarole** or curly endive that has been washed, dried, and torn into small pieces, or spring mix

⅓ tight-packed cup fresh **basil leaves**, torn

16 large fresh **sage leaves**, torn

5 large **garlic cloves**, coarse chopped

⅓ cup good-tasting **extra-virgin olive oil**

¼ teaspoon **red pepper flakes**

1 tight-packed tablespoon **brown sugar** (light or dark)

Salt and fresh-ground **black pepper**

PASTA AND FINISH

1 pound imported **bow-tie pasta**

½ cup **half-and-half**

1 to 1½ cups (about 6 ounces) shredded **Asiago cheese**

(recipe continues)

1. Slip one large or two smaller shallow sheet pans into the oven. Preheat the oven to 450°F. Bring the salted water to a boil.

2. In a big bowl, toss together all the ingredients for the roasted vegetables. Be generous with the salt and pepper.

3. Pull out the oven rack holding the sheet pan. Taking care not to burn yourself, turn the squash blend onto the hot sheet pan and spread it out. Bake for 25 minutes, or until the squash is tender, turning the vegetables two or three times during roasting.

4. As the squash becomes tender, drop the pasta into the boiling water and cook it until tender, but with some firmness to the bite. Drain in a colander.

5. Once the squash is tender, turn on the broiler to caramelize it. Watch the vegetables closely, turning the pieces often. Anticipate about 5 minutes under the broiler. You want crusty brown edges on the squash and wilted, almost crisp greens.

6. Scrape everything into a serving bowl. Add the half-and-half, hot pasta, and 1 cup of the cheese. Toss to blend, tasting for salt and pepper. Add more cheese if desired. Serve hot.

Variation
FENNEL GARLIC ROAST

Heat a shallow roasting pan in a 450°F oven as directed above. Instead of squash, use 2 fennel bulbs, cored and sliced thin, 2 large onions sliced thin, and 8 garlic cloves, crushed. Omit the greens, basil, sage, and brown sugar. Toss the vegetables with the oil in the recipe, the red pepper flakes, and 3 tablespoons whole fennel seeds, ½ teaspoon salt, and ½ teaspoon black pepper. Roast them for 15 minutes.

Stir in a drained 14-ounce can of whole tomatoes (crushed), and continue roasting until the fennel is tender and slightly browned. Eliminate the half-and-half. Instead, toss the vegetables with the cheese, and serve them over spaghetti, linguine, bucatini, ziti, penne, or fusilli.

The first thing to do when you walk into the kitchen is slip a big shallow sheet pan (or two smaller ones) into the oven and turn it to 450°F. Then prep the dish.

Peeling winter squash the easy way: **Tough skin and hard flesh make winter squash annoying to peel, but there is a relatively easy way to sidestep most of the work and the dangerous knife slips: With a chef's knife, halve the squash lengthwise. Flip it cut side down onto your cutting board and cut it crosswise into 1-inch-thick slices. Now it's easy to trim away the peel and seeds from each slice. Cut the crescents of squash into 1-inch chunks, and you are done.**

Eden in Iowa
SEED SAVERS EXCHANGE

We were recording in a vault—not filled with money, but filled with 24,000 seeds, one of the world's largest collections of genetic material. We'd come to northeastern Iowa to Seed Savers Heritage Farm, the country's largest nonprofit center for saving living biodiversity. They are in the business of growing out endangered heirloom food seeds from gardeners across the nation. It's a living museum and a seed bank that opens its orchards and gardens to the public.

Seed Savers creates an outstanding annual publication for its members. They call it their "Yearbook," and it is based on the model of an old-time gardeners' exchange. Instead of swapping your favorite tomato seeds over the back fence, you do it through this nonprofit organization. **They offer more than 12,000 rare and sometimes very wacky varieties of plants from amaranth to watermelon.** When gardeners are seeking the new and unusual, this is the place to go.

Members receive three publications a year, detailing the available offerings. This is an invaluable resource for those interested in preserving our gardening heritage. For those of us who may never touch a trowel, the yearbook reads like a storybook; for instance, check out Hannah's Good for Nothing Apple. For information on Seed Savers, go to www.seedsavers.org.

OVER-THE-HILL GREENS

Throwaways—the drooping lettuce, the wilted kale, the limp parsley—all present opportunities, provided you get to them before slime sets in.

- **Roast them** with vegetables as in the butternut squash pasta recipe (page 169), or with potatoes, carrots, cauliflower, and peppers. Use the greens as though they are herbs.
- **Flash-sauté greens** to top bruschetta, pasta, and baked potatoes.
- Create fritters by **wilting the greens** in hot water, squeezing them dry, and then mixing the chopped leaves with cheese, egg, and bread crumbs. Shape into small patties and pan-fry.
- **Freeze the greens** in a freezer bag with other vegetable and meat bits for homemade broth.

TWO BROCCOLIS WITH CAVATAPPI AND RAISIN–PINE NUT SAUCE

| Serves 4 as a main dish | 15 minutes prep time; 15 minutes stove time | The sauce can be made 1 hour before serving |

This is broccoli on broccoli. You take your typical head of everyday broccoli and marry it to its assertive Italian cousin, broccoli raab (a.k.a. broccoli rabe, *broccoli di rapa*, *cime di rapa*, or *rapini*).

This pasta is so practical; the broccolis and the pasta cook in the same pot. The vegetables are almost melting by the time the pasta is done. When the trio is tossed with the sauté of chiles, salami, pine nuts, and raisins, you have a pasta like few others.

8 quarts **salted water** in a 10-quart pot
1 to 1½ pounds **broccoli**
1 large bunch (1 to 1¼ pounds) **broccoli raab** (broccoli *di rapa, cime di rapa, rapini*)

THE SAUTÉ

Good-tasting **extra-virgin olive oil**
1 medium **red onion**, cut into ¼-inch dice
Salt and fresh-ground **black pepper** to taste
2 ounces **Genoa salami**, sliced ¼ inch thick and cut into ¾-inch dice
2 **jalapeños**, fine chopped (seeded if you want less heat)
4 large **garlic cloves**, fine chopped
1 heaping tablespoon **tomato paste**
1 cup **water**
⅓ cup **raisins**

1 pound imported **cavatappi**, rotini, or fusilli

⅓ cup **pine nuts**, toasted

1 to 1½ cups shredded **Stella Fontinella**, Asiago, or young sheep cheese

1. Bring the salted water to a boil.

2. Peel the broccoli stalks, and cut them into ¼-inch-thick diagonal slices. Quarter the florets. Trim the broccoli raab stems to within an inch of where the leaves begin. Pile up the stalks and slice them into ¼-inch pieces.

3. Generously film the bottom of a straight-sided 12-inch sauté pan with olive oil, and set it over high heat. Add the onion and generous sprinkles of salt and pepper. Sauté until the onion is golden brown, stirring often. Halfway through the sauté add the salami and jalapeños. Once the onions are browned, blend in the garlic and tomato paste. Cook for 1 minute.

4. Stir in ½ cup of the water and boil it down to nothing as you use a wooden spatula to scrape up everything from the bottom of the pan. Repeat with the remaining ½ cup water. Once it is boiled off, stir in the raisins and pull the pan off the heat. Cover and set aside.

5. Drop the pasta into the boiling water. Cook, stirring often, for 3 minutes. Stir in the two broccolis and boil until the pasta is just tender. Scoop ½ cup of the pasta water out of the pot and set it aside. Immediately drain the pasta and vegetables in a colander.

6. Reheat the onion sauté over medium-high heat. Blend in the reserved pasta water, and add the pasta and vegetables and the pine nuts. Toss over the heat for 1 to 2 minutes, or until the pasta is lightly coated with the moistened sauté. Taste the pasta for seasoning. Turn it into a serving bowl. Pass the cheese separately.

Buy leafy broccoli raab using the same standards as you do for broccoli: it should be bright green, the florets should be mostly unopened, and there should be no aroma of over-the-hill cabbage.

SUMMER ZUCCHINI PASTA

Serves 4 as a main dish | *10 minutes prep time; 10 minutes stove time* | *The pasta can be served hot or at room temperature*

Every single year for as long as I have known Sally, she has planted zucchini. She is typically a very sensible person, but somehow she is unable to remember in May exactly how many zucchini will appear in July.

This pasta is her retaliation. It's cooked in one pot, with mostly raw ingredients, and is perfect on a hot summer night or served at room temperature for a "pasta salad" that even the Italians would approve of.

5 quarts **salted water** in a 6-quart pot
1 pound small **zucchini** (about 4 or 5)
1 pound imported **penne**
4 tablespoons good-tasting **extra-virgin olive oil**
¼ teaspoon **red pepper flakes**, and more to taste
4 large **garlic cloves**, coarse chopped
2 cups **grape tomatoes**, halved; *or* 2 cups other fresh
   tomatoes, coarse chopped
1 to 1½ cups (6 ounces) **feta cheese**, crumbled
⅓ tight-packed cup fresh **basil leaves**, coarse chopped

1. Bring the salted water to a boil.
2. Trim off the ends of the zucchini. Cut the squash into sticks about the size of the penne.
3. Drop the pasta into the boiling water. In the last 3 minutes of boiling (check pasta package for timing), drop the zucchini into the pot. Boil, stirring often, until the penne are tender but still have a little bite. Scoop out 1 cup of the pasta water and reserve it. Immediately drain the pasta and zucchini in a colander.

4. Return the pasta pot to the heat, turning it down to low. Film the bottom of the pot with the olive oil. Add the red pepper flakes and garlic, and gently sauté just until the garlic is fragrant, 30 seconds to 1 minute.

5. Remove the pot from the heat, and add the drained pasta and zucchini, the tomatoes, feta, basil, and as much of the reserved pasta water as necessary to lightly coat the pasta. Toss gently, taste for seasoning, and serve.

While penne works nicely, there is nothing sacred about using that particular shape (see below).

Bridegrooms for Butterflies
Swapping Pasta Shapes

Rarely is the pasta called for in the recipe already in the cupboard. So what do you do? Follow your own good sense.

If hollow tubes of ziti (which translates as "bridegrooms") are called for, it means the saucing is substantial enough for a bold, bigger pasta, like farfalle ("butterfly" in Italian), or rigatoni, gemelli, fusilli, cavatappi, radiatori, cornetti, orecchiette, or even ridged penne. If angel hair (capellini, capelli d'angelo) is needed, thin spaghetti (spaghettini), tagliarini, or vermicelli could take over the job. To get out of the spaghetti rut, substitute linguine, bucatini, trenette, or bigoli.

Just remember: the chunkier and gutsier the sauce, the bigger and/or more convoluted the pasta can be; the more delicate and brothlike the saucing, the finer and lighter the pasta.

PASTA WITH CHOPPING-BOARD PISTACHIO PESTO

Serves 4 to 6 as a main dish | *10 minutes prep time; 10 minutes stove time* | *Equally good hot from the pot or at room temperature*

Pistachios, scallions, garlic, and fresh herbs: who would think this adds up to a pasta dish? This is actually a riff on an Umbrian home sauce. You do it all with your trusty knife and one pot. Call it green spaghetti, and the kids will be all over it. It's also good hangover food.

5 quarts **salted water** in a 6-quart pot

THE PESTO

¼ teaspoon **salt**

⅛ teaspoon fresh-ground **black pepper**, or to taste

2 large **garlic cloves**

1 tight-packed cup coarse-chopped fresh **chives** or scallion tops

4 tight-packed tablespoons fresh **basil leaves**

2 tablespoons fine-chopped **red onion**

⅓ cup shelled **salted pistachios** or almonds

2 tablespoons good-tasting **extra-virgin olive oil**

PASTA AND FINISH

1 pound imported **spaghetti** or linguine

1 tablespoon good-tasting **extra-virgin olive oil**

2 tablespoons fine-chopped **red onion**

1 cup (4 ounces) grated **Asiago** or Stella Fontinella cheese

1. Bring the salted water to a boil.

2. To make the pesto, pile the salt and pepper on a chopping board. Crush the garlic into it with the side of a large knife, and fine chop. Add the chives, basil, and onion, and continue chopping until the pieces are cut very fine. Add the nuts to the pile and continue cutting until they are coarse chopped. Directly on the board, blend in the oil. Taste for salt and pepper.

3. Drop the pasta into the boiling water and cook at a fierce boil, stirring often, until it is tender but still a little firm to the bite. Scoop out 1 cup of the pasta water and set it aside. Quickly drain the pasta.

4. Film the empty pasta pot with the 1 tablespoon olive oil. Place it over medium heat, and sauté the fine-chopped onion in it for 1 minute. Stir in the pesto. Warm it for only a few seconds over medium heat to let the flavors blossom—do not cook it. Stir in about ⅓ cup of the reserved pasta water to stretch the sauce. Immediately pull the pot off the heat.

5. Add the drained pasta to the pot, and toss with the pesto and the cheese, adding more pasta water if the mixture seems very dry. Taste again for seasoning, and serve.

(variation follows)

{ **COOK** *to* Cook }

This pasta proves a pet theory: chop ingredients together and not only do you save a lot of time, but their flavors also blend in a unique way.

MONDAY-NIGHT BALSAMIC SPAGHETTI

This pasta dinner is built on the same technique as pistachio pesto. Instead of onion cooked just before serving, garlic is mellowed by gentle cooking ahead of time. With this foundation you create a dish that is close to the pistachio pesto, but with a burst of sweet, tart, and savory from adding balsamic vinegar.

Film the bottom of a straight-sided 12-inch sauté pan with olive oil. Add 1/3 cup water to the pan and 12 large garlic cloves that have been coarse chopped, with a generous sprinkling of salt and fresh-ground black pepper.

Place the pan over medium heat and cover it. Cook for 5 minutes, or until the garlic is soft but not colored; add more water if needed. Set the pan aside while you boil the pasta as directed above. Just before draining the pasta, remove 2/3 cup pasta water from the pot.

As the pasta drains, add the reserved pasta water to the sauté pan, and simmer it down for a few seconds over medium-high heat.

Blend in 1 tight-packed cup mixed fresh herbs (basil, parsley, scallions, etc.) and 1 cup coarse-chopped grape tomatoes.

Add the cooked pasta, 1 cup fresh-grated Parmigiano-Reggiano cheese, and 6 tablespoons balsamic vinegar to the pan. Toss to blend thoroughly, and serve hot.

> With pasta, you turn a pile of ingredients into a fantastic dish in minutes.
>
> —*Jamie Oliver*

LYNNE'S RETRO GARLIC BREAD

Serves 4 to 8

5 minutes prep time; 15 minutes oven time

You can assemble the bread a day ahead; flip on the oven when you get home and bake it off. Leftovers rewarm well.

You never outgrow your love of garlic bread. In high school this recipe separated me from the home-ec Bisquick types. Garlic bread was a big deal then—it signaled your sophistication to your friends. Then it went into the closet. Garlic bread became "so '70s," and therefore nothing you would ever admit to eating. Well, I am here to tell you garlic bread is back. This is treat food, up there with hot biscuits saturated in butter, cupcakes with buttercream, and pan-crisped grilled cheese sandwiches—home food of the first order.

3 tablespoons good-tasting **extra-virgin olive oil**
3 tablespoons **unsalted butter**
¼ cup **water**
5 large **garlic cloves**, minced
1 generous teaspoon **dried basil**
1 generous teaspoon **dried oregano**
¼ teaspoon **salt**, or to taste
Fresh-ground **black pepper** to taste
1 large crusty **baguette** (whole-wheat preferred)
1 tight-packed cup (5 to 6 ounces) shredded **Asiago** *or*
   Parmigiano-Reggiano cheese

1. Preheat the oven to 400°F. In a small saucepan, combine all the ingredients except the bread and cheese, and set over medium-low heat. When the butter melts, cover the pan and cook for 10 minutes to soften the garlic. Take care not to brown it. Once the garlic is soft, uncover the pan and simmer until you hear the mixture sizzling. This is the cue that the water has cooked off. Pull the pan off the heat immediately.

2. Split the baguette in half horizontally. Divide the garlic blend between the two halves. Sprinkle each with half of the cheese. Set them on a foil-covered baking sheet, cheese side up, and bake for 15 minutes, or until the cheese is bubbly. Slice, and serve hot.

THE TRUE
FETTUCCINE ALFREDO

Serves 3 to 4 as a main dish; 6 to 8 as a first course

5 minutes prep time; 10 minutes stove time

It's best to make this pasta and eat it right away. A salad served afterward offers a nice balance.

Fettuccine Alfredo is splendidly lavish, absurdly simple, and utterly delicious. It has nothing to do with the gloppy mess sweeping sports bars, family buffets, pseudo-Italian restaurant chains, and online recipe collections.

Fettuccine Alfredo is a great way to understand the Italian way with pasta. Pasta recipes fall into two categories: a prepared sauce goes over the pasta or, as in Alfredo, the sauce is prepared with the pasta in the pan.

With Alfredo, the sauce is melted butter, cream, and Parmigiano-Reggiano cheese. That is it. (And some purists argue that the cream should be eliminated. This is how simple a pasta saucing can be.) You mix them all together with the ribbon-shaped fettuccine in a skillet until the noodles have absorbed the cream.

Interestingly, as pure Italian as this may seem, it isn't a dish of long tradition. Roman restaurateur Alfredo De Lelio created it in the 1920s. As the story goes, he first made the pasta for movie stars Mary Pickford and Douglas Fairbanks. It might even be true. One way or the other, this was Alfredo's dish, a theatrical version of the homey favorite of pasta merely tossed with cheese.

> 5 quarts **salted water** in a 6-quart pot
> 1 pound imported **fettuccine**
> 6 tablespoons **butter**
> 1 cup **heavy whipping cream**
> 1½ to 2 cups fresh-grated **Parmigiano-Reggiano cheese**
> **Salt** and fresh-ground **black pepper**

1. Bring the pot of salted water to a boil, drop in the pasta, and boil it, stirring often, for 7 minutes, or until the pasta is slightly under-cooked. Immediately drain it in a colander.

2. As soon as the pasta goes into the water, put the butter in a straight-sided 12-inch sauté pan and place it over medium heat. Melt the butter, taking care not to let it color. Set the pan aside until the pasta is done.

3. Once the pasta is draining, reheat the butter over medium-high heat. Turn the pasta and the cream into the sauté pan, and toss to thoroughly coat the noodles. Continue to toss the pasta for 2 to 3 minutes, so the cream can permeate the pasta. There should be very little cream in the bottom of the pan.

4. Finally toss in the cheese, starting with 1½ cups and adding more to taste. Toss for 20 seconds. Season the pasta to taste with salt and fresh-ground black pepper. Immediately turn it into a serving bowl and serve it hot.

Life is a combination of magic and pasta.

—Federico Fellini

21ST-CENTURY MAC 'N' CHEESE

Serves 4, and doubles easily | *8 to 10 minutes prep time; 30 minutes oven time* | *You could assemble the dish a day ahead to bake when you walk in the door*

Never underestimate the healing power of macaroni and cheese at the end of a day from hell. Make this as rich as you'd like by selecting milk, half-and-half, or heavy cream.

3 quarts **salted water** in a 4-quart pot
½ pound (2 cups) imported **elbow macaroni** or penne pasta
1 large **egg**
1 cup **milk**, half-and-half, or heavy cream
1 small **garlic clove**
¾ medium **onion**, coarse chopped
1 generous cup (5 ounces) shredded good-quality extra-sharp **cheddar cheese**
5 ounces **cream cheese**, crumbled
⅔ cup (3 ounces) shredded **Gruyère**, Appenzeller, or Manchego cheese
Generous ⅛ teaspoon **red pepper flakes**
Generous ⅛ teaspoon **salt**
Generous ⅛ teaspoon fresh-ground **black pepper**
Generous ¼ teaspoon **sweet paprika**, Hungarian or Spanish
3 tablespoons **unsalted butter**
12 **saltines**, coarse crumbled

1. Bring the salted water to a boil. Drop in the macaroni or penne. Boil, stirring often, until the pasta is tender but still with a little firmness. Drain in a colander.

2. Preheat the oven to 350°F. Butter a shallow 1½-quart baking dish, and add the cooked macaroni.

3. In a blender or food processor, combine the egg, milk, and garlic. Process for 3 seconds. Add the onion, cheeses, red pepper flakes, salt, black pepper, and paprika, and blend for 10 seconds, or until the onion is cut down to small pieces and the ingredients are blended. Turn the mixture into the dish, folding it into the macaroni. (The casserole could be covered with plastic wrap and refrigerated for up to 24 hours at this point.)

4. To bake, bring the casserole close to room temperature if it has been refrigerated. Melt the butter in a small saucepan, add the saltine crumbles, and coat them with the butter. Spread them over the top of the casserole. Bake for 20 to 25 minutes, or until thick yet creamy. If the top is not golden brown, slip the casserole under the broiler for a minute. Remove it from the oven, let it stand for 5 minutes, and serve.

Variation
16TH–CENTURY MAC 'N' CHEESE

Back in the days when pasta was the exclusive property of the rich and the royal, this dish was showing up on tables from London to Rome.

As in the recipe above, this can be made ahead. Use wide ribbons of pasta like tagliatelle or fettuccine. Eliminate all the other ingredients.

Butter the baking dish generously. Spread one-third of the cooked pasta in the dish, and pour about ⅓ cup heavy whipping cream over it. Dust it generously with ¼ teaspoon cinnamon, ¼ teaspoon fresh-ground black pepper, several strips of thin-sliced prosciutto, ¼ cup crushed salted almonds, and ¼ cup fresh-grated Parmigiano-Reggiano. Repeat the layers two more times, ending with the Parmigiano-Reggiano on the top.

Cover the dish with foil, and bake at 350°F for 20 minutes, or until bubbling. Uncover and bake for another 5 minutes.

{ **COOK** *to* Cook }

This streamlined version sidesteps the need to make the usual cream sauce base. A quick whir in the blender or processor gives you what you need. Egg and cheese stand in for the usual flour thickener. To my mind, thickening with flavorful ingredients brings more to the dish than using flavorless starch.

HOISIN CHINA NOODLES WITH FOUR FLAVORS

Serves 4 as a main dish | *15 minutes prep time; 10 minutes stove time* | *This dish is best cooked and served immediately*

A favorite dish from an old teacher, this is a Chinese pasta with meat sauce. It evolved from two of my favorite recipes by Chinese cookbook author Gloria Bley Miller.

There's a curious juxtaposition in Chinese food. Marrying flavors into a complex whole is a technique the Chinese do best, yet no other cuisine plays opposing textures with the precision that they do. You'll taste it all in this suave hoisin-scented pork with slippery noodles and crunchy water chestnuts, all finished with crisp raw vegetables.

Before there were cooking schools and Chinese food experts on television, there were the books. Through her writing, author Gloria Bley Miller was one of my first teachers. Her *Thousand Recipe Chinese Cookbook* was a classroom in itself. She stayed at my bedside for years.

BUILDING
THE **LIBRARY**

THE THOUSAND RECIPE
CHINESE COOKBOOK
BY GLORIA BLEY MILLER (GROSSET
AND DUNLAP, 1970)

THE FOUR FLAVORS

1½ cups thin-sliced **radishes**

1½ cups **bean sprouts**

1½ cups peeled, seeded, and diced **cucumbers**

1½ cups thin-sliced fresh **spinach leaves**

NOODLES

5 quarts **salted water** in a 6-quart pot

¾ pound narrow **Chinese egg noodles** or imported spaghetti

STIR-FRIED "SAUCE"

1 pound **ground pork butt**

3 tablespoons **dry sherry**

1 large **garlic clove**, minced

1 teaspoon **sugar**

2 tablespoons **soy sauce**

2 tablespoons **hoisin sauce**

½ teaspoon **hot chile paste** or hot chile powder (use more or less to taste)

3 tablespoons expeller-pressed **canola oil** or other neutral-tasting oil

Heaping ½ cup thin-sliced whole **scallions** (about 4)

½ cup sliced **water chestnuts**

¾ cup **Cheater's Homemade Chicken Broth** (page 48) or canned chicken broth

1. Place each of the "four flavors" in a separate small serving bowl.

2. Bring the salted water to a boil. Drop the noodles into the boiling water and boil, stirring often, until tender but still firm to the bite. Drain them in a colander and rinse thoroughly with cold water. Set aside.

3. In a medium bowl, use a fork to blend the pork with the sherry, garlic, and sugar. Let stand while prepping the rest of the dish.

4. In a small bowl, blend together the soy sauce, hoisin sauce, and chile paste.

5. Heat a wok or a large skillet over high heat. Swirl in the oil. When it is hot, add the pork and stir-fry for 3 minutes, breaking up any chunks. The meat is ready when it is no longer pink and most of its liquid has cooked off. Add the scallions and water chestnuts. Stir-fry for 45 seconds more.

6. Stir in the soy sauce mixture, and stir-fry for 1 minute. Add the broth and heat quickly. Then cook, stirring, for 2½ minutes over high heat.

7. Add the noodles and stir-fry for 1 minute to permeate the noodles with the sauce. Turn the noodles into a large bowl. Serve them immediately, with the bowls of the four flavors.

{ **COOK** *to* Cook }

The secret of success for every stir-fry is to have each ingredient prepped and ready to go before touching the wok, and to watch the timing carefully. (See The Rhythm of a Stir-Fry, page 249).

I favor the pork shoulder cut called butt for its excellent flavor and proper balance of fat to lean for Chinese dishes.

If you can find fresh water chestnuts, their special sweetness and juicy crispness will greatly enhance the dish. They will need peeling.

HOISIN-SCALLION FRIED RICE WITH EGG

Follow the recipe, substituting 3 cups cooked rice for the noodles. Eliminate the pork and its flavorings and the chicken broth. Make the sauce blend of soy sauce, hoisin sauce, and chile paste as directed in the recipe above.

Heat the wok and oil as directed above. Stir-fry the rice with the scallions and water chestnuts for 2 minutes. Add 2 beaten eggs, and continue stir-frying the rice until the eggs are in firm threads.

Add the soy sauce mixture and cook for another 30 seconds. Serve the rice accompanied by the four flavors.

The Sound of Chopsticks— Elizabeth Andoh

We know the Japanese revere the sight, the taste, the smell, the complete aesthetic of their food. But did you know that sound plays an equal role? When we interviewed Japanese food scholar Elizabeth Andoh, we were open-mouthed when she talked about the sound the chopsticks made on the side of a rough rice bowl rather than a smooth one. Yes, in Japan you would consider that, too, as you set the table for supper.

How to Buy a Wok
CAPTURING THE SPIRIT
of the Chinese Stir-Fry

What a beguiling thought: a pot that breathes with its own spirit. In a discussion on the show, Grace Young explained the Chinese term *wok hay. Hay* means *chi:* energy or breath. It is used to describe the pinnacle of stir-fry, a coveted taste and aroma that comes only from searing food in a very hot wok. The Cantonese are the consummate masters of *wok hay.* But it can be done at home. To begin, you need the right wok. **These are Grace's guidelines:**

Buying

- Cheap is good; a fine wok costs $20 to $25. You can pick up a sound wok in many Chinese groceries and equipment stores.

  The wok needs to be carbon steel or Chinese-made cast iron (which differs from American cast iron). These are prized because they heat up quickly and retain the heat. You will not achieve *wok hay,* nor an edible stir-fry, with nonstick, stainless-steel, aluminum, electric, or enameled woks.
- Big is good. Buy a 14- to 16-inch wok with a flat bottom. This allows more direct contact with the burners of our Western-style stoves. A long wooden handle makes maneuvering it easier.
- Woks need to be seasoned, or broken in. This is as easy as washing, heating, and cooking:

  1. Scrub away the wok's protective oil coating with hot soapy water and a scouring pad.
  2. Dry the wok over low heat. Use a wad of paper towel to wipe off any additional oil appearing on the surface.
  3. Season the wok with an oily stir-fry of ginger, garlic, scallions, and about ½ cup vegetable oil: Heat the wok over high heat, swirl in the oil to coat the entire interior of the wok, and stir-fry the aromatics. The wok will absorb the flavors as well as some oil. Pour out the oil and aromatics, and dry the wok with paper towels.
  4. From this point on, clean your wok with hot water, rubbing it with a coarse cloth. Don't use anything abrasive. Wash it with soapy water only occasionally. Dry the wok over low heat. In a short time the wok will be nonstick and black as night, exactly as it should be.

Cooking

- Live by the mantra "hot wok, cold oil." Always heat the empty wok first. When a drop of water evaporates on the wok's surface in 2 seconds, it is ready for cooking. This is the time to swirl in the oil.
- Make sure the vegetables and meat are bone-dry and are not overcrowded in the wok. For a 14-inch wok, you want to cook no more than 4 cups of vegetables at one time.
- Meats, fish, and poultry are often marinated or moistened in some way before cooking. This is why you want to stir-fry no more than 1 pound (about 2 cups) of them at a time. They need the space to crisp.

Main
DISHES

FEATURING

POULTRY

ROASTED CHICKEN BREASTS WITH PRESERVED LEMON

Flash Chicken Sauté with Cider and Almonds

JERRY TRAUNFELD'S TARRAGON CHICKEN BREASTS WITH BUTTERY LEEKS

Oven-Roasted Chicken Cacciatora

CHICKEN CURRY WITH GENTLE SPICES

Filipino-Style Chicken Adobo
(Chicken in Tart Garlic Sauce)

TOMATO-CHEDDAR-PACKED TURKEY BURGERS

Crisp Brick-Fried Chicken with Rosemary and
Whole Garlic Cloves

SEAFOOD

SALMON PAN ROAST WITH GARLIC SHAVINGS AND BASIL ON FRESH GREENS

Lemon-Garlic Roast Salmon on New Potatoes

FLASH-ROASTED TROUT ON GREEN HERBS

Plumped Ginger-Caramel Shrimp

NORTH SHORE SHRIMP SCAMPI

Santa Fe Summer Pot with Avocado and Shrimp

PAN-BROWNED SCALLOPS ON A BED OF BACON AND BRUSSELS SPROUTS

Vintage Bistro Mussels

MEATS

TAMARIND-GLAZED PORK CHOPS

Oven-Crisped Pork, Peppers, and Greens

PORK TENDERLOIN PAN ROAST WITH BLACK OLIVES AND ORANGE

Stir-Fry of Hoisin Lamb with Cashews and Snow Peas

LAMB CHOPS WITH CROSSOVER SPICE CRUST

Black Pepper-Honey Steak

SCANDINAVIAN SPICED MEATBALLS WITH CARAMELIZED APPLES

Ask your child what he wants for dinner only if he's buying.

—Fran Lebowitz

Some nights supper is a bowl of popcorn, a glass of wine, and the TV. Some nights you debate whether to cook or not to cook for

all kinds of reasons, not the least of which is guilt, be it about health, money, or feeding the kids yet another frozen pizza.

All the dishes in this chapter had to clear two hurdles. First, they all had to be made of basic cuts—chops, fillets, tenderloins, breasts, etc.—that are readily available at the market. Second, the recipes had to take a reinvigorated look at beloved traditions or offer unexpected variations on basic themes.

We're globalists at heart. We never tire of tracking down new tastes, especially from India and the entire Pacific Rim. And it should be clear by now that you will never pull us out of the Mediterranean. That said, we can't have spent all the years we have in Minnesota without developing genuine feelings for Scandinavian flavors.

We think of these recipes as centerpiece meals, perfect for real weeknight eating but also expansive enough for the special guest or a party.

Chickens
THE FREE, THE NATURAL,
and the Organic

In writing recipes I used to specify free-range chickens until I learned that by regulation, "free range" simply means the bird could see outside the henhouse and had to have access to the outdoors. "Free range" has nothing to do with what they are eating, nor does it guarantee that the birds run free in the fresh air.

It made me question the other labels on chickens in the market—"natural," "antibiotic and hormone free," and "certified organic." What did these really mean?

In talking with experts of every stripe, including distinguished nutrition authority Professor Marion Nestle, it became clear that only the label "certified organic" was regulatory, meaning by law it ensures the chicken ate a diet containing no animal by-products, no chemical pesticides or fertilizers, nor any genetically engineered feed. In addition, you can be certain an organic chicken has not met up with a hormone, or been confined indoors.

BUILDING
THE LIBRARY

WHAT TO EAT: AN AISLE-BY-AISLE GUIDE TO SAVVY FOOD CHOICES AND GOOD EATING
BY MARION NESTLE (NORTH POINT PRESS, 2006)

Poultry is for the cook what canvas is for the painter.

—*Jean Anthelme Brillat-Savarin*

ROASTED CHICKEN BREASTS WITH PRESERVED LEMON

Serves 6 to 8

10 minutes prep time; 45 minutes oven time

The chicken can be cooked 2 days ahead and reheats well

Once you've tasted good preserved lemons in a dish, they haunt you. You can't pin down if they are solely salty, purely lemon, only bitter, or deliciously oily. They do beautiful things to chicken. This recipe also borrows a seasoning mix from one of the lemons' home countries: Morocco.

You can find preserved lemons on grocery and specialty store shelves. Once opened, the lemons will keep for 6 months in the refrigerator if kept covered with fresh lemon juice.

Slow roasting keeps the chicken breasts moist. If you have the time, roast them for close to an hour at 300°F.

½ to ¾ **preserved lemon**, lightly rinsed
⅓ cup good-tasting **extra-virgin olive oil**
½ light-packed cup fresh **coriander** sprigs
2 large **garlic cloves**
1 generous teaspoon whole **cumin seeds**
6 large bone-in, skin-on **chicken breasts**
   (3 to 4 pounds; organic if possible)
Fresh-ground **black pepper**

1. Turn the oven to 450°F. In a food processor, finely chop together the lemon (start with ½ lemon), olive oil, coriander, garlic, and cumin. Taste for saltiness, adding the rest of the lemon if you'd like.

2. Cover a large, shallow roasting pan (a half-sheet pan is ideal) with a sheet of heavy-duty foil. Arrange the chicken breasts on the foil, and spread the lemon mixture over them. Grind a generous amount of pepper over the chicken, and put the pan in the oven. Turn the heat down to 325°F.

3. Roast the chicken for 45 minutes, basting it with its pan juices. When the chicken reaches 170°F on an instant-reading thermometer, it is done. If you'd like, brown the chicken under the broiler for 2 to 3 minutes per side.

4. Pile the chicken on a platter, and serve it hot or warm. A bundle of fresh coriander is a nice finish on the plate.

FLASH CHICKEN SAUTÉ WITH CIDER AND ALMONDS

Serves 4 | *5 minutes prep time; 15 minutes stove time* | *Serve immediately. Reheats well.*

The way America is eating chicken breasts, the day of the "Franken-chicken," one big breast staggering around on toothpick legs, cannot be far off.

Truth be told, chicken breast is often the most neutral of neutrals. It carries flavors with little contribution of its own. Some of us feel this is an opportunity, not a liability.

This recipe addresses the flavor issue head-on: sauté the breast fast, and let the pan juices do the heavy lifting. Boiling pan juices down with vinegar and garlic is an infallible flavoring technique. Gild the lily with almonds.

1½ cups **Cheater's Homemade Chicken Broth** (page 48)
    or canned chicken broth
Good-tasting **extra-virgin olive oil**
4 boneless, skinless **chicken breasts** (organic if possible)
Salt and fresh-ground **black pepper**
6 large **garlic cloves**, thin sliced
1 cup **cider vinegar**
2 teaspoons **unsalted butter**
2 tablespoons whole **salted almonds**, coarse chopped

   1. In a 10-inch sauté pan (preferably not nonstick), boil down the broth until it is reduced by about two-thirds. Pour it into a container and set it aside. Rinse and dry the pan.

   2. Lightly film the pan with oil. Heat it over high heat. Slip the chicken breasts into the pan, sprinkling them with salt and pepper. Lightly brown them on both sides. Lower the heat to medium low, and cook, uncovered, for 4 minutes per side, or until they are firm but not springy when pressed. Remove the chicken to a serving platter and keep it warm.

(recipe continues)

3. Make the pan sauce by adding the garlic and vinegar to the pan. Boil, scraping up the brown bits in the pan, until the vinegar is boiled down to ¼ cup. Stir in the reserved broth and boil for 2 minutes, or until the sauce is rich-tasting (it need not be thick). Adjust the salt and pepper. Stir in the butter until it's barely melted, and immediately pour the sauce over the chicken, topping it with the almonds.

Variation
LEAN CHICKEN PICCATA WITH YELLOW PEPPERS AND ONIONS

Follow the recipe to the point where the chicken is browned. As you turn the heat down to medium low, add 1 thin-sliced medium onion and 1 thin-sliced yellow bell pepper to the pan.

Replace the vinegar with 1 cup white wine, and finish the recipe as written. Instead of almonds, squeeze the juice of ½ lemon over the meat.

This recipe is a good place to audition different vinegars—nutlike Spanish sherry vinegar; inky, sweet, smoky Chinese black vinegar (look for "Chinkiang" or "Shanxi" on the label); the Philippines' brisk palm vinegar; England's mellow malt vinegar; and, of course, the ubiquitous balsamic.

COOKING WITH VINEGAR

I collect vinegars the way some people collect stamps. Salad dressings are only starters.

Just as you can boil down wine into those sautés at the beginning of so many pan sauces, soups, and stews, you can reduce a vinegar to create a layer of savoriness that can't be achieved any other way.

Curiously, as vinegar boils down, it loses its acid bite and actually sweetens. A few tablespoons will do the job, and each type of vinegar brings a different accent to the mix.

Peter Mayle
HOW TO BEHAVE
IN FRANCE

The French feel of the tarragon chicken recipe on page 200 brings to mind the man who may be the ultimate Francophile, Peter Mayle. We have had him on *The Splendid Table* an embarrassing number of times and will continue to do so. Peter's sideways insights into French life never fail to amuse.

When we asked Peter what advice he had for getting on well with the French, he said: **"It is very important to go some way toward trying to speak their language,** for two reasons. First, it indicates a certain courtesy to the host country, and secondly, it gives you an opportunity to make a fool of yourself, which the French love because then they get to correct you. You get the sex of the carrot wrong and they say, *'Ce n'est pas ça.'* Then they get to put you right on the gender of the carrot, and your relationship blossoms."

BUILDING THE LIBRARY

PETER MAYLE IS THE AUTHOR OF MANY BOOKS ON FRANCE, INCLUDING **FRENCH LESSONS: ADVENTURES WITH KNIFE, FORK, AND CORKSCREW** (KNOPF, 2002)

JERRY TRAUNFELD'S TARRAGON CHICKEN BREASTS WITH BUTTERY LEEKS

Serves 4

5 minutes prep time; 25 minutes stove time

Serve immediately or reheat gently

For chef Jerry Traunfeld, herbs are where you begin a dish, not merely what you add as a grace note. His recipes range from utterly simple to sophisticated—from herb-infused sugars to be used in baking, to mussels with mint pesto, to this dish bedding chicken in butter-braised leeks and tarragon.

Tarragon doesn't like to fight for attention; it sings out best when it stands alone or in the quiet company of delicate flavors. This recipe, which takes just 25 minutes to prepare, shows how to put tarragon's singular nature in the spotlight.

2 cups thin-sliced **leeks**, white and light green parts only (1 large or 2 small)

2 cups **Cheater's Homemade Chicken Broth** (page 48) or canned chicken broth

4 tablespoons **unsalted butter**

4 boneless, skinless **chicken breasts** (about 1½ pounds; organic if possible)

Kosher **salt** and fresh-ground **black pepper**

2 teaspoons fresh **lemon juice**

2 tablespoons coarse-chopped fresh **tarragon leaves**

1. Place the leeks in a large skillet with the chicken broth and 2 tablespoons of the butter. Cook at a gentle boil over medium heat until they are tender and the broth has boiled down far enough that the leeks are no longer completely submerged. This should take about 8 minutes.

2. Sprinkle both sides of the chicken breasts with salt and pepper. Place them on top of the simmering leeks, spoon some of the leeks over

the chicken, and cover the pan tightly. Reduce the heat to low. After 10 minutes, test the chicken for doneness: it should feel firm when you press it. If the breast pieces are large, it could take as much as 15 minutes, but don't overcook them.

3. When the chicken is done, transfer it to a warm platter. Increase the heat under the leeks to high, and stir in the lemon juice, the remaining 2 tablespoons butter, and the tarragon. When the butter melts, season to taste. Pour the leek sauce over the chicken, and serve.

Variations
HERBAL IMPROVISATIONS

Instead of the tarragon, stir in 2 tablespoons chopped fresh marjoram leaves or ½ cup chopped fresh dill or chervil.

Variations
LEEKS ON THEIR OWN

- For a leek side dish, prepare Jerry's recipe only through the first step, cooking the leeks with the broth and butter or olive oil until tender, and sprinkling them with fresh tarragon and coarse salt.
- For a leek and carrot side dish, prepare the same dish using half leeks and half thin-sliced carrots with some crushed garlic. Finish them with a squirt of fresh lemon juice but omit the tarragon.
- For a take on a classic vichyssoise, simmer the leeks with 1 diced medium potato, 1 sliced garlic clove, a sprig of fresh thyme, and a bay leaf in the chicken broth. Remove the bay leaf, then puree, strain, and finish the soup with cream. Serve it hot or chilled.

BUILDING THE LIBRARY

THE HERBFARM
COOKBOOK
BY JERRY TRAUNFELD
(SCRIBNER, 2000)

OVEN-ROASTED CHICKEN CACCIATORA

Serves 6, and doubles easily. If doubling, bake in two pans.

10 minutes prep time; 45 minutes oven time

This can be made 2 days ahead and reheats well

This Tuscan one-pan meal neatly sidesteps the traditional time-consuming stovetop browning with its usual mess. For big, unstoppable flavors roast the chicken pieces in a cloak of garlic and herbs along with tomato, peppers, and meaty black olives. These aromatics become the sauce.

2½ to 3 pounds bone-in, skin-on **chicken thighs** (8 thighs; organic if possible)

⅓ cup pitted **Kalamata olives**

4 thin slices **cacciatore** or Genoa or hard salami, cut into 1-inch squares

1 large **red bell pepper**, cut into 1-inch pieces

1 large fresh **tomato**, or 3 drained canned ones, coarse chopped

1 medium to large **red onion**, coarse chopped

Leaves from two 4-inch sprigs fresh **rosemary**

10 fresh **sage leaves**, torn

4 large **garlic cloves**, minced

1 teaspoon **fennel seeds**, lightly crushed

¼ cup **dry red wine**

¼ cup good-tasting **extra-virgin olive oil**

Salt and fresh-ground **black pepper**

Juice of 1 **lemon**

1. Turn the oven to 400°F. Arrange the chicken on a large, shallow roasting pan (a half-sheet pan is ideal), and scatter all the ingredients except the lemon juice over the chicken.

2. Roast the chicken for 30 minutes. Baste with the pan juices, turn the chicken pieces over, and continue roasting for another 10 to 15 minutes, basting and turning occasionally. When the chicken reaches 170°F on an instant-reading thermometer, it is done. If you'd like, brown the chicken under the broiler.

3. Turn the contents of the pan into a big bowl. Adjust the seasonings, and squeeze the lemon juice over it. Serve hot.

Variation

CUMIN-CINNAMON-SCENTED CHICKEN

Follow the recipe as written, spreading the chicken on the pan. Instead of the ingredients above, scatter 2 red onions, cut into wedges, 3 chopped garlic cloves, ½ teaspoon salt, 2 teaspoons ground cinnamon, 2 teaspoons ground cumin, 2 teaspoons Crossover Spice Blend (page 128), ¼ cup *each* olive oil and apple cider, and 3 tablespoons cider vinegar over the chicken. Roast as directed in the recipe.

Variation

LEMON-OREGANO CHICKEN ROASTED WITH ONION AND CARROT

Follow the recipe as written, spreading the chicken on the pan. Instead of the other ingredients, use 2 thin-sliced medium carrots, 1 coarse-chopped onion, 1 thin-sliced small lemon, and 4 crushed garlic cloves. Sprinkle everything generously with olive oil, lemon juice, fresh oregano, salt, and fresh-ground black pepper. Roast as directed in the recipe.

Feel free to pile up the herbs and vegetables and chop them together. This cuts the prep time by half.

Cacciatore, or "hunter's salami," are the size of sausages, taste winey and meaty, and originated in the Lombardy region of northern Italy. Some domestic brands to check out (for this and other salami) are Fra' Mani, Biellese, Salumi, Molinari, The Fatted Calf, and Oldani.

CHICKEN CURRY WITH GENTLE SPICES

| Serves 4 to 6 | 15 minutes prep time; 25 minutes stove time | The curry keeps for 4 days in the refrigerator and reheats well |

The term "curry" conjures images of sturdy sauces dense with spice, and some are just that. But they can also be light, fresh, and surprisingly gentle in their spicing.

For we of the Western world, yogurt plays a new role in this recipe. We don't think of simmering down yogurt into a sauté the way we'd reduce wine or stock, but it's an old technique in India. Yogurt calms and softens the nip of chile, black pepper, and spice.

Make the fresh curry paste in the food processor. There is no need to pre-brown the chicken. Serve it with Dumbed-Down Rice (page 297).

CURRY PASTE

1 large **onion**, cut in half

6 large **garlic cloves**

One 3-inch piece fresh peeled **ginger**

Generous ½ tablespoon **Crossover Spice Blend** (page 128), or a blend of ground coriander, ground cumin, and fresh-ground black pepper

½ teaspoon **salt**

½ teaspoon **ground cinnamon**

2 medium-sized ripe **tomatoes**; *or* 3 or 4 canned tomatoes

1 or 2 **jalapeños**, stemmed and seeded (or not, if you like it hot)

½ cup **water**

CHICKEN

Cold-pressed **vegetable oil**

2 cups organic **plain whole-milk yogurt**

(recipe continues)

2 pounds boneless, skinless **chicken thighs** (organic if possible), cut into bite-sized pieces

⅓ cup **water**

Salt and fresh-ground **black pepper**

2 tight-packed tablespoons fresh **coriander leaves**, chopped

1. In a food processor, combine one of the onion halves with the garlic, ginger, spice blend, salt, cinnamon, tomatoes, jalapeño, and the ½ cup water. Puree, and set aside.

2. Thin-slice the remaining onion half. Film the bottom of a straight-sided 12-inch sauté pan with the oil, and heat it over medium-high heat. Add the sliced onion, and sauté until it begins to color. Add the curry paste, reduce the heat to medium, and sauté for 10 minutes, stirring often with a wooden spatula, until the oil separates from the curry. Don't rush this step. Thoroughly sautéing the curry paste sets up the foundation of the dish.

3. Blend ⅔ cup of the yogurt into the curry sauce and simmer, stirring and scraping up the curry paste from the bottom of the pan, until the yogurt thickens and then nearly cooks away, 8 to 10 minutes.

4. Stir in the chicken, and add the remaining yogurt and the ⅓ cup water. Bring the mixture to a slow simmer. Cook, uncovered, for 8 minutes, or until the chicken is cooked through and tender.

5. Lift the chicken out of the pan with a slotted spoon, and place it in a serving bowl. Raise the heat until the sauce is boiling. Boil it down until once again it is so thick that the oil separates from the curry paste. Taste the sauce for seasoning, and pour it over the chicken. Sprinkle the curry with the fresh coriander.

{ **COOK** *to* **Cook** }

Whole-milk yogurt is essential here. There are three dependable organic brands I look for: Brown Cow, Seven Stars, and Stonyfield Farm.

Also essential to the curry are Steps 2 and 3 in the recipe: sautéing the curry paste until the sauce "breaks" (the oil separates out from the rest of the sauce) and reducing the first addition of yogurt. Please follow the instructions to the letter; in these two steps lies the success of the curry.

THE LUNCHMEN OF
Mumbai

A tiffinwallah is the lunch delivery man of Mumbai. This service in India isn't like our office sandwich shop delivery. It is far closer to a combination relay race and post office.

The service developed 125 years ago when workers from different regions came to then Bombay. It flourishes today for two reasons. First, Mumbai trains are so crowded during commutes that there is literally no room for workers to carry even a lunch pail. Second, homemade food holds a place of prime importance in Indian life, especially in Mumbai, with its ethnic and religious diversity. If you are an orthodox Hindu, you must eat food cooked by your own caste. If you are a Muslim, you have to avoid pork, and then there are the general concerns of hygiene. **So how do Indians eat a homemade lunch if they can't carry it with them?** Enter the tiffinwallah.

This service is for the average worker, not for the affluent. It costs about $7 a month. But the workings of the tiffinwallah system are the best part of the story.

In the morning your tiffinwallah shows up at your house to pick up your tiffin (lunch pail), which is filled with your homemade lunch. On his bicycle, he sails through the neighborhood collecting tiffins, then peddles fiercely to the train station, where the tiffins are sorted on a sidewalk and loaded onto a train headed to the center of Mumbai.

As the trains continue to roll, more tiffins come aboard. At their destination, the tiffinwallahs unload, re-sort, and load more bicycles. They then careen through Mumbai traffic, bearing each client's lunch to his office door. When lunch is over, the empty tiffin is placed outside the door and the tiffinwallah does everything in reverse.

According to Margo True, former editor of *Saveur* magazine, who told us this story, India's tiffinwallah system sometimes surpasses the Six Sigma efficiency standard for corporations, making 3.4 mistakes per 1 million tasks. A CEO's dream.

FILIPINO-STYLE CHICKEN ADOBO (CHICKEN IN TART GARLIC SAUCE)

Serves 4 to 6

10 minutes prep time; 24 hours marinating time; 35 minutes stove time

Adobo is outstanding the day after it is cooked

I loved this dish the first time I tasted it, years ago. With its simmer sauce of vinegar, garlic, and soy sauce, adobo is the hallmark dish of the Philippines. It came back into my life while we were taping a show in Honolulu. The Maunakea Marketplace in Honolulu's Chinatown has a food court of Filipino cooks cooking for Filipino shoppers. There I had my first adobo in decades, and I was hooked all over again.

The marinade makes the recipe. You marinate the chicken overnight, turn everything into a pot, and simmer it. The cooking technique that sets Filipino adobo apart is that you brown the meat after it is cooked, not before. That aroma of a browning marinade-saturated chicken can drive you mad.

¼ cup **soy sauce**

10 large **garlic cloves**, coarse chopped

1 tablespoon fresh-ground **black pepper**

1¼ cups **Filipino palm vinegar**, cider vinegar, or white distilled vinegar

1 cup whole canned **tomatoes** with their liquid

2 **bay leaves**, broken

3 pounds bone-in, skin-on **chicken thighs** (about 8; organic if possible)

Good-tasting **extra-virgin olive oil**

2 medium **onions**, thin sliced

2 whole **scallions**, thin sliced (optional)

1. The day before you will be cooking the chicken, take a large glass or stainless-steel bowl and combine in it the soy sauce, garlic, black pepper, vinegar, tomatoes (break them up with your hands as you add them to the bowl), and bay leaves. Add the chicken, making sure it is almost completely submerged in the marinade. Lightly cover and refrigerate for 18 to 24 hours.

2. When you are ready to cook the chicken, turn the mixture into a heavy 4-quart pot. Bring it to a gentle bubble, cover, and cook for 25 minutes, or until the center of a chicken thigh registers 175°F on an instant-reading thermometer.

3. With tongs, remove the chicken to a plate. Skim as much fat as possible from the cooking liquid, increase the heat, and start briskly boiling it. You want to reduce it by half.

4. While the liquid reduces, film a straight-sided 12-inch sauté pan with the olive oil. Heat it over medium-high heat. Arrange the chicken pieces, skin down, in the pan and let them brown (stand back because they will spatter). Adjust the heat so the chicken doesn't burn.

5. When the chicken pieces are a deep, rich brown on one side, turn them over and scatter the onions around them. Continue browning the chicken, moving the onions around so they don't burn. Then, with a slotted spoon, transfer the chicken and onions to a serving bowl. Pour the boiled-down pan juices over them, and serve. Garnish the adobo with the scallions if you like.

COOK *to* Cook

You can find palm vinegar from the Philippines in some Asian markets. It is made throughout the Pacific Rim from the sap of palm trees and tastes particularly tart and brisk. Cider or white vinegar is a good substitute.

TOMATO-CHEDDAR-PACKED TURKEY BURGERS

Makes 4 generous burgers; multiplies easily

15 minutes prep time; 15 minutes stove time

You could assemble the burgers a day ahead and chill them until ready to cook

These are the burgers from Bountiful. Gloriously juicy, messy, and satisfying, they could put the beef burger out of business. The great trick is blending browned onions and garlic into the meat. The duo makes that lean turkey lush and juicy.

4 tablespoons good-tasting **extra-virgin olive oil**

1 large **onion**, fine chopped

1 cup **grape tomatoes**, halved; *or* 1 large ripe tomato, diced

Salt and fresh-ground **black pepper**

2 large **garlic cloves**, fine chopped

1 pound **ground turkey** (organic, and half light and half dark meat if possible)

¼ cup **dry white or red wine**

2 to 3 ounces extra-sharp **cheddar cheese**, cut into ¼- to ½-inch cubes

4 large **hamburger buns**

1. Heat 2 tablespoons of the oil in a 12-inch nonstick skillet over high heat. Add the onions and tomatoes with generous sprinkles of salt and pepper. Sauté over high heat, stirring frequently, until the onions begin to brown, about 3 minutes. Add the garlic and sauté for 1 more minute. Remove the skillet from the heat. Scoop half of the onion mixture into a large bowl and the rest into a small one. Rinse the skillet and dry it.

2. Add to the large bowl the ground turkey, ¼ teaspoon salt, ⅛ teaspoon pepper, and the wine. Blend well, and shape the mixture into 4 balls. Make a deep hole in each ball with your thumb, and insert one-fourth of the cheese into each hole. Pinch the holes closed, and flatten the balls into

¾- to 1-inch-thick patties with no sign of cheese on the outside. The patties will be very soft and sticky.

3. Heat the remaining 2 tablespoons olive oil in the same skillet over medium-high heat. Sear the burgers for about 30 seconds on each side, until they are browned. Turn them carefully with a pancake spatula, as they are quite fragile.

4. Lower the heat to medium low and cook the burgers for about 5 minutes per side, or until there is no pink at the center and an instant-reading thermometer measures at least 150°F. Serve them hot on the buns, topping each one with some of the reserved onions and your favorite condiments.

This is where a nonstick pan shines. Tender and fragile, the raw burgers need the slip of nonstick for easy handling.

Variation
KEFTA KEBABS WITH POMEGRANATE SYRUP

Prepare the recipe as written, eliminating the cheese. When you season the turkey in Step 2, add 2 tablespoons chopped fresh parsley and 1 teaspoon Crossover Spice Blend (page 128). Shape the meat into small balls (you could also cook them on skewers), and pan-fry them until cooked through. Turn them onto a serving platter, and drizzle with pomegranate molasses or syrup (find this sweet-tart concentrate of pomegranate juice in Mediterranean shops and some supermarkets). Scatter chopped scallions over the kebabs.

You can find your way across this country using burger joints the way navigators use stars.

—*Charles Kuralt, journalist and creator of the* On the Road *TV news series*

CRISP BRICK-FRIED CHICKEN WITH ROSEMARY AND WHOLE GARLIC CLOVES

Serves 3 or 4 | *10 minutes prep time; 30 minutes stove time* | *Serve and enjoy immediately*

Author and regular contributor Sally Schneider is a crack cook with an easy way in the kitchen. She sees classic dishes through modern eyes, preserving the recipe's essentials but streamlining it for today's cooks.

This recipe is an example. Sally could see a fast weeknight meal in this traditional Italian technique of cooking a whole chicken under a brick. You need only a large skillet and some weights.

As Sally says, "The result is succulent chicken—both white meat and dark—with a delectable crisp skin, and with much more flavor than the ubiquitous boneless breast; loss of bones always means loss of flavor."

The dish takes about 10 minutes of actual work and about 30 minutes unattended cooking time, during which time, Sally says, "You can have a cocktail and put the rest of your meal together, as your home fills with a lovely fragrance."

BUILDING THE LIBRARY

THE IMPROVISATIONAL COOK
BY SALLY SCHNEIDER
(MORROW, 2006)

One 3-pound **chicken** (organic if possible), rinsed, dried, and butterflied

1 tablespoon **kosher salt**

Fresh-ground **black pepper**

4 large sprigs fresh **rosemary** or thyme

1 tablespoon **extra-virgin olive oil**

8 **garlic cloves**, unpeeled, lightly smashed

1. Tuck the bird's wings back and under themselves so that they lie flat against the breast. Sprinkle both sides of the chicken with the kosher salt and pepper. Rub, and then press, the rosemary into both sides so it remains in contact with the meat.

2. Heat the olive oil in a large nonstick skillet over medium heat. Put the chicken in the skillet, skin side up. Place one or two foil-wrapped bricks on top of the chicken; or use a heavy skillet, about 2 inches smaller in diameter than the skillet you are cooking in. (If you don't have a heavy enough pan—4 to 5 pounds—use another smooth-bottomed item, such as a saucepan. Balance it on the bird and add heavy objects to weight the pan down, such as a can or two, or a 5-pound bag of sugar, or a rock.)

3. Cook the chicken for 10 minutes, or until the underside is brown. Remove the weights, and with tongs, turn the chicken over; replace the weights. Nestle the garlic cloves around the bird, and continue cooking until the skin is crisp and brown, about 12 minutes. The bird is done when an instant-reading thermometer reads 170°F in the thigh. Transfer the chicken to a cutting board and let it rest for 5 minutes. If desired, pour the pan juices over the bird when serving.

THE ART OF THE BUTTERFLY

Butterflying is a simple task that speeds up and tidies up cooking a chicken. With a whole chicken resting solidly on a cutting board, breast side down, cut along both sides of the backbone with sharp scissors. Flip the bird skin side up, flatten it out, and press down on the breast to crack the bone. You just butterflied a bird.

Butterflying boneless cuts like thick chicken breasts and chops is even easier. You can cut cooking times in half by slicing a long deep cut and opening the meat up like a book. Flatten and sauté.

Seafood
THE WATCHDOGS

Should we eat Chilean sea bass or not? What about farmed salmon or wild swordfish? Conflicting information about what we should and should not be eating seems to come in waves, and much of it is confounding. Nowhere is it more baffling than in the world of fish and shellfish.

When you are confused about what is good for the environment, what is endangered, and whether your choice should be farmed or wild, the Seafood Watch program at the Monterey Bay Aquarium (www.seafoodwatch.org) is an invaluable resource. Their website provides printable pocket-sized guides that break down fish choices by geographic regions. EACH GUIDE HAS THREE LISTS: "Best Choices," "Good Alternatives," and "Avoid." They fold to the size of a credit card to slip into a wallet.

For answers about which fish have issues of contamination, one sound resource is Environmental Defense (www.environmentaldefense.org). Although they have not researched everything that swims, their list includes much of what is in the market, is comprehensive and constantly updated.

"Carpe diem" does not mean "fish of the day."

—Anonymous

SALMON PAN ROAST WITH GARLIC SHAVINGS AND BASIL ON FRESH GREENS

Serves 4 | *5 minutes prep time; 10 minutes stove time* | *Cook and serve immediately*

Good old salmon in a white wine sauce gets a major makeover when shaved garlic and torn fresh basil go into the pan. Skip making a side dish by bedding the salmon on a pile of greens and sugar snaps. The garlic-basil pan sauce doubles as a salad dressing. Use this trick with anything from meat to vegetables to tempeh.

GREENS

One 5-ounce bag (or 4 handfuls) fresh **spring greens**
　　or mesclun mix
¼ pound (or a handful) fresh **sugar snap peas**, coarse chopped
12 fresh **basil** leaves, torn into large pieces

SALMON ROAST

4 small wild **salmon steaks**, cut 1 inch thick (or fillets),
　　or other firm-fleshed fish
Good-tasting **extra-virgin olive oil**
¼ teaspoon **salt**
⅛ teaspoon fresh-ground **black pepper**
3 large **garlic cloves**, sliced paper-thin
12 fresh **basil leaves**, torn into large pieces
⅔ cup **dry white wine**
Lemon wedges

1. Divide the greens among four dinner plates. Scatter the sugar snap peas and the 12 torn basil leaves over them.

2. Rinse the salmon and pat it dry. Examine the fish for any tiny bones and remove them.

(recipe continues)

3. Lightly film a slant-sided 12-inch skillet with the oil, and heat it over medium-high heat. Season the salmon steaks on both sides with the salt and pepper. Slip them into the skillet, and sear for 1 minute. Turn the fish with a metal spatula, taking care not to break it, and sear for 1 minute on the other side.

4. Sprinkle the garlic and the basil leaves around the fish. Turn the heat to medium low, cover the skillet, and cook for 6 to 7 minutes, turning the steaks midway through cooking, or until the salmon is just firm when pressed. The flesh should be barely opaque near the center.

5. Remove the fish from the skillet and keep it warm. Add the wine to the skillet, turn the heat to high, and stir, scraping up any brown bits from the bottom. Simmer until the pan juices are sizzling and syrupy.

6. Drizzle the hot sauce over the greens and top them with the salmon. At the table, squeeze the lemon over the fish and greens.

Variation
THAI SEAFOOD SAUTÉ

Follow the recipe above, eliminating the greens, snap peas, and basil. Sear your fish of choice in the oil, then remove it from the pan. Stir in the thin-sliced garlic and 1 minced jalapeño. Sauté for 1 minute, then blend in a teaspoon of jarred Thai curry paste (red will be the hottest, while green is usually the mildest—but be warned, all Thai curry pastes are hot).

Swirl in a small can (about 6 ounces, or ¾ cup) of coconut milk. Boil until the sauce is smooth and rich-tasting.

Add a few handfuls of shredded napa cabbage and 2 tight-packed tablespoons of fresh coriander leaves. Boil for 30 seconds.

Slip the fish back into the pan. Simmer it gently over medium-low heat until it is just firm when pressed. The sauté is good on its own or over rice noodles.

{ **COOK** *to* Cook }

The steak cut is easier to handle than the fillet, but if a fillet is the only option, heat extra oil in the pan and slip in the fillet, skin side down. Cook until the skin is crisp, and then loosen the fillet with a metal spatula and turn it to finish cooking on the other side.

Finned Perfection from

Chef Thomas Keller

A legendary perfectionist, chef Thomas Keller believes that fish should be stored in the kitchen the way they swim in the water. **Flatfish should be stored flat,** the way they move around in the ocean, and an oval-shaped fish should be stored upright, with the belly down. As Keller explained on the show, "I store them that way not only out of respect, but for the logical reason that storing them in an unnatural posture will stress out the flesh." We think there is dignity in the detail.

LEMON-GARLIC ROAST SALMON ON NEW POTATOES

Serves 4 generously, and multiplies easily | *10 minutes prep time; 20 minutes for marinating; 10 minutes oven time* | *The dish is best eaten hot out of the oven*

Lemon, garlic, and olive oil roasted into seafood and new potatoes. Could there be any question that this dish will be a winner? It's the old story of why certain combos show up over and over, and why we never tire of them: what grows together goes together. That trio trumpets the Mediterranean. You roast and serve the salmon from the same dish, and some have been known to eat directly from it, too.

POTATOES

10 to 12 small **red-skin potatoes**, unpeeled
3 quarts boiling **salted water** in a 4-quart pot

MARINADE

½ cup good-tasting **extra-virgin olive oil**
5 large **garlic cloves**
Juice of 1 large **lemon**
Salt and fresh-ground **black pepper**

THE FISH

Four 1-inch-thick **salmon steaks** (wild if possible),
    Pacific cod, or halibut
2 generous teaspoons **capers**, drained and rinsed
Leaves from 2 or 3 sprigs fresh **parsley**

1. Slip the potatoes into the boiling water and simmer for 15 minutes, or until they are still slightly firm when they are pierced with a knife. Drain them in a colander and rinse under cold running water to stop the cooking.

2. While the potatoes are cooking, heat the oven to 400°F. In a food processor, combine the olive oil, garlic, lemon juice, and salt and pepper; puree. Place the salmon steaks in a shallow bowl. Pour the marinade mixture over them, and refrigerate for 20 to 30 minutes.

3. Peel and thin-slice the potatoes. In a shallow baking dish that can hold the salmon steaks with some room to spare, overlap the potato slices to cover the bottom of the dish. Moisten the potatoes with a little of the marinade, and sprinkle with half of the capers. Top the potatoes with the salmon steaks, the rest of the marinade, and the remaining capers.

4. Roast the salmon in the oven for 8 to 10 minutes, or until the fish is just firm when pressed. The flesh should be barely opaque near the center; make a small cut to check. If the fish is cold when it goes into the oven, it could take longer to cook. Serve the salmon and potatoes in their baking dish, sprinkled with the parsley leaves.

Variation
CHUTNEY ROAST FISH

Make the marinade as in the recipe, but cut the olive oil to ¼ cup. After pureeing it with the lemon juice, garlic, and salt and pepper, stir in ¼ to ⅓ cup fruit chutney. Finish the recipe as directed, omitting the capers.

FLASH-ROASTED TROUT ON GREEN HERBS

| *Serves 4* | *5 minutes prep time; 10 minutes oven time* | *Roast and eat immediately* |

Roasting trout on a tangle of fresh herbs makes the kitchen smell like a wild hillside in Provence. The herbs do all the work in this recipe. They scent the fish and make a great rustic-looking presentation at the table. Carry this idea over to roasting anything—from chicken breasts on herbs and orange slices, to eggplant on parsley, tarragon, and shallots.

Good-tasting **extra-virgin olive oil**

6 or 7 sprigs *each* of **fresh herbs** similar to *herbes de Provence* (thyme, parsley, oregano, lavender, basil, sage, and only 2 sprigs rosemary), a total of about 38 sprigs

4 whole **scallions**, coarse chopped

4 whole farmed **rainbow trout** (organic if possible), rinsed inside and out and patted dry

4 **garlic cloves**, crushed

Salt and fresh-ground **black pepper**

Juice of 1 **lemon**

1 large **lemon**, cut into 4 wedges

1. Preheat the oven to 450°F. Lightly oil a large shallow roasting pan (a half-sheet pan is ideal), and slip it onto the middle rack of the oven to preheat. As it heats, rinse the herbs and scallions, and dry them on paper towels.

2. Make three slashes in each side of the trout, not quite all the way through to the bone. Rub a liberal amount of olive oil on the outside of the fish and into the slashes, as well as into the cavity. Place one-fourth of the crushed garlic inside each trout. Salt and pepper the fish on both sides.

3. When ready to cook, scatter the herbs and scallions on the heated pan to create a nest for the fish (they protect the fish from sticking to the pan). Lay the fish on top of them, with ample room between. Roast for 8 to 12 minutes, or until the fish is nearly opaque or white to the bone. Immediately remove the pan from the oven.

4. With two metal spatulas, lift the trout, with their beds of herbs, onto a serving platter. Arrange some of the roasted herbs around them, then squeeze the lemon juice over them. Garnish the platter with the lemon wedges, and serve.

Variation
ROAST FISH WITH GINGER-TOMATO GLAZE

Use any fillet, steak, or whole fish for this recipe.

Follow the recipe as written, substituting for the herbs an equal amount of sprigs of fresh coriander, mint, and chives or scallions. Instead of the olive oil, puree together 1 inch of fresh ginger, the 4 garlic cloves, 4 grape tomatoes, 1 teaspoon *each* of honey and oil, and salt and pepper to taste. Rub the puree inside and outside the fish. Roast the trout as directed above.

Variation
ROAST FISH WITH PRESERVED LEMON AND GARLIC

Use any fillet, steak, or whole fish for this recipe.

Follow the recipe as written, substituting for the herbs a bed of sliced onion, fresh coriander, and sliced orange. In a food processor, puree together the olive oil and the garlic called for in the recipe, with one-fourth of a preserved lemon and ⅛ teaspoon fresh-ground black pepper. (Find preserved lemons at groceries and Middle Eastern shops.) Rub the puree inside and outside the fish. Roast the trout as directed above.

> Although prequalified by virtue of their brain size, trout have no politics.
>
> —*J. A. Kissane*

Flatfish
AND ROVING EYEBALLS

Flatfish like sole, fluke, flounder, and turbot swim on their sides, with both eyes on the top of their heads. But they begin life looking like every other fish, with roundish bodies and eyes on either side of their heads.

At some mysterious point in their growth, flatfish flip to one side and stay that way. Their bodies flatten out, and one of their eyeballs migrates to the other side, keeping things in balance.

Even odder is the fact that fish whose eyes migrate to the right side of their bodies can only swim straight or to the right, and fish with left-side eye migration can only turn left.

Fish and visitors stink in three days.

—Benjamin Franklin

IS IT FRESH?
Looking a Fish in the Eye

Looking a fish in the eye is the one foolproof way of determining its freshness. When the eyes are clear and rounded, the fish is in prime condition. Flat or clouded eyes reveal that it has been out of the water too long.

Be leery when you see counters stocked with beheaded whole fish. Your first thought should be, "What are they hiding?"

That said, most of us live in the world of fillets and steaks sold at supermarket counters. There are clues there as well. **Avoid the following:**

- Liquid in the package.
- Splits in the fillet or steak.
- Dry-looking cuts.
- Bruising and discolorations.
- Smelly fish.

- Soft fish. Fresh fish is firm and resilient. With your finger, gently press the fish through the plastic wrapping. If the indentation springs back, it is fresh. If the depression remains, save your money.

STORING At home, keep fresh fish in ice—that is, on a bed of ice and covered in ice. A shallow plastic storage container works best for this. Use fresh fish within 24 hours of buying it.

HOW TO COOK FISH

With fish, timing is everything. Overcooked tastes awful, and undercooked is a hard sell for most people.

For quick results, no matter how you cook your fish, calculate your timing at 8 minutes per inch of thickness of the fish.

This method is the safest way to begin. It makes up for variables like how cold the fish is when it goes into the oven, the temperature you're cooking at, inconsistent oven temperature, etc.

Test for doneness by pressing the fish gently. Properly done fish is almost firm. When you think you are close, make a small slit to see the piece's center. You want no sign of raw fish. The flesh should be opaque, but it should not flake. Flaking fish is overcooked fish.

If you have any doubt, it is better to slightly undercook the fish and then let it stand for 10 minutes before serving. It will continue cooking and will be perfectly done.

PLUMPED GINGER-CARAMEL SHRIMP

Serves 4 generously | *20 minutes prep time; 5 minutes stove time* | *Cook and eat immediately*

If there is one recipe in this book that is guaranteed to have your family moaning with gratitude, this is it. After eating these shrimp, a five-year-old has been known to say, "Wow, Mom, thanks!" And they've driven a grown woman to shamelessly lick her plate— in front of everyone. Our only caution is follow the directions to the letter. There is a fine line between caramelization and cremation.

BRINE

- ½ cup **kosher or sea salt** (not iodized)
- ⅓ cup **sugar**
- ⅓ cup medium-hot **chile powder**
- 2 quarts **warm water**
- 1½ pounds large **frozen shrimp** (in or out of their shells; organic if possible)

SAUTÉ

- 4 large **garlic cloves**
- One 4-inch piece fresh peeled **ginger**
- 4 tablespoons expeller-pressed or cold-pressed **canola oil** or other mild oil
- ¼ to ½ teaspoon fresh-ground **black pepper**
- **Salt**
- 4 teaspoons **sugar**

1. In a medium stainless or glass bowl, blend the salt, sugar, and chile powder in the warm water. Drop in the shrimp, and let stand at room temperature for 20 minutes while you set up the rest of the meal.

(recipe continues)

2. Drain the shrimp, peel off their shells if necessary, and pat the shrimp dry.

3. Chop the garlic and ginger together into ⅛-inch pieces. Heat the oil in a straight-sided 12-inch sauté pan over medium-high heat. Stir in the garlic-ginger mixture, the pepper, and a sprinkle of salt. Cook for 1 minute, stirring with a wooden spatula. Blend in the sugar and keep stirring until the garlic is pale gold. Do not let the pieces get dark brown.

4. Immediately drop in the shrimp and stir for another 1 to 2 minutes, or until the shrimp are turning pink and are barely firm. Turn the shrimp into a serving bowl. Taste them for seasoning, adjust as necessary, and serve hot or warm.

Variation
SHRIMP STIR-FRY WITH CHICKPEAS AND GREENS

Follow the instructions for brining, peeling, and drying the shrimp as directed above.

Substitute for the garlic and ginger: 1 medium onion, 2 yellow bell peppers, 2 seeded jalapeño or serrano chiles, and ⅓ cup pitted Kalamata olives. Chop together into ¼-inch pieces.

Using 4 tablespoons extra-virgin olive oil instead of the canola oil, stir-fry the shrimp. When just firm, spoon them from the pan to a large serving bowl.

Swirl a little more olive oil into the pan, add a can of rinsed and drained chickpeas, the chopped onion mixture, and a couple handfuls of salad greens. Stir-fry over high heat for 1 to 2 minutes, seasoning the vegetables to taste as you cook.

Once they are tender-crisp, add the vegetables to the shrimp and serve. This is excellent over No-Cook Whole-Wheat Couscous (page 296) or tossed with pasta.

COOK to Cook

Frozen shrimp are called for as a convenience. Certainly you could use fresh or thawed. If you do, use ice-cold water instead of warm and marinate the shrimp in the refrigerator.

One-third cup of chile powder is not an error. In a brine you need this much to end up with a subtle boost of flavors. Try it once, then tell us we are crazy.

Brining:
UPPING THE FLAVOR
Quotient

Consider brining "do-it-yourself" culinary home improvement: It makes fish juicier and plumps up lean or tough meats and poultry. And because brining is about salt, it improves flavor. **To brine, cover the food with salted (and flavored, if you'd like) cold water and refrigerate.** Take care not to overdo. Brining too long gives you oversalted, spongy meats that taste pickled. Where most recipes have us time our brining by the weight of the meats, the fact is you want to brine by the meat's thickness; this way you cannot overmarinate. **Here is a guide:**

The Essentials

- Use kosher or sea salt. Iodized salt leaves a hot or bitter aftertaste.
- Be sure the liquid is ice-cold when the food goes into it.
- Always brine in the refrigerator.
- When seasoning a brine, overdo it. For instance, for 2 quarts of brine you would want $1/3$ cup hot chile powder, or 20 crushed garlic cloves, or 2 cups fresh basil. We're not kidding; you need quantities like these to have any distinctive flavor permeate the meat.

The Timing

- Meats and poultry that are close to an inch thick, like pork chops or chicken breasts, can brine for 45 minutes to 4 hours.
- Whole chickens and Cornish hens need 4 to 8 hours, depending on size.
- Turkeys weighing from 12 to 20 pounds need 2 days.
- Roasts demand $1\frac{1}{2}$ to 2 hours per inch of thickness.
- Fish and seafood are the exceptions to these rules. Their structures are delicate, so brine small pieces like shrimp, fillets, and steaks no longer than 30 minutes. Large whole fish or 3- to 4-inch-thick cuts could take an hour.

NORTH SHORE SHRIMP SCAMPI

Serves 3 to 4, and doubles easily | *10 minutes prep time; 24 hours marinating time; 4 minutes stove time* | *Eat immediately*

After years of hounding everyone about doing a show on America's most overlooked food town, *The Splendid Table* crew finally got to Honolulu. I didn't oversell: they were blown away.

On our way to surfer's nirvana, the north shore of Oahu, we stopped for lunch at Giovanni's Shrimp Truck for an island favorite: the most garlicky, luscious shrimp scampi we'd ever eaten. This is my divination of the recipe. The shrimp truck serves it in true Hawaiian plate-lunch style, with two scoops of rice. Dumbed-Down Rice (page 297) makes that easy.

For the big flavors that make this scampi so good, you have to marinate the shrimp overnight.

MARINADE

⅓ cup good-tasting **extra-virgin olive oil**
1 tablespoon fresh **lemon juice**
6 or 7 large **garlic cloves**, minced
¼ teaspoon **salt**
¼ teaspoon fresh-ground **black pepper**
1½ pounds raw extra-large or jumbo **shrimp**, shelled
   (if frozen, see Giving Flavor to Frozen Shrimp, page 35)

COOKING THE SHRIMP

3 tablespoons **butter**
Salt and fresh-ground **black pepper**
¼ cup **dry white wine**
Juice of ½ large **lemon**
2 tablespoons fresh **parsley leaves**, chopped (either flat or curly)

1. In a medium bowl, gently combine the olive oil, lemon juice, garlic, salt, pepper, and shrimp. Cover and refrigerate overnight.

2. About 15 minutes before serving, set a 12-inch skillet over medium-high heat. In the skillet melt 2 tablespoons of the butter with a little salt and pepper. Add the shrimp with its marinade, stir once or twice, and turn the heat down to medium low. Cover the skillet, and cook the shrimp for 3 to 4 minutes, or until they are barely firm. With tongs, transfer them to a heated serving platter. Taste a shrimp for seasoning.

3. Turn the heat under the skillet up to medium high. Stir the wine into the pan juices, and boil it for 1 minute, or until it has evaporated and the pan juices are rich-tasting. Off the heat, stir in the remaining 1 tablespoon butter. Scrape the contents of the skillet over the shrimp. Drizzle the lemon juice over them, and scatter with the chopped parsley. Serve hot.

Hawaii is not a state of mind, but a state of grace.

—Paul Theroux

SANTA FE SUMMER POT WITH AVOCADO AND SHRIMP

| *Serves 4* | *10 minutes prep time; no stove time* | *This can wait, chilled, for 30 to 40 minutes* |

A summer pot is primal summer—flashy colors, bright tastes, all crunchy and raw. It is what I think of as a supermarket dish: a cool stew you put together with a few things you pick up on the way home. Don't bother turning on the stove.

¼ cup fresh **lime juice**
½ medium **red onion**, fine chopped
1 large **garlic clove**, minced
½ **jalapeño**, seeded and minced
½ teaspoon **Crossover Spice Blend** (page 128) or a blend of ground coriander, ground cumin, and fresh-ground black pepper
1½ pounds ripe delicious **tomatoes**, coarse chopped (do not peel); *or* one 28-ounce can whole peeled tomatoes
2 sprigs fresh **coriander**
1 small **cucumber**, peeled and diced
1 ripe **avocado**, diced
1 pound cooked, peeled **shrimp**, or firm tofu *or* leftover poultry (organic if possible), diced
Handful **tortilla chips**, lightly crushed
2 **limes**, each cut into 8 wedges

1. In a small bowl, combine the lime juice, onion, garlic, jalapeño, and spice blend. Let marinate for 10 minutes.

2. Place the tomatoes and coriander sprigs into the bowl of a food processor, and pulse until the mixture is chunky. Add the onion mixture, and pulse five times.

3. Divide the cucumber, avocado, and shrimp among four bowls. Spoon the tomato blend into the bowls. Garnish with the crushed tortilla chips and lime wedges.

You would never know it by going to a supermarket, but children are supposed to eat the same food as their parents.

—Dr. Marion Nestle

PAN-BROWNED SCALLOPS ON A BED OF BACON AND BRUSSELS SPROUTS

Serves 4	*10 minutes prep time;* *35 minutes stove time*	*Serve immediately*

You have to love the sturdiness of these Brussels sprouts next to the yieldingness of the scallops, the bitter against the sweet, and the nubbins of bacon and onion that get picked up with every forkful. The French have been in on this for years.

1 cup **water**
1 pound small **Brussels sprouts**, rinsed, trimmed,
   and halved
3 slices good-quality **bacon**, fine chopped
Salt and fresh-ground **black pepper**
2 tablespoons **extra-virgin olive oil**
1 medium **onion**, fine chopped
2 tight-packed tablespoons fresh **tarragon leaves**,
   plus 1 teaspoon for garnish
1 pound **sea scallops**

   1. In a straight-sided 12-inch sauté pan, combine the water, Brussels sprouts, bacon, and salt and pepper to taste. Bring the mixture to a boil over high heat. Cook until the water has boiled off and the bacon is beginning to render some of its fat, 6 to 7 minutes.

   2. Lower the heat, add 1 tablespoon of the oil, the onion, and the 2 tablespoons tarragon, and continue sautéing. Give the ingredients plenty of room in the pan so they will brown. Do not overstir. They need to sit in one place and brown.

   3. When the sprouts are nicely browned on all sides and the bacon is crisp, pull the pan off the heat, scoop the mixture into a large bowl, and set it aside.

4. Wipe out the sauté pan with a wad of paper towels, and return it to the stove. Heat it over medium-high heat, and add a scant 1 tablespoon olive oil. Then add the scallops, again leaving plenty of room between them so they will brown. Season them with salt and pepper. Let them sear in one spot for 1 to 2 minutes, then check them for a rich brown color. If nicely browned, turn them, reduce the heat to medium, and continue cooking on the other side for 1 minute.

5. Return the Brussels sprout mixture to the pan and continue to cook until the scallops are still a little soft when pressed. Scoop them out of the pan onto a serving platter, then spoon the sprouts and their seasonings over the scallops. Garnish with the remaining tarragon, and serve hot.

The success of this dish totally depends on the size of the pan. Use the largest sauté pan you have. To get a golden sear, it is essential not to crowd the Brussels sprouts or the scallops.

If the skillet is too crowded (you will see the sprouts or scallops throwing off water), cook them in batches and return everything to the pan for a final quick reheat just before serving.

When I am talking about food I am talking about life.

—Nigella Lawson

VINTAGE BISTRO MUSSELS

Serves 3 to 4

10 minutes prep time; 10 minutes stove time

Cook and eat these hot, or chill the mussels and serve them without their cooking liquid

Some dishes taste so good generation after generation that it's a sin to fool with them. This is especially true when the recipe is as straightforward as mussels steamed with white wine and shallots. When you clatter those mussels into the pot, you'll join a parade of hungry Frenchmen who've been sopping up the broth of their *moules à la marinière* since long before Marie Antoinette.

Good-tasting **extra-virgin olive oil**
4 large **shallots**, fine chopped
2 sprigs fresh **thyme**
Salt and fresh-ground **black pepper**
1 small **garlic clove**, minced
⅔ cup **dry white wine**
1 cup **water**
4 pounds **mussels**, well rinsed and debearded
1 light-packed tablespoon fresh **parsley leaves**, minced

1. Lightly film a 6-quart pot with olive oil. Set it over medium-high heat and stir in the shallots, thyme, and a light sprinkling of salt and pepper. Reduce the heat to medium low, cover the pot, and steam the shallots for 4 to 5 minutes, or until they're soft and clear. Don't let them brown.

2. Return the heat to medium high. Stir in the garlic and wine. Boil the wine until two thirds of it has evaporated. Pour in the water, bring it to a simmer, and add the mussels. Cover the pot, turn the heat down to medium, and cook them for 5 minutes.

3. Once the shells open an inch, the mussels are ready. Using tongs, immediately lift them out and transfer them to soup bowls. Continue cooking any not fully opened mussels for another 2 minutes. At this point, discard any unopened ones. Pile the remaining mussels in the soup bowls, pour in their cooking liquid, sprinkle them with the parsley, and enjoy.

Variation
SAFFRON-TOMATO MUSSELS

Follow the recipe as written, adding 1 chopped tomato and a pinch of saffron with the wine. Swirl 1 tablespoon butter into the mussel broth before pouring it into the soup bowls.

Variation
SOUTH CHINA SEA MUSSELS

Follow the recipe as written, substituting 1 chopped medium onion for the shallots. Instead of the thyme, use a spoonful of Indian curry paste or Crossover Spice Blend (page 128) and minced fresh hot chile to taste. For the wine substitute ½ cup coconut milk, 2 minced garlic cloves, and 2 teaspoons minced fresh ginger. Finish the mussels with chopped fresh coriander or garlic chives.

Mussels' classic accompaniments are rough bread, soft butter, and a glass of Muscadet, the wine so crisp it crackles. Lemony iced tea could stand in.

BUYING MUSSELS

Mussels come from two main sources: They are gathered in the wild, where they grow attached to rocks and pilings, or they are farmed. Farmed mussels make more sense than the wild ones. They are raised attached to ropes, and therefore they do not become sandy, nor do they have the gritty beard they sport in the wild.

Convenience aside, farmed mussels are checked for pollutants. You can ask to see their inspection tag, with its date and location of harvest. Buy mussels where the turnover is fast and where they are sold loose or in net bags, never sealed in plastic sacks. If any are gaping wide open and will not close, or give off a fishy odor, go elsewhere. One spoiled mussel in a sack can ruin its neighbors.

Cook mussels the day you buy them. Until you are ready to cook, keep them cold in an open bowl in the refrigerator. Once they are cooked, throw away any unopened ones.

Meats
Plumped and Colored
BUYER BEWARE

Labels in the supermarket meat department have become fascinating reading. Scan a couple, and you might be surprised to find that a good part of what you are paying for is water, preservatives, salt, and coloring. I am not talking about ham; this is what is happening to our steaks, chops, ribs, and roasts.

It began with America's obsession with lean meat, which led to so little fat in our meat that modern cuts cook up dry and flavorless. The meat industry's solution to the problem is to inject salted liquids and preservatives into the meat.

Up to 12 percent of what we pay for in a pork tenderloin, for example, could be water with a mix of sodium, phosphate, and preservatives.

In the case of beef, similar liquids are pumped into the meat, along with red food coloring to make it appear fresher (when beef is exposed to air, it darkens, which we consumers don't like).

Relief is in sight. We still need to check labels, but as the carnivores' backlash continues to grow, there will be more and more encouraging words on those labels. Grass-fed meat, meat from local small-scale farmers, and meat from specific breeds are worth trying. At this moment the most legally reliable and reassuring term you can find on a label is "certified organic."

TAMARIND-GLAZED PORK CHOPS

Serves 2 to 4 | *10 minutes prep time; 5 to 10 minutes grill time* | *These are best eaten hot off the grill*

Tamarind, all on its own, gives barbecue sauce a run for its money. Toss in garlic and chile, especially the fruity-hot Aleppo or velvety ancho. These thin-cut chops, hot off the grill, are like eating crisp cookies right from the oven.

GLAZE

A backlash against bland pork is in high gear. All over the country you'll find farmers bringing back excellent pork, be it breed-specific, organic, and/or open-range. Some breed names to look for on labels are Berkshire, Duroc, Gloucestershire, Large Black, Red Wattle, and Tamworth.

3 generous tablespoons **tamarind concentrate**
2 tablespoons **ground Aleppo pepper** (or other sweet dried chile like ancho)
6 **garlic cloves**
2 teaspoons **Asian fish sauce** (*nam pla* or *nuoc nam*)
1 teaspoon **sugar**
2 tablespoons **dry white wine**
3 tablespoons **water**, or more as needed

PORK CHOPS

4 thin-cut, bone-in **pork chops** (organic if possible)
Good-tasting **extra-virgin olive oil**

1. If you are grilling, prepare the grill.

2. In a food processor, puree the tamarind, Aleppo pepper, garlic, fish sauce, sugar, and wine. Thin the paste with water as needed to get to the consistency of thick maple syrup. Set it aside.

3. Grill the chops over a medium fire until nicely browned, or alternatively film a large sauté pan with olive oil and sear the pork over medium-high heat for 3 to 5 minutes.

4. In the last few minutes of grilling (or searing), baste the chops with the marinade, turning them once to coat both sides. You want it to bubble and caramelize. Serve the chops, with the extra marinade alongside.

OVEN-CRISPED PORK, PEPPERS, AND GREENS

| Serves 4 | 10 minutes prep time; 25 minutes oven time | Serve immediately |

Sometimes the obvious escapes us. You see a roast and immediately assume it demands an hour in the oven. True enough if it's left whole, but small pieces cook faster than big ones. Cut that roast down to size, and you instantly slash the cooking time.

You can cut cooking time as well by giving pieces ample room to really roast and brown, and by putting your side dish right in the pan, so everything cooks together.

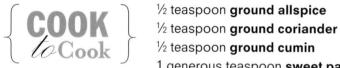

Tender lamb from the leg or loin can stand in for the pork. The finish for this roast is the combo of Turkish Almond Sauce and No-Cook Whole-Wheat Couscous. Both are easily prepared while the meat cooks.

THE ROAST

½ teaspoon **ground allspice**
½ teaspoon **ground coriander**
½ teaspoon **ground cumin**
1 generous teaspoon **sweet paprika**
¼ teaspoon **salt**
¼ teaspoon fresh-ground **black pepper**, or to taste
2 large **garlic cloves**, minced
1 or 2 **pork tenderloins** (total of 1¼ to 1½ pounds), cut crosswise into ½-inch-thick slices; or 2 pounds tender leg of lamb (organic if possible), cut into 2-inch cubes
1½ pounds **mixed peppers** (my mix: 2 red bells, 1 Anaheim, 2 jalapeños), seeded and thin sliced
2 big handfuls (about 5 ounces) organic **mixed greens**
1 small to medium **onion**, thin sliced
¼ cup good-tasting **extra-virgin olive oil**

FOR SERVING

1 recipe **No-Cook Whole-Wheat Couscous** (page 296)
1 recipe **Turkish Almond Sauce** (recipe follows)

1. Slip one large or two smaller shallow baking pans into the oven (a half-sheet pan is ideal). Turn the oven on to 450°F.

2. In a large bowl, toss all the roast ingredients together, making sure they are coated with the oil. Spread everything out on the hot baking pan, taking care not to burn yourself. Make sure the pieces are generously spaced, to help the crisping process.

3. Roast for 20 to 25 minutes, turning the meat and vegetables occasionally. The greens should be crisp, and the pork firm.

4. Serve the roast around a mound of No-Cook Whole-Wheat Couscous, and pass the Turkish Almond Sauce at the table.

TURKISH ALMOND SAUCE

Makes 2 cups | *10 minutes prep time* | *Keeps for 2 days in the refrigerator*

A cream sauce Turkish-style, this is so much more modern than Alfredo or béchamel. The crunch of almonds and the tang of yogurt is pure mommy food in the eastern Mediterranean. Turn the sauce into a dip, dress a salad with it, or use it to gussy up takeout.

1 large **garlic** clove, minced
3 tablespoons fine-chopped **sweet onion** (Walla Walla, Vidalia, Maui)
2 tablespoons **white wine vinegar** or distilled white vinegar
¼ cup good-tasting **extra-virgin olive oil**
Salt and fresh-ground **black pepper**
1 cup **plain whole-milk yogurt**
1 cup whole **salted almonds**, coarse chopped
2 tight-packed tablespoons fresh **coriander leaves**, chopped (optional)

1. In a serving bowl, combine the garlic, onion, and vinegar. Let stand for 10 minutes.

2. Beat in the olive oil until the sauce is creamy. Add salt and pepper, and stir in the yogurt. Add the almonds (and coriander if using) just before serving to keep them crunchy.

How to Read a Meat Label
OR, FINDING THE KINDEST CUTS

Tough or tender? That's the puzzle of the meat case. Fortunately a code is written on nearly every meat package, and once you crack it, the puzzle is solved. The name of the cut usually includes a telltale word revealing where on the animal the meat comes from. **As in real estate, location is everything.**

In those parts of the animal where the most movement occurs (shoulder, hips, neck, legs), the meat ranges from chewy to occasionally tender. You find the tenderest cuts where little movement happens: the top center of the animal, from the shoulders to the hips.
Here are the code words to look for:

- **Chuck, shoulder, Boston butt:** These are all the shoulder area. "Chuck" means "shoulder" in beef. With lamb, the shoulder is actually called "shoulder" and pork shoulder is divided into cuts that usually have "shoulder" in their names. Boston butt is a specific cut of pork shoulder (and an excellent choice for roast pork).

  All these cuts share rich flavor, generous amounts of flavorful fat, and the occasional tender pocket. Use shoulder cuts for braising, roasting, burgers, chops and steaks.

- **Leg and round (top, bottom, and eye of round):** These are from the animal's rear, or rump, end and the top part of its leg.

  In beef, the rear and leg are called the round. In lamb, veal, and pork, it is simply called the leg. These cuts range from pot roast, to steaks, to osso buco, to leg of lamb.

  Beef round cuts like tri-tip roast, London broil, and top round steak are more tender. Avoid the eye of round roast. It looks like the tenderloin but has the texture of iron and the flavor of cardboard.

- **Loin, tenderloin, sirloin, top loin, and rib and back rib:** Between the shoulder and hip are the tenderest cuts of all—from standing rib roast, to ribeye steaks and chops, to sirloins, T-bones, and porterhouses.

  The exception is pork. No longer is pork loin roast moist and tender. The meat is far too lean; instead use pork shoulder roasts and chops for roasting and grilling.

- **Shank, flank, skirt, strip, brisket, short rib, spare rib:** The world loves these cuts—*carne asada* in Mexico, the archetypal Jewish brisket, Italy's osso bucco, the lamb shanks of France, the Middle East's lamb riblets, and the multitude of America's barbecued ribs.

  These are the legs, bellies, and sides of the beasts. Most are best slow-cooked, stewed, or slow-roasted. These pieces love marinades, brines, and rubs, and a few can be bargain substitutes for expensive steaks. Flank, skirt, hanger, and strip steaks have unstoppable flavor. Marinate them, fast-grill to rare, then cut into thin slices at an angle across the grain.

The 450°F Oven

Walk in the door and turn the oven to 450°F. Even if you have no idea what you are going to be eating, this single act starts supper. Roast thin-sliced chicken in minutes, caramelize a mess of vegetables in half an hour, transform a piece of stale bread into garlic-laden slices topped with oozing cheese. **That single turn of a knob opens you to culinary serendipity.**

PORK TENDERLOIN PAN ROAST WITH BLACK OLIVES AND ORANGE

| *Serves 2, and doubles easily* | *10 minutes prep time; 30 minutes stove time* | *Serve immediately. Rewarms well.* |

Sizzled strips of orange zest, roasted olives, white wine, and garlic restore to today's pork what it is lacking: lusciousness. When fat was bred out of the meat, so was its flavor. But you can tease goodness out of a tenderloin with high seasonings like these. This recipe uses of a tried-and-true restaurant trick for speeding up roasting: brown first in a skillet on the stovetop and then finish cooking in a hot oven.

2 large **garlic cloves**
Shredded zest and juice of 1 small **orange**
1 tablespoon good-tasting **extra-virgin olive oil**, plus more
    for browning
1 teaspoon **dried basil**
Salt and fresh-ground **black pepper**
1 **pork tenderloin** (about ¾ to 1 pound; organic
    if possible)
About 10 pitted black **Kalamata olives**
½ cup **dry white wine**
Water

1. Preheat the oven to 450°F. In a blender or food processor, mince together the garlic, orange zest, a few tablespoons of the orange juice (save the rest for basting), the olive oil, basil, and light sprinklings of salt and pepper. Make about 8 deep slits in the meat, and stuff them with the minced mixture.

2. Lightly film a 12-inch skillet (with an ovenproof handle) with olive oil. Sear the pork on all sides over medium-high heat (it doesn't have to actually brown). Add the olives, remaining orange juice, and the wine to the pan, and slip it into the oven.

3. Roast for 20 minutes, or until an instant-reading thermometer inserted in the center of the tenderloin reads 150°F. As the pork cooks, the pan juices will brown, which is what you want. You don't want burning, however, so add about ½ cup water to the pan if burning threatens. Baste the tenderloin several times with the pan juices.

4. Carefully remove the pan from the oven (watch the handle—it will be very hot), and let the meat rest for 5 to 10 minutes. Slice the meat into ½-inch-thick rounds, swiping it through the pan juices as you go. Serve it moistened with the pan juices, piling the olives on the slices.

An equipment note: a pan with an ovenproof metal handle is essential for this kind of recipe.

WHEN TO SALT

Salt when you begin to cook, and you win on two counts. If you salt the meat or onions at the start of a sauté, or salt the vegetables or the fish as they go into the oven for roasting, you use less salt in the end and build deeper flavors.

With onions, for instance, salting at the very beginning of a sauté speeds up browning. The salt encourages the onions to give off their liquid. Among other things, that liquid contains sugars which encourage browning, so the sauté goes faster. At the same time, the salt infiltrates the onion, which makes it taste better. Talk about a win-win situation.

STIR-FRY OF HOISIN LAMB WITH CASHEWS AND SNOW PEAS

Serves 3 to 4

20 minutes prep time; 6 minutes stove time

Serve and eat immediately

Tender lamb, sweet and savory hoisin sauce, crunchy water chestnuts and fresh snow peas—all give you a fast supper that's far beyond the usual takeout. Lamb is one of the hallmarks of northern Chinese cooking, especially Mongolian. It is logical when you think of the vast steppes of the region where sheep and goats thrive where little else will.

This recipe speaks of the new China, where regions sometimes fuse. Here Mongolia's lamb and southern China's beloved hoisin sauce meet with the Cantonese stir-fry.

THE LAMB

1 to 1¼ pounds tender **lamb** (organic if possible; lamb steaks are ideal), trimmed of fat and connective tissue, and cut into ½-inch by 1-inch chunks

1 teaspoon **Chinese five-spice powder**; *or* ½ teaspoon anise seeds or fennel seeds, bruised

¼ to ½ teaspoon **red pepper flakes**

½ teaspoon **salt**

1 tablespoon **cornstarch**

1 tablespoon **dry red or white wine**

VEGETABLES

One 1-inch piece fresh peeled **ginger**, minced

1 **garlic clove**, minced

¼ to ½ teaspoon **salt**

1 medium **red onion**, cut into 1-inch dice

½ cup **water chestnuts**, quartered or sliced

1 handful **snow pea pods**, trimmed

(recipe continues)

SAUCE

- 3 tablespoons **hoisin sauce**
- 1 tablespoon **soy sauce**
- 1 tablespoon **rice vinegar**
- 2 tablespoons **rice wine** or dry white wine

STIR-FRY

- 3 tablespoons cold-pressed **vegetable oil**
- ½ cup **salted cashews**, roughly broken

1. Measure out, cut, and group together each section's ingredients: In a bowl, toss the lamb with its seasonings, including the cornstarch and wine, so it is thoroughly coated. Have the ginger and garlic ready to go into the wok, and have the onion, water chestnuts, and snow peas piled on a piece of paper towel, ready to go. In a small bowl, blend the sauce ingredients together. With this lineup, the stir-fry will easily come together in a few minutes.

2. Set a 14- to 16-inch wok or a straight-sided 12-inch sauté pan over high heat. When it is hot, swirl in 1½ tablespoons of the vegetable oil. Add the lamb and stir-fry for 90 seconds. Spread the lamb out as you cook it, so all its sides sear. Immediately remove the lamb to a clean bowl. Wipe out the wok with a thick wad of paper towels.

3. Heat the wok again over high heat. Swirl in the remaining 1½ tablespoons oil. Stir in the ginger and the garlic, and stir until fragrant (maybe 5 seconds), sprinkling with the salt. Immediately add the vegetables. Stir-fry for 1½ to 2 minutes. Add the sauce mixture, and continue stir-frying for another 90 seconds.

4. Turn the lamb into the wok, and stir-fry for about 10 seconds to heat it through. Stir in the cashews, and turn the mixture into a serving bowl. Serve immediately.

{ COOK *to* Cook }

See The Rhythm of a Stir-Fry (opposite) before putting the wok on the stove. Once you start cooking, nothing takes more than 2 minutes.

Five-spice powder is found in many supermarkets. If it's unavailable, use anise or fennel seeds.

Tender beef is good here, too.

The Rhythm of a STIR-FRY

It is reassuring to know that nearly all stir-fries follow the same steps, or rhythm. With this scheme you can improvise on your own. Never dump everything into the wok at once.

Here is the rhythm:

1. Season the hot oil by first stir-frying the recipe's aromatics for a few seconds.
2. Add the meat, fish, or tofu. Stir-fry, and remove.
3. Add more oil, and stir-fry the vegetables.
4. Leaving the vegetables in the wok, add the liquid ingredients. Bring them to a boil, return the meat to the pan to blend the flavors, and reheat. Serve the stir-fry immediately.

BUILDING THE LIBRARY

THE BREATH OF A WOK: UNLOCKING THE SPIRIT OF CHINESE WOK COOKING THROUGH RECIPES AND LORE
BY GRACE YOUNG AND ALAN RICHARDSON
(SIMON & SCHUSTER, 2004)

LAMB CHOPS
WITH CROSSOVER SPICE CRUST

| *Serves 4* | *5 minutes prep time; 10 minutes stove time* | *Serve immediately* |

Lamb chops are the big treat at our house. These are flavored with our Crossover Spice Blend. Nothing could be easier, or as simple and satiating. The quantity of spices may seem like a lot, but they are surprisingly gentle with the lamb, so be generous with them.

2 tablespoons **Crossover Spice Blend** (page 128)
1 tablespoon coarse **kosher or sea salt**
Four 1-inch-thick loin **lamb chops** (organic if possible)
Good-tasting **extra-virgin olive oil**
½ **lemon**

1. Combine the Crossover Spice Blend with the salt in a small bowl. Rub a generous amount of the blend on both sides of the chops, and set the extra spice blend aside.

2. Film the bottom of a 12-inch skillet with the olive oil, and heat it over medium-high heat. When the oil looks wavy, sear the chops on one side for about 3 minutes, until they have a golden brown glaze. Turn them over, reduce the heat to medium, and continue cooking, turning the chops occasionally, until they are done to your liking, about 9 or 10 minutes for medium rare (125° to 130°F on an instant-reading thermometer).

3. Dust the chops with additional spice blend and sprinkle with a squeeze of lemon.

Don't take a butcher's advice on how to cook meat. If he knew, he'd be a chef.

—Andy Rooney

BLACK PEPPER–HONEY STEAK

| Serves 3 to 4 | 5 minutes prep time; 15 minutes stove time | Serve immediately; makes great leftovers |

Honey gives this recipe its edge. Once the steak is cooked, you taste only the barest hint of sweetness, yet the sugar opens up all the meat's bold beefiness. Each mouthful delivers fabulous crustiness and a hum of black pepper.

Flavors are released by chemical reactions. One family of tastes opens up with water, another in fat; alcohol releases both these families and more. This is why the wine is in this recipe, and in so many others.

3 tablespoons **dry red wine**

3 tablespoons **honey**

3 large **garlic cloves**, minced

1 teaspoon fresh-ground **black pepper**, plus more as needed

1½ to 2 pounds **steak** (chuck, ribeye, porterhouse, T-bone, top loin, New York strip, Delmonico, *or* Kansas City strip; organic if possible), cut 1¼- to 1½-inches thick and trimmed of excess fat

2 tablespoons **extra-virgin olive oil**

Salt

1. Combine the wine, honey, garlic, and pepper in a shallow dish. Add the steak, turning to coat it with the mixture. Let it stand at room temperature while you set up the rest of the meal.

2. Heat the olive oil in a 12-inch sauté pan over medium-high heat. Pat the steak dry, add it to the pan, and brown it quickly on both sides, sprinkling salt and grinding more pepper over both sides as they cook. (A splatter screen will protect the stovetop from being a total mess.)

3. Turn the heat to medium low and cook, turning the steak often, for 10 minutes, or until it reaches an internal temperature of 125° to 130°F (for medium rare). Remove it to a platter and let it rest for 5 to 10 minutes. The steak finishes cooking, collects itself, and is much juicier for the wait.

The
SECRET STEAK

A couple wrote in to the "Ask the Splendid Table" newspaper column. They had just moved into their first home and had invited their big family over for the day. Grilling steak was the family tradition, but the couple's budget was more McDonald's than steakhouse. What could they serve?

I recommended this elusive cut of beef, which I've been using for years but never talked about because it is not always easy to find in the meat case. It is a cut of chuck that equals porterhouse and ribeye in flavor at less than half the price. Chuck is a little chewy, but slow grilling to medium rare and thin slicing pretty much solve that problem.

Meat scientists explained to me that this cut comes from a particular muscle on the steer. They've also told me that most butchers won't know what you are talking about. So what you need to know is what to look for on the package label and *in* that package.

The package in the meat case will be labeled "chuck roast" or "chuck pot roast." The entire roast will look like a big rectangle and will be divided into separate sections by long ribbons of white fat. It should be about 3 inches thick. The section you are looking for is a long triangular-shaped piece that is marbled with white squiggles and dashes of fat.

Turn this section into 4 steaks by cutting that triangle away from the rest of the roast (freeze the leftover meat for stew or pot roast). It will be a 3-inch-thick cut of beef. Cut it in half horizontally to get two I^1/$_2$-inch-thick pieces. Then halve each one vertically to get 4 separate steaks.

Red meat is not bad for you. Now blue-green meat, that's bad for you!

—Tommy Smothers

SCANDINAVIAN SPICED MEATBALLS WITH CARAMELIZED APPLES

Serves 4

20 minutes prep time; 20 minutes stove time

The meatballs can be assembled ahead, and the completed dish reheats beautifully

Chunks of tart apple caramelized in red wine coat these little balls. They're plied with bits of prune, scallion, and unexpected spice. We don't associate Spice Islands spices like ginger, nutmeg, and coriander with Scandinavia, but the Scandinavians were great traders; they've used them for centuries.

Making meatballs takes more time than flipping a steak on the grill, but the payback is tenfold.

MEATBALLS

½ medium **onion**

⅓ cup **dry red wine**

1 large **egg yolk**

1 large **garlic clove**

Generous ¼ teaspoon **fresh-grated nutmeg**

1 generous teaspoon **ground ginger**

1 teaspoon **salt**

2 teaspoons **Crossover Spice Blend** (page 128) or a blend of ground coriander, ground cumin, and fresh-ground black pepper

1 pound **ground beef** (85% lean; organic if possible)

½ pound **ground chicken** or turkey thigh (organic if possible)

5 large *or* 10 small pitted **prunes**, cut into ⅛-inch dice

3 large whole **scallions**, thin sliced

(recipe continues)

SAUTÉ AND SAUCE

Good-tasting **extra-virgin olive oil**
Salt and fresh-ground **black pepper**
½ teaspoon **caraway seeds**, bruised
1 medium **Granny Smith apple**, cored (not peeled) and cut into ¼-inch dice
½ medium **onion**, cut into ¼-inch dice
½ cup **dry red wine**
¾ cup **Cheater's Homemade Chicken Broth** (page 48) or canned chicken broth
11 or 12 fresh **parsley leaves** (garnish)

1. In a food processor, puree together the onion, red wine, egg yolk, garlic, nutmeg, ginger, salt, and spice blend. Add the beef and chicken, and pulse 5 times. Scrape everything into a bowl, and thoroughly blend in the prunes and scallions. Shape the mixture into twenty-five or twenty-six 1¼-inch balls.

2. Lightly film a straight-sided 12-inch sauté pan with oil, and heat it over medium-high heat. Add the meatballs, taking care they don't touch. Brown them well on one side. Gently turn them over with a metal spatula, and sprinkle them with salt, pepper, the caraway seeds, the apples, and the diced onion. Reduce the heat to medium low, cover the pan, and cook for 8 minutes, or until there is no pink in the center of the meatballs.

3. With a slotted spoon, transfer the meatballs to a serving dish, leaving the apples behind. Turn the heat up to high. Boil down the pan juices, stirring with a wooden spatula, until the apples are sizzling and browning. Blend in the red wine and keep boiling until the wine has totally evaporated. Stir in the broth, and boil it down by half. Taste the sauce for seasoning; then scrape the sauce over the meatballs. Scatter them with the parsley, and serve.

Poultry thigh, rather than breast, is the secret weapon in the quest for moist and tender meatballs.

CHINESE GINGER-SCALLION MEATBALLS

For the ingredients in the processor, substitute a ½-inch piece of fresh peeled ginger, 3 whole scallions, 1 tablespoon soy sauce, 1 egg yolk, a little sugar, and ½ cup dry red wine. Puree, and then add the meat as directed above. Once it has been pulsed 5 times, turn the mixture into a bowl and stir in the scallions. Instead of the prunes, blend in 8 to 10 diced water chestnuts.

Brown the meatballs as directed with ½ diced medium onion, 1 diced red bell pepper, and ½ cup thin-sliced bamboo shoots. For the pan sauce ingredients, substitute ⅓ cup rice wine or dry white wine, 1 cup chicken broth, and 1 tablespoon hoisin sauce.

You don't sew with a fork, so I see no reason to eat with knitting needles.

—Miss Piggy

Sides

FEATURING

THREE-PEA TOSS

Wine-Braised Carrots with Fried Sage Leaves

SUGAR SNAPS AND SCALLIONS
WITH CODDLED LETTUCE

Melting Greens

GREEN BEANS WITH LEMON, GARLIC, AND
PARMIGIANO GREMOLATA

Smothered Broccoli with Peppers, Onions, and Raisins

GARLIC-CAULIFLOWER "MASHED POTATOES"

"Drippy" Mexican Sweet Corn on the Cob

PROVENÇAL OVEN ONION SAUTÉ

Sweet Yams in Ginger-Stick Curry

BUTTER-STEAMED LEEKS WITH
FRESH TARRAGON

Greek Pot-Crushed Potatoes

ALMOND-TURMERIC POTATOES

Mushroom Ambrosia with Miso

WORKING MOTHER'S BARLEY

No-Cook Whole-Wheat Couscous

DUMBED-DOWN RICE

Scallion-Dill Pilaf

Part of the secret in life is to eat what you like and let the food fight it out inside.

–Mark Twain

This chapter

could be called "Overcook Your Vegetables." While the crisp of salads and the snap of fresh carrots and radishes are fine, cooking vegetables down until they are meltingly suave lends them a sophisticated edge—kind of a Catherine Deneuve makeover of the produce section.

The dishes in this chapter are meant to accent suppers, and they vary in intensity to give you ample room to mix and match. They are also fast and simple, which is what you should expect from a side dish. Some, like Smothered Broccoli with Peppers, Onions, and Raisins (page 273), could be a main dish. Serve it with a chunk of bread, a nice cheese, and a glass of wine. What could be missing? You will also find insanely easy techniques for basic staples like barley, rice, and couscous.

Over the years the show has turned up a choice collection of places to go to when one needs to be reminded that the world is really okay. Nothing beats Crying While Eating and the Museum of Burnt Food. Oh, and for you gardeners, we give you the only weapon you will ever need (and the last one you'll ever want) against bunnies and Bambi.

THREE-PEA TOSS

Serves 4 to 6

10 minutes prep time; 5 minutes stove time

Serve hot or at room temperature

A beauty queen of the first order, this dish flies in the face of the old saying "Like two peas in a pod." The truth is, no two peas are ever the same.

1 to 1¼ cups **sugar snap peas**
2 tablespoons **extra-virgin olive oil**
1 medium **red onion**, cut into ½-inch dice
Generous pinch of **sugar**
Salt and fresh-ground **black pepper** to taste
1 to 1¼ cups **snow pea pods**
1 cup frozen **baby peas**
2 tight-packed tablespoons fresh **mint leaves**, chopped
½ cup salted whole **almonds**, coarse chopped

A wok is the best way to cook these peas. Have everything cut and measured before turning on the heat.

1. String the sugar snap peas with a small, blunt knife: grasp the stem between your thumb and the blade, and pull down the length of the pea pod. Rinse the pea pods and dry them thoroughly.

2. Heat a wok or a straight-sided 12-inch sauté pan over high heat. Swirl in the oil. Add the onion, sugar, and salt and pepper, and toss over high heat for 1 minute.

3. Add the sugar snaps and toss for 30 seconds. Stir in the snow peas and cook for 30 more seconds. Finally add the frozen peas and stir-fry for another 30 seconds, or until they are thawed. Turn the peas into a serving bowl, and toss with the mint and almonds. Serve immediately.

WINE-BRAISED CARROTS WITH FRIED SAGE LEAVES

| *Serves 3 to 4, and doubles easily* | *8 minutes prep time; 20 minutes stove time* | *Serve the carrots hot or warm. They hold for 4 days in the refrigerator, so make extra.* |

Being married to a tomato-obsessed Italophile, my carrot-loving husband moans, "Carrots must not be an Italian vegetable." In the interest of marital relations, I dug deep into my childhood memories of those interminable family holiday dinners. Out of them came fried sage leaves and carrots cooked in wine, certainly not a dish I appreciated then.

2 tablespoons good-tasting **extra-virgin olive oil**
20 large fresh **sage leaves**
Salt and fresh-ground **black pepper**
1 to 1¼ pounds **carrots**, cut on the diagonal into
    ¼-inch-thick pieces
½ medium **onion**, minced
½ cup **dry white wine**
Water

1. Heat the oil in a 12-inch skillet over medium-high heat. Add all but 6 of the sage leaves to the pan with some salt and pepper. Sauté them until they crisp, turning the leaves with tongs, a total of 30 seconds to 1 minute. Pick them out of the pan with the tongs and drain them on paper towels.

2. Keep the heat at medium high as you add the carrots and onions to the skillet, along with the 6 remaining sage leaves (tearing them as they go in). Sauté for 3 minutes, or until the onions are picking up color. Pour in the wine and enough water to barely cover the carrots. Bring to a lively bubble and cover the pan.

3. Cook the carrots for 10 minutes, or until they are nearly tender. Uncover and boil off all the liquid so the carrots are coated in a light glaze. Taste them for seasoning, and turn them into a serving dish. Scatter the fried sage leaves over the carrots.

CARROTS WITH CURRY
AND COCONUT MILK

Follow the recipe, eliminating the sage leaves. Add the carrots and onions to the pan as directed above. Once the onions color, add 1 teaspoon to 1 tablespoon Thai or Indian curry paste. Substitute half water and half coconut milk for the wine. Finish the recipe as directed above.

People who eat white bread have no dreams.

—*Diana Vreeland*

SUGAR SNAPS AND SCALLIONS WITH CODDLED LETTUCE

Serves 3 to 4 | *10 minutes prep time; 10 minutes stove time* | *The dish is best eaten right away*

Gentle flavors, quiet tarragon, and sweet butter are what make this trio work. When I imagine cooking spring vegetables I picture them gentled along, never shocked by excessive heat or overwhelming seasonings. The sense is not so much cooking as protecting them. Using tender spring lettuce to moisten peas as they cook is an old French technique, and the white and pale green parts of the scallions stand in for the more traditional leeks.

12 **scallions**
1 to 2 tablespoons **unsalted butter**
1 tight-packed teaspoon fresh **tarragon leaves**, chopped
¾ pound **sugar snap peas**, stringed and washed
Salt and fresh-ground **black pepper**
6 leaves **romaine** or Bibb lettuce, cut into thin shreds
Shredded zest of ½ large **orange**
¼ cup **water**
½ teaspoon **sugar**

1. Trim away the scallions' roots and cut away their dark green stalks. You should now have 2- to 2½-inch-long pieces of white to pale green stalks.

2. In a straight-sided 12-inch sauté pan set over medium heat, melt the butter with the tarragon until the butter is creamy. Stir in the sugar snaps and scallions, sprinkle them with salt and pepper, and sauté for 2 to 3 minutes.

3. Blend in the lettuce and the orange zest, reduce the heat to medium low, and stir for 30 seconds to 1 minute. Add the water and sugar, and continue cooking for 2 minutes, or until the water has evaporated and the peas are just tender. Serve hot.

The Museum of
Burnt Food

It all started by accident, with a pot of apple cider left cooking on the stove. When curator and founder Debra Henson-Conant returned, "art" had been made. It was a freestanding apple cider structure about 6 inches tall. Thus the Museum of Burnt Food began. As it says on the museum home page, "It's wonderful to wake up and realize art has happened."

Some exhibition highlights:

Before and After Whole wheat bread—one slice burned, one not.

But Is It Jewish? A burned bagel.

The Forever Shrimp Kebab Incinerated shrimp on a stick.

Hot Apple Cinder, Opus II, from the Gary Dryfoos Foundation for Research on the Ability to Cook While Sleeping.

Check it out for yourself at www.burntfoodmuseum.com.

MELTING GREENS

Serves 2, and doubles easily | *5 minutes prep time; 10 minutes stove time* | *Serve hot or at room temperature*

Sally claims there is something therapeutic about a simple bowl of greens. "This dish is my tonic," she says. "Whenever I feel a cold coming on, or I am tired and my thirteen-year-old insists on baking a cake at nine p.m., I haul out a bunch of greens (even if they are in dubious condition) and wilt them in a pan with garlic and olive oil. The wisdom of the old advice to use fresh greens as a spring tonic comes through loud and clear—you feel purified."

Good-tasting **extra-virgin olive oil**
4 **garlic cloves**, coarse chopped
1 whole dried **red chile**
1 bunch **Swiss chard** or a combination of greens (chards, kales, sturdy lettuces), washed, stripped from center ribs, and torn into pieces (about 5 cups)
⅓ cup **Cheater's Homemade Broth** (page 48), canned chicken or vegetable broth, or water
Salt and fresh-ground **black pepper**

1. Generously film the olive oil over the bottom of a large saucepan with a tight-fitting lid, and heat it over medium-high heat. Add the garlic and the chile. Sauté them very briefly—no more than 30 seconds.

2. Add the greens and the broth. The pan will look heaping, but prepare yourself—the greens shrink shockingly as they cook down.

3. Reduce the heat to medium low, cover, and cook the greens for 10 minutes, or until they are tender. Check occasionally to make sure the greens are not burning, adding more liquid if needed. Sturdier greens like kale may take 5 to 10 minutes longer.

4. Just before serving, remove the chile and season the greens generously with salt and pepper and more of the olive oil if desired.

Variations

- Follow the recipe, but begin by browning 3 tablespoons chopped pancetta, bacon, or salami in the oil before adding the garlic and chile.
- Follow the original recipe, adding a chopped tart apple to the pot with the greens.
- Finish the cooked greens with 3 or 4 generous spoonfuls of fresh ricotta.
- Finish the greens with 2 teaspoons soy sauce, 2 teaspoons sesame seeds, and 1 teaspoon Asian sesame oil.

When making a quick pot of greens, be sure to pull the leaves from the center ribs and stems, which take too long to tenderize in a fast sauté.

THE GARDENER'S SECRET REPELLENT

Silence is deadly on the air. To date it's happened only once on *The Splendid Table.* Who knew the response to a simple gardening question could stop me in my tracks?

I was interviewing Master Gardener Shepherd Ogden, of the Cook's Garden seed catalog. Sally had prompted me to ask him how to stop deer and rabbits from wiping out her vegetable garden (Sally was desperate—she'd lost three successive plantings to the creatures).

Shepherd's solution left me open-mouthed and speechless. He said, "Surround the garden with porous rocks, like cinder blocks. Collect the urine of a carnivore (as in yours, if you are not a vegetarian). Douse the rocks, and no creature big or small will cross the pee line."

After the interview, off the air, he suggested to Sally that her husband or son might be best suited to the task, but having taken the losses personally, Sally did the deed herself. It worked. Regular reapplication is necessary.

GREEN BEANS WITH LEMON, GARLIC, AND PARMIGIANO GREMOLATA

Serves 4 | *10 minutes prep time; 15 minutes stove time* | *Serve the beans hot or at room temperature*

A mince of lemon zest, garlic, and parsley, gremolata is the traditional final tease of Milan's osso buco. That same mix brings a double impact to green beans. I used to first boil the beans, then reheat them with the gremolata, until Mediterranean food authority Paula Wolfert pointed out how silken beans become when they're left to cook slowly in a skillet. Best of all, it's one less pan to wash.

BEANS

Good-tasting **extra-virgin olive oil**
1½ pounds **green beans**, stem ends trimmed
Salt and fresh-ground **black pepper**
½ cup **water**

GREMOLATA

Shredded zest of 1 large **lemon** (organic preferred; after all,
   you are eating the entire rind)
½ tight-packed cup fresh **flat-leaf parsley leaves**
3 large **garlic cloves**
½ teaspoon **salt**
¼ teaspoon fresh-ground **black pepper**

CHEESE

½ cup fresh-grated **Parmigiano-Reggiano cheese**

1. Lightly film the bottom of a straight-sided 12-inch sauté pan with the oil. Heat it over medium-high heat. Add the beans and generous sprinklings of salt and pepper, and sauté for 2 minutes. Add the water, immediately cover the pan, and turn the heat to medium low. Cook the beans for 15 to 20 minutes, checking them often for burning and adding a little water if necessary. You want the beans to become very tender.

2. As soon as the beans are covered, make the gremolata: In a food processor, mince together the lemon zest, parsley, garlic, salt, and pepper. Stir half of the mixture into the cooking beans. Blend the rest of the gremolata into the grated cheese.

3. When the beans are tender, uncover them, cook off any liquid in the pan, and turn them into a serving bowl. Toss the beans with the cheese-gremolata mixture.

Variation

GREEN BEANS WITH PRESERVED LEMON AND BLACK OLIVES

Follow the recipe as written, substituting for the gremolata and cheese ¼ cup minced preserved lemon, ⅓ cup coarse-chopped pitted Italian or Greek olives, and ⅓ cup chopped fresh coriander. Add half the seasonings to the cooking green beans and stir in the other half just before serving.

Variation

GREEN BEANS WITH SALAMI AND ALMONDS

Follow the recipe as written, cooking ¼ cup chopped Genoa salami, cacciatore, or hard salami with the beans and the gremolata. Complete the recipe as written, adding ⅓ cup coarse-chopped toasted whole almonds with the cheese-gremolata mix.

SMOTHERED BROCCOLI WITH PEPPERS, ONIONS, AND RAISINS

Serves 6 to 8 | *10 minutes prep time; 10 minutes stove time* | *Serve hot or at room temperature*

Broccoli takes on great character when cooked beyond crisp. I like it nearly melting and smothered in this sauté of raisins, rosemary, and peppers with the unexpected crunch of pine nuts.

1½ to 2 pounds **broccoli**
Salt and fresh-ground **black pepper**
Good-tasting **extra-virgin olive oil**
1 medium **red bell pepper**, cut into thin strips
1 medium **red onion**, thin sliced
Leaves from a 4-inch sprig of fresh **rosemary**, chopped
⅛ teaspoon **red pepper flakes**, or to taste
¼ cup **raisins** (golden preferred)
2 tablespoons **pine nuts**, toasted

1. Peel the broccoli stalks. Cut the florets into 1-inch pieces, and slice the stalks into ½-inch-thick rounds.

2. Place a steamer basket in a 6-quart pot. Add water up to the base of the steamer. Cover and bring to a boil over high heat. Add the broccoli, cover, and steam for 4 minutes, or until a stalk barely resists being pierced with a knife. Immediately turn the broccoli into a colander and drain it. Transfer the broccoli to a serving platter and season with salt and pepper.

3. Place the empty pot back on the burner, lightly film it with the olive oil, and set it over medium-high heat. Once it is hot, stir in the bell peppers, onions, rosemary, red pepper flakes, and some salt and black pepper. Sauté for 3 minutes, or until the onions pick up color. Stir in the raisins. Cook another moment to soften them. Pour everything over the broccoli. Scatter the pine nuts over the vegetables, and moisten them with a little olive oil if needed. Serve hot or at room temperature.

GARLIC-CAULIFLOWER "MASHED POTATOES"

| *Serves 3 to 4* | *5 minutes prep time; 8 minutes stove time* | *This reheats well, and holds in the refrigerator for 4 days* |

The French caught on to the genius of pureeing cauliflower about two centuries ago. With the new millennium, Americans discovered the *pièce de résistance* of the low-carb diet. We have finessed the idea by cooking garlic with the cauliflower, as well as the cauliflower's greens, and pureeing them with a little sweet butter and good olive oil.

A workhorse dish of the first order, this cauliflower goes anywhere a potato can and reheats like a trouper.

1 large **cauliflower** with its green leaves
About ¼ teaspoon **salt**
5 large **garlic cloves**, thin sliced
1 tablespoon **butter**
1½ tablespoons good-tasting **extra-virgin olive oil**
Generous ⅛ teaspoon **fresh-grated nutmeg**
Fresh-ground **black pepper**
2 to 3 tablespoons **water**, or as needed

1. Add water to a 6-quart pot fitted with a steamer. Cover, and bring the water to a boil over medium-high heat.

2. Meanwhile, wash the cauliflower and its leaves. Cut the cauliflower leaves into thin strips. Thin-slice the cauliflower's core, and break the rest of the cauliflower into florets.

3. Drop the cauliflower leaves and core onto the steamer first, salting them lightly. Add half of the florets, all of the garlic, a sprinkle of salt, then the rest of the florets. Cover, and steam over medium-high heat for 8 minutes, or until the cauliflower is so tender that it is easily pierced with a knife.

4. Drain the entire contents of the pot in a colander, then transfer it to a food processor. Add the butter and oil, and puree. Season with the nutmeg, pepper, and more salt if needed. If the puree seems dry, puree in some water. Serve immediately, or reheat later.

Overcooking the cauliflower is the key to this dish. It should be nearly falling apart.

THE ORPHANS OF WINTER

While potatoes rule as the moguls of the root world, rutabagas, turnips, celery root, and parsnips remain the snubbed, unsung heroes of winter. Your great-grandmother understood them. These denizens of her root cellar ended up as many a save-the-family side dish that would fill you up and push expensive meats from the center of the plate—not a bad thought for today's dinner plate, either.

When in doubt, roast roots in high heat, with onion, garlic, olive oil, and your seasonings of choice. Caramelizing them neutralizes their earthiness. Root vegetables love warm spices—think cinnamon, nutmeg, allspice, black pepper, and chiles.

Potatoes, like wives, should never be taken for granted.

—Peter Pirbright

"DRIPPY" MEXICAN SWEET CORN ON THE COB

| *Serves 6* | *10 minutes prep time; 8 minutes grill time* | *The corn is best grilled, dipped, and eaten hot* |

At the El Burrito Market in St. Paul's Mexican community, you can tell it's corn season when you pull your car into the parking lot and see people clustered around the smoking outdoor grill. They're all in this odd posture, bending out from the waist, eating corn. The bend is self-protection from the chile-tinted butter, cream, and cheese dripping off the cobs.

6 to 8 ears fresh sweet **corn**, husks removed
12 tablespoons (1½ sticks) **salted butter**, melted
Salt and fresh-ground **black pepper**
2 cups **Mexican *crema*** or sour cream
About 3 cups fresh-grated **Mexican Queso Anejo** or
  Parmigiano-Reggiano cheese
½ cup hot **chile powder**

1. Prepare an outdoor grill. When the coals are completely covered with gray ash, grill the corn about 4 inches from the coals, turning the ears often with tongs and brushing them several times with the butter. After about 5 minutes, or when the corn is beginning to color, remove the ears to a platter. Sprinkle them lightly with salt and pepper.

2. Place the *crema* in one shallow bowl, the cheese on a large plate, and the chile powder in a salt shaker.

3. Let the corn cool until it is easy to handle but still warm. Roll the ears of corn in the *crema*, draining off some of the excess. Then roll them in the cheese. Finish the ears by sprinkling them with chile powder to taste, and drizzling each one with a little more *crema* and melted butter.

Variation

CHILE-LIME CORN ON THE COB

At the other end of the spectrum from the lavish drippy corn is to grill the corn, brushing the ears with butter, then roll each one simply in fresh-squeezed lime juice (about 1 cup) and sprinkle it liberally with hot chile powder.

Some people like to temper the heat of the chile with a squeeze of lime juice over the ear of corn.

In a pinch, the corn can be cooked on a stovetop grill or under the broiler.

I believe in the forest, and in the meadow, and in the night in which the corn grows.

—Henry David Thoreau

PROVENÇAL OVEN ONION SAUTÉ

Serves 3 to 4 | *10 minutes prep time; 20 minutes oven time* | *Holds well in the refrigerator for 5 days*

Think of this as a hot tapenade, a side dish, a topping, and a sauce of sorts. Pile some on fish, lamb, or chicken, on bruschetta, or on grilled vegetables, or toss it with pasta.

5 or 6 oil-packed **anchovies**, rinsed
1 tablespoon **red wine vinegar**
3 tablespoons good-tasting **extra-virgin olive oil**
4 large **garlic cloves**, coarse chopped
½ large **orange**
¼ teaspoon **fennel seeds**, bruised
½ to ⅔ cup pitted **Kalamata olives**, coarse chopped
1 medium ripe **tomato**, diced; or 2 canned tomatoes, drained and crushed
3 medium to large **red onions**, sliced ¼ inch thick
Coarse salt and fresh-ground **black pepper** to taste
1 to 2 tablespoons fresh **lemon juice**

For speed and fewer tears, slice the onions in a food processor.

1. Preheat the oven to 450°F. Cover a large pan (a half-sheet pan is ideal) with foil and slip it into the oven to preheat.

2. In a large bowl, mash the anchovies into the vinegar, olive oil, and garlic. Shred the zest of the orange half right into the bowl (you get more of the orange's fragrant oils this way). Add the fennel seeds, olives, tomato, onions, salt, and pepper, tossing to blend.

3. Spread the mixture over the hot pan. Roast, stirring occasionally, for 15 to 20 minutes, or until the onions are coloring but still have a little crunch. The tomato pieces should be cooked down. Stir in the lemon juice to taste. Serve hot, warm, or at room temperature.

Crying
WHILE EATING

Food, angst, and art all intersect on a website we and our listeners have learned to love, **"Crying While Eating."** The brainchild of Dan Engber, "Crying" is a collection of short movies based on the theme of eating and weeping. Nothing puts a bad mood in its proper place like www.cryingwhileeating.com.

A few samples from the site:

WHO: Byl
WHAT HE IS EATING: Fresh mozzarella
WHY HE IS CRYING: "Parenthood is like being pecked to death
by small chickens."

WHO: Carlee, Eric, and Justin
WHAT THEY ARE EATING: Chicken taco with lime, chicken burrito
with mild sauce
WHY THEY ARE CRYING: Gentrification

WHO: Daniel L.
WHAT HE IS EATING: A bagel with hummus
WHY HE IS CRYING: Inconsistent weather

WHO: Kayleah
WHAT SHE IS EATING: A head of lettuce
WHY SHE IS CRYING: Not comfortable with human contact

SWEET YAMS IN GINGER-STICK CURRY

Serves 4 as a side dish; 2 as a main dish

20 minutes prep time; 20 minutes stove time

The yams are best at room temperature and improve with several days in the refrigerator

Yams and sweet potatoes are so often baked that we forget how fast they cook when sliced thin and boiled. Sturdy, distinctive, and gorgeous, they can go far beyond the marshmallow-and-cinnamon treatment.

Make no mistake: this is a creation for ginger and chile lovers. Slices of green chile, golden sticks of fried ginger, and bronzed shallots spooned over yams the color of a sunset turn out a movie star of a dish. Jewel or Garnet yams are the best choices for this recipe.

YAMS

4 quarts **salted water** in a 6-quart pot

2 large Garnet or Jewel **yams** (about 1¾ pounds), peeled, halved lengthwise, and cut into ¼-inch-thick half-rounds

CURRY

Cold-pressed **vegetable oil** or extra-virgin olive oil

One 1-inch piece fresh **ginger**, peeled and sliced into paper-thin matchsticks

4 large **garlic cloves**, sliced paper-thin

1 **jalapeño**, sliced very thin (for milder flavor, seed the chile)

2 whole **scallions**, cut into 1-inch lengths

2 large **shallots**, thin sliced

Salt and fresh-ground **black pepper**

½ light-packed cup fresh Thai, holy, or regular fresh **basil leaves**, coarse chopped

Juice of 1 **lime**, or more to taste

(recipe continues)

1. Bring the salted water to a boil.

2. Once the water is bubbling fiercely, drop in the yams and cook them at a hard bubble for 10 minutes, or until tender. Drain in a colander and turn into a serving dish. Set the pot back on the stove.

3. Generously film the pot with the oil. Set it over medium-high heat and add the ginger, garlic, jalapeño, scallions, shallots, and generous sprinklings of salt and pepper. Sauté for 2 minutes, stirring often. Then cover the pot tightly, reduce the heat to medium low, and cook for 5 to 8 minutes, or until the ginger has softened.

4. Stir in the basil and cook, uncovered, for no more than 30 seconds. You want it to release its fragrance and soften a little, but still stay bright green. Spoon the curry sauce over the yams. Taste them for seasoning, then squeeze the lime juice over the finished dish.

Cutting the ginger into paper-thin matchsticks may seem fussy, but there is method to what seems to be madness. That shape changes how you taste the ginger in this dish. Crushed or chopped ginger would taste different—an interesting thing to remember when you see very specific instructions like these in Chinese recipes. There's always a reason.

THE ALUMINUM POT CONSPIRACY

Never cook in an unlined aluminum pot. Aluminum on the outside of a pot conducts heat well; inside the pot it is a setup for failure.

Our strong stance was inspired by yet another experience with aluminum sabotage: In shooting the photos for this book, the bright orange yams for Yams in Ginger-Stick Curry turned dull and brownish when boiled in an aluminum pot. We cooked another batch in a stainless steel–lined pot, and the bright orange sang through.

Aluminum reacts with dairy products, eggs, and acids, including wine and tomatoes, discoloring them and adding a metallic taste.

BUTTER-STEAMED LEEKS WITH FRESH TARRAGON

Serves 3 to 4 | *15 minutes prep time; 15 minutes stove time* | *The leeks hold in the refrigerator for 2 days and reheat well*

Gentle and timeless, leeks braised with tarragon, butter, and wine are considered the training-wheels recipe for these most-ignored members of the onion family.

4 large or 6 small **leeks**, white part only
1 tablespoon **butter**
One 6-inch sprig fresh **tarragon**
Salt and fresh-ground **black pepper**
2 tablespoons **white wine**
½ cup **Cheater's Homemade Broth**, chicken or vegetable
   (page 48)
About ⅓ cup **water**
1½ tablespoons **heavy whipping cream**, sour cream, or
   plain whole-milk yogurt
1 teaspoon chopped fresh **tarragon leaves**

1. Trim away the leeks' roots and greens. You want the white and very palest green parts of the stalk. If the outer layer of white is tough, trim that away as well. To clean, make a deep vertical cut down the length of each stalk to allow water between the layers. Soak them in cold water for 10 to 15 minutes. Dry with paper towels.

2. Heat the butter in a 12-inch skillet over medium-high heat, and add the leeks, tarragon, and salt and pepper. Sauté to barely browned on all sides. Blend in the wine and broth. Cover, reduce the heat to medium low, and cook for 5 to 10 minutes, or until the leeks are tender.

3. When the leeks are done, carefully lift them to a platter. Add the water to the skillet, and boil down the pan juices until they are almost syrupy. Add the cream and simmer for 30 seconds. Pour the sauce over the leeks, and sprinkle with the chopped tarragon.

GREEK POT-CRUSHED POTATOES

Serves 4 to 6 | 10 minutes prep time; 15 minutes stove time | These hold in the refrigerator for 2 days and reheat well. Refresh the lemon after reheating.

These potatoes will be the brightest taste on the plate. The flavors are clean and pure—new potatoes creamed in the pot, bright parsley, mellowed garlic, with a big shot of puckery lemon. They pair beautifully with anything grilled or roasted.

4 quarts **salted water** in a 6-quart pot
8 large **garlic cloves**
2 pounds **red-skin potatoes**, unpeeled
Good-tasting **extra-virgin olive oil**
Salt and fresh-ground **black pepper**
Pinch of **red pepper flakes**
A few spoonfuls of **water**
1 tight-packed teaspoon fresh **oregano leaves**, torn
⅓ cup fresh **flat-leaf parsley** or curly parsley leaves
4 whole **scallions**, thin sliced
Juice of 1 to 1½ **lemons**

1. Bring the salted water to a boil.
2. Thin-slice the garlic in a food processor; remove and set it aside, then thin-slice the potatoes. Drop the potatoes into the boiling water and simmer for 6 to 8 minutes, or until tender. Drain the potatoes in a colander, shaking away any excess water.

3. Put the empty pot back on the stove (don't worry if there are traces of potato starch), film it with the olive oil, and set it over medium heat. Add the sliced garlic, salt and black pepper, red pepper flakes, and water. Cook, uncovered, over medium heat for 5 minutes to soften the garlic, adding more water if necessary to keep the garlic from browning.

4. Add the oregano and cook until it is fragrant, about 30 seconds. Return the potatoes to the pot. Lightly crush the potatoes while blending them with the sautéed garlic, and season to taste. Fold in the parsley, scallions, and lemon juice. Turn into a bowl, and serve.

The addition of water to a sauté of garlic may seem odd, but adding a small amount of water lets the garlic mellow and soften without any chance of it becoming burned or bitter. This is a technique to take into any recipe where you want a caramel-like, soft garlic flavor with no bite.

Mashed potato is the gentile's chicken soup. It's nature's tranquilizer. I take it instead of Valium.

—Andrew Payne

WOMEN WHO EAT DIRT
GEOPHAGY

Naturalist Susan Allport wrote an article for the journal *Gastronomica* that piqued our interest. Considering that *The Splendid Table* is about the pleasures of food, it was an unusual subject, but it was about a practice that is medicinal, ancient, and pleasurable to many.

She explained that people all over the world eat dirt and look upon it as a normal and healthful custom. In truth what is eaten is clay that is dug from the layer that lies below the Earth's surface. That layer of clay is not contaminated by any organic materials, making it both nutritious and safe, according to Susan.

Women eat dirt more frequently than men because women have a harder time meeting their nutritional needs. Dirt contributes minerals, particularly calcium and iron. Dirt also detoxifies foods. For instance, in the Peruvian Andes the local wild potatoes are full of toxins. The dirt the Andeans eat helps purify the tubers so the body can absorb their nutrients without taking in their toxins. The clay absorbs and carries the poisons out of the body.

In Africa people are aficionados. There, clays are carefully shaped, dried in blocks, and baked over smoldering fires. They are rumored to have a wonderful earthy taste—no pun intended.

Here in the United States, clay is often baked in the stove and sometimes seasoned with vinegar, salt, or sugar. Tradition in some parts of the country has women carrying small sacks of their clay tied to their belts.

Perhaps what we don't realize is that clay (also known as kaolin) is a mainstay in our modern drugstore. **Ever heard of Kaopectate?**

What the PLANTS KNOW

During an interview, author, journalist, and gardener Michael Pollan told us the story of the day he was working in his garden alongside a bumblebee when he realized that "the bee and I were both working for the plants. The plant fooled us both into thinking we were getting the better end of the deal, but we were wrong."

He went on to explain: "The bee makes off with the nectar, but he has unknowingly picked up pollen on his legs and is moving it around the garden. That plant has evolved to trick that bee into spreading its genes throughout the world, which is exactly what domesticated plants have done to us."

It's an unusual view of co-evolution (and the theme of his book *The Botany of Desire*). Michael believes that "plants have taken up in their own identities, our values. In the case of an apple, our values for

BUILDING THE LIBRARY

THE BOTANY OF DESIRE: A PLANT'S-EYE VIEW OF THE WORLD
BY MICHAEL POLLAN
(RANDOM HOUSE, 2001)

sweetness. In the case of a flower, a look at what we think is beautiful." If we're smart, Michael believes, we should use plants as a mirror to ourselves.

ALMOND-TURMERIC POTATOES

Serves 2 to 3 as a main dish; 4 to 5 as a first course

5 minutes prep time; 20 minutes stove time

The finished potatoes can wait, covered, in their pot for an hour or more. They are excellent at room temperature.

If you cook no other potato recipe in your lifetime, you must try this one. A small amount of turmeric brings out the earthiness, and somehow the sweetness, of potatoes. This is kind of an upside-down potato casserole with the caramelized onions on the bottom rather than the top. A final handful of crisp almonds takes these potatoes over the top.

The recipe is a takeoff on a dish from Viana La Place's *Unplugged Kitchen*, a book Sally goes to again and again. She says it reminds her of the things she loves most about cooking—using her hands and slowing down.

BUILDING THE LIBRARY

UNPLUGGED KITCHEN
BY VIANA LA PLACE
(MORROW, 1996)

Good-tasting **extra-virgin olive oil**

1 medium yellow or white **onion**, peeled and thin sliced

¼ teaspoon **ground turmeric**

Salt and fresh-ground **black pepper**

1½ to 2 pounds **Yukon Gold potatoes**, unpeeled, sliced as thin as possible

2 tablespoons **Cheater's Homemade Chicken Broth** (page 48), canned chicken or vegetable broth, or water, plus more if needed

⅓ cup sliced **almonds** or hazelnuts, toasted

1. Generously film the olive oil over the bottom of a 4-quart saucepan with a tight-fitting lid. Set the pan over medium-high heat. Layer in the onion, turmeric, some salt and pepper, the potatoes, and more salt and pepper. Let the mixture cook, without stirring, until the onion starts to soften and brown. Don't stir, but peek under them to look for color.

(recipe continues)

2. Add the broth or water, cover, and reduce the heat to low. Again, don't stir, but shake the pan occasionally, and check to make sure there is still some liquid on the bottom of the pan. Add more liquid as needed. Cook for 15 to 20 minutes, until there is a syrupy brown glaze on the bottom of the pan, the onion is coloring, and the potatoes are tender. Pull the pan off the heat and let it stand, covered, for 5 minutes.

3. Taste for seasoning. Just before serving, sprinkle with the toasted nuts. Spoon down to the bottom of the pan to get some of the glaze for each serving.

Do not let one drop of the golden oil from the potatoes and onions go to waste. This is why bread was created.

POOR MAN'S SAFFRON

If you prize saffron for both its flavor and its color, it's hard to replace it with less expensive seasonings. But when color alone is wanted, you have several options.

Turmeric in small quantities is used in India and Southeast Asia; annatto seed (also known as achiote and usually heated in oil) is used in Mexico, Central America, and the Caribbean; and don't overlook (unsprayed) marigold petals plucked from flowerpots. Each of these substitutes brings a different flavor to a dish; none are going to throw off most creations.

HUNGER

—Composer and humorist Peter Schickele

Got up this morning, couldn't fit in my jeans,
I need to lose a lot of weight and you know what that means,
It means hunger, hunger, it means hunger.

All it takes is a couple of weeks on the road,
And I come back looking like Mr. Toad,
'Cause of hunger, hunger, 'cause of hunger.

Now I really hate being so gol'durn fat,
But there's something else I may hate worse than that,
And that's hunger, hunger, that's hunger.

Still in all you know it doesn't make sense,
To be a dictionary picture of the adjective "immense,"
'Cause of hunger, hunger, 'cause of hunger.

MUSHROOM AMBROSIA WITH MISO

Serves 2 to 3

10 minutes prep time; 10 minutes stove time

Serve immediately

You needn't publicize the miso in this recipe, unless you know it will be greeted with enthusiasm. For the uninformed, the miso here tastes like bits of browned chicken. In fact, eaten blindfolded, the mushrooms taste like chicken, too.

One of the easiest ways to clean mushrooms is to fill a salad spinner with water, quickly plunge the mushrooms in and out, then drain the water away and spin the mushrooms dry as you would lettuce. Depending on how sandy the mushrooms are, you may need two changes of water before spinning dry.

3 tablespoons **butter**

1 pound mixed **mushrooms** (such as white buttons, cremini, and shiitake), trimmed, washed, dried, and sliced ¼ inch thick

½ medium **onion**, minced

Salt and fresh-ground **black pepper**

1 heaping tablespoon **miso** (white or light-colored preferred)

½ cup **water**

1 teaspoon chopped fresh **chives** (garnish)

1. In a straight-sided 12-inch sauté pan, melt the butter over medium heat, taking care not to burn it. Add the mushrooms and the onion, season with salt and pepper, and increase the heat to medium high.

2. Sauté the mushrooms until they begin to throw off their liquid and start to brown (don't worry if the pan looks dry when they start to cook), 6 to 7 minutes.

3. Mix the miso in the water with a fork or whisk. It will not dissolve fully; some small chunks are fine.

4. When the mushrooms are lightly browned and all of their moisture has evaporated, add the miso water and continue to cook until all the liquid has evaporated, about 2 minutes. Taste for seasoning, and serve the mushrooms with a scattering of the chopped chives.

There are old mushroom hunters and there are bold mushroom hunters, but there are not old and bold mushroom hunters.

—*Anonymous*

WORKING MOTHER'S BARLEY

Makes 3½ to 4 cups | *30 minutes stove time* | *Holds in the refrigerator for 5 days and reheats beautifully*

Sometimes we wonder if people stay away from grains because they feel bullied by the cooking directions. Anything that says "simmer covered until the liquid is gone" is scary. We've all had the burned pots to prove it.

Well, we're here to say, "Forget it." We are fans of the boil-like-hell-in-lots-of-water method of grain cookery. They are tough; they can take it.

Barley is the essence of simplicity—toothy, rustic, and nutty. We like it with a little bit of firmness, but you can keep cooking it until you get to your desired texture. And by the way, tossed with a little butter, it's an easy sell to kids.

Pearl barley is what you want for this recipe. It's widely available, and because the hull and most of the grain's bran have been polished away, it cooks quickly.

1 cup **pearl barley**, rinsed and drained
1 recipe **Cheater's Homemade Broth** (page 48), chicken or vegetable; *or* two 14-ounce cans broth
2 to 3 cups **water**
¼ teaspoon **salt**, or to taste

1. Place the barley, broth, 2 cups of the water, and the salt in a 4-quart saucepan. Bring to a boil. Reduce the heat and simmer, uncovered, for 25 minutes, or until tender. If the barley starts to dry out before it's fully cooked, simply add more water.

2. Drain in a strainer. Serve hot or at room temperature.

Supertasters

Science now explains why some of your pals can't take hot chiles. They aren't wimps, and no amount of encouragement will help them develop a tolerance. They are supertasters who possess an acute, and sometimes painful, sense of taste. They are part of the 25 percent of us who have heightened sensitivity to sugar, salt, chile heat, and acids.

Taste researcher Dr. Linda Bartoshuk's early work revealed that the number of taste buds on our tongues divides us into supertasters, medium tasters, and nontasters. **Medium tasters are often the food lovers among us,** and nontasters do actually taste, but do so on a muted level.

In a discussion on the show, Dr. Bartoshuk taught us this simple test to determine where we fall on the scale: Soak a cotton swab in blue food coloring and swab your tongue. Then take a loose-leaf reinforcement (the hole is 6 millimeters across) and place the edge of the hole on the midline of your tongue. Count the number of pink circles you see in the hole (you may need a magnifying glass). Thirty or more indicate that you are a supertaster; five and below means you are a nontaster. Mediums are in between.

NO-COOK WHOLE-WHEAT COUSCOUS

Serves 4 | *10 to 15 minutes soaking time*

This is the all-embracing side dish. Couscous is already cooked when we buy it. All you need to do is rehydrate the grains. My Moroccan-born French teacher showed me this technique. You could do this hours ahead and keep it covered until you are ready to eat. Serve the couscous at room temperature or heat in a 350°F oven in a covered baking dish for 15 minutes.

Regular semolina couscous can be handled the same way.

2 cups **whole-wheat couscous**
½ teaspoon **salt**
2 to 3 cups **water**

1. In a medium bowl, combine the couscous and salt. Drizzle with about ½ cup water. Gently toss and rub the couscous between your palms to moisten it evenly. Let it stand for a few minutes so the grains can fully absorb the water.

2. Repeat the process at least four times, tasting the grains as you go. When they are close to tender, stop adding water. Once they absorb the last addition, they will be fluffy and light.

DUMBED-DOWN RICE

Serves 3 to 4 | *15 to 20 minutes stove time*

There's a reason boil-in-bag rice and all its mutations sell so well: few things intimidate cooks like achieving "the perfect rice." Forget it. If you can boil water, you can make great rice. Treat it like pasta—boil it in lots of water, drain it just before it's done, and let it stand, covered, for a few minutes. Perfect fluff.

All rices work here; only the cooking times vary from one rice to another. You could skip the 10 minutes rest for the rice by cooking it to tender in the boiling water, draining, and serving.

Fragrant rices like basmati and jasmine should be rinsed several times before cooking to remove the extra starch and ensure that the grains cook up separate and fluffy.

3 quarts **salted water** in a 5- to 6-quart pot
1 cup **long-grain white rice**

1. Bring the salted water to a boil.
2. Drop the rice into the water and boil for 8 to 10 minutes, or until it is slightly undercooked. Drain it in a sieve, return it to the pot, and let it rest, covered, for 5 to 10 minutes. Fluff with a fork and serve.

SCALLION-DILL PILAF

Serves 3 to 4

10 minutes prep time; 15 minutes stove time

The pilaf holds for a couple of days in the refrigerator and reheats well

This rice looks like spring in a bowl and tastes even better than you can imagine.

RICE

3 quarts **salted water** in a 5- to 6-quart pot
1 cup **long-grain white rice**

AROMATICS

To reheat rice, put it in a shallow baking dish, moisten with ¼ cup water, cover with foil, and bake in a 325°F oven for 10 to 15 minutes.

Good-tasting **extra-virgin olive oil**
6 whole **scallions**, thin sliced
1 **garlic clove**, fine minced
½ tight-packed cup fresh **dill leaves**, chopped
1 to 2 teaspoons grated **lemon zest**, or to taste
Salt and fresh-ground **black pepper**

1. Bring the salted water to a boil.

2. Drop the rice into the water and boil for 10 minutes, or until it is slightly undercooked. Drain the rice thoroughly and return it to the pot. Cover the pot and set it aside.

3. While the rice is resting, film a small sauté pan with a generous amount of olive oil, and sauté the scallions over medium heat until they begin to soften, about 1 minute. Stir in the garlic, and pull the pan from the heat.

4. Add the scallion-garlic sauté to the pot of rice, along with the dill and lemon zest. Combine gently, taste for seasoning, and cover. Let rest for an additional 5 minutes, and serve.

Carolina Gold
AN AMERICAN
LEGACY

If you don't live in the South, you probably don't realize that **America once grew the rice that was one of the highest-priced and most-coveted commodities in Europe for seventy-some years.** That variety, named Carolina Gold, was grown in South Carolina and Georgia from the eighteenth century to the early 1900s. It was rumored to taste of almonds and green tea.

As geography professor Judith Carney told us on the air, the rice came from Africa. Carolina Gold's rice empire was built on the skills and labor of slaves from the Gambia and Angola rice regions. The knowledge these people brought with them made nearly six generations of plantation gentry rich, while the slaves did the deadly work of cultivating the rice, with the ever-present snakes and diseases.

When the Civil War brought an end to slavery and plantation life, Carolina Gold gradually disappeared. Other rices that were easier to process took its place.

Well, Carolina Gold is back, thanks to Richard Schulze, who told us the story of how he uncovered some of the original grains in a seed bank in 1986 and planted them on his plantation near Charleston. The taste lives up to the lore. Today Carolina Gold comes from several sources. The Carolina Gold Rice Foundation (www.carolinagoldricefoundation.org) is a good place to begin tracking it down. It's worth the effort. September is harvest time. Get the new crop and keep it in the freezer.

BUILDING THE LIBRARY

BLACK RICE: THE AFRICAN ORIGINS OF RICE CULTIVATION IN THE AMERICAS
BY JUDITH CARNEY
(HARVARD UNIVERSITY PRESS, 2001)
THE CAROLINA RICE KITCHEN: THE AFRICAN CONNECTION
BY KAREN HESS (UNIVERSITY OF SOUTH CAROLINA PRESS, 1998)
CAROLINA GOLD RICE: THE EBB AND FLOW HISTORY OF A LOWCOUNTRY CASH CROP
BY RICHARD SCHULZE
(THE HISTORY PRESS, 2005)

Sweets

FEATURING

RUSTIC JAM SHORTBREAD TART

Dark and Moist Gingerbread

LITTLE FRENCH FUDGE CAKES

Farmhouse Panna Cotta

SALLY'S COCONUT MACAROONS

Old-Time Bittersweet Hot Fudge

EDNA LEWIS'S SUGARED RASPBERRIES

Rosemary Figs with Honeyed Fresh Cheese

PINEAPPLE-GINGER SORBET

The Duke's Hot Chocolate

Money talks, chocolate sings.

–Anonymous

Truth be told, weeknight dessert for most of us is often something that takes place at an open freezer door with a spoon

in one hand and a carton of ice cream in the other.

This chapter is for those nights when we want a bit more—to celebrate a good report card, to ignite a little romance, or just to feel like a civilized human who has actual time to linger over the end of supper.

These desserts work for both weeknights and big-deal dinners. They are home sweets. Nothing here tastes like a fast substitute for the real thing. These recipes *are* the real thing.

When we first started working on this chapter, we banned baking, believing no one would bake on a work night. Then Sally showed off her mother's macaroons, which took all of 10 minutes, that were delicious and downright decadent. The ban was lifted: of course you can bake on a weeknight—the oven's usually on anyway.

Between recipes are our guests' stories. They range from a neurologist who tells about a man who could actually taste shapes, to an art historian with an unexpected look at milk and its links to the French Revolution.

Take on these recipes and reads for pleasure and for a break from that freezer door. After all, we all need something sweet once in a while.

RUSTIC JAM SHORTBREAD TART

Serves 4 to 6 | 10 minutes prep time; 30 minutes oven time | Keeps for 2 days, tightly wrapped, on the counter

Cut into buttery little pieces, this cross between a tart and a cookie crumbles and then melts away as you eat it. The shortbread comes together in a blur. You sidestep a rolling pin by patting the crust into the pan with your fingers, and the filling is as easy as taking jam straight from the refrigerator.

Shortbread is a gift to all the pastry-shy of this world. Its generous amount of butter and lack of liquid protects the dough from toughening. Shortbread is also the first cousin of the dreaded pie crust.

Learn to make shortbread and any pie crust will fall at your feet. There is one key step in this recipe that will ensure success with any pie-crust dough you ever attempt: Once all the ingredients are together in the processor, pulse them only until they begin to gather together in small clumps—better to stop processing early than late.

Zest of ½ **lemon**
¼ cup whole **almonds**
¾ cup **unbleached all-purpose flour**, organic preferred
  (measured by dipping and leveling; see page 307)
¼ cup **sugar**
Generous pinch of **salt**
6 tablespoons cold **unsalted butter**, cut into 6 chunks
1 large **egg yolk**
½ teaspoon **almond extract**
¾ cup **jam** (tart cherry and wild blueberry are especially
  good)

(recipe continues)

1. Preheat the oven to 400°F. Butter a 9-inch round silver-colored cake or tart pan. (If using a dark-colored pan, you will want to cut baking time by about 5 minutes.)

2. With the food processor running, drop in the lemon zest and almonds, and grind them fine. Stop the machine, scrape down the sides, and add the flour, sugar, salt, butter, egg yolk, and almond extract. Pulse until they are blended and starting to come together in small clumps at the bottom of the processor. (They should look like clusters of peas.)

3. Turn the pastry dough into the pan. With your hands, pat it out to evenly cover the bottom of the pan. Give the tart a standing rim by nudging the dough ½ inch up the sides of the pan. Don't worry if it looks a little ragged.

4. Bake the crust in the center of the oven for 13 to 16 minutes, or until its edges are golden and the center is starting to color. The rim will sink down a little, which is fine.

5. Remove the pan from the oven, and turn the heat up to 500°F. Carefully spread the jam over the tart, and immediately return it to the oven (don't wait for the temperature to reach 500°). Bake for another 5 to 10 minutes, or until the jam is bubbly.

6. Cool the tart on a rack, slice it into squares or wedges, and serve. Serve the tart warm—but not hot, because hot jam can burn.

COOK to Cook

You can take this filling in many directions. For instance, mix together bits of jam from the bottoms of the jars in the refrigerator, use sweet chutneys and conserves, add citrus zest and spices, or merely dust the pastry with cinnamon and sugar before baking.

When you bake with almonds, as in this shortbread, remember that the ones sold in the baking aisle are often flavorless. It's better to use nuts from the snack section. Don't worry if they are salted or not skinned—they will be fine in this recipe.

The Baker's Pitfalls

NOT MEASURING THE FLOUR RIGHT: Depending upon how you measure the flour, a baking recipe can fly or fail. A single, leveled measuring cup of flour can hold $3\frac{1}{2}$ to 5 ounces of flour, a huge difference. It may seem picky, but it really is all about how the flour gets into the measuring cup. So you see the trap that awaits us when we don't know how the recipe's creator measured the flour.

All our recipes use the "dip and level" method, which yields a 5-ounce cup. You get there by dipping the cup down into the flour sack, lifting it out heaped with flour, then sweeping a straight edge (like the back of a knife) over the cup to level it off. Don't tap the cup on the counter or you will pack in more flour, which will undermine the recipe's success.

NOT USING THE RIGHT FLOUR: **All our recipes call for unbleached all-purpose flour, and truth be told, we use organic.**

Because the amount of protein in flour determines much of how your baking will turn out, you should know that all these recipes were created with a flour containing 3 grams of protein per $\frac{1}{4}$ cup of flour. Depending upon where you live in the country, that percentage may vary. To figure out the percent of protein in your flour, look at the nutrition label on the side of the flour sack. Look for flour with at least 3 grams of protein per $\frac{1}{4}$ cup.

You cannot substitute bread flour, bleached flour, whole-wheat flour, cake flour, pastry flour, or self-rising flour for unbleached all-purpose flour. Each one will change how the recipe turns out because of differing amounts of protein, leavening agents, and/or possible chemical additives.

THE BOTTOM LINE IS: Always use the flour called for in any recipe, even if it means another trip to the store.

Oven
BETRAYAL

Nearly every oven I've known was inaccurate. The worst part is that most of us blame ourselves when the dish doesn't turn out right. It's a constant cry we hear from callers to the show: "It must be me. I did something wrong." It is not you; most likely it is your oven.

Give yourself absolution and solve the problem of oven betrayal by buying an accurate oven thermometer. For a modest amount of money you can find a type we have depended upon for years. It is a rectangular metal plate printed with a temperature gauge. Attached to it is what looks like a glass tube containing mercury, but in fact it is a harmless temperature-sensitive substance. Hang it in the center of the oven, let the oven preheat for 20 minutes, and check the temperature. Then adjust the oven's setting as necessary.

THE COLOR OF SUCCESS: THE RIGHT BAKING PAN

More Future Bakers of America have been defeated in the first round, convinced of their ineptitude, because of the color of their pan. Unbeknownst to them, that color affects the results of a recipe. Light-colored pans, like aluminum, are usually what recipe writers use to develop a dessert; their baking time is the standard. Dark-colored pans (including nonstick) bake faster and give darker crusts. And glass is the maverick, baking hottest of all. Often it is suggested that you lower your oven temperature 25 degrees when using a glass baking dish. If using a dark pan, lower it a bit as well.

All of our recipes specify the pan to use.

Freezer Pastry
AND CONTROL ISSUES

An easy way to get a jump-start on the sweet course is to stockpile the foundation of tart and pie pastries in the freezer. Since these hold for several months, you could have a season's worth of desserts ready to go. Cold gives you an added edge in making pastry: it protects the dough from toughening.

We've found that freezing butter (or other fat) gives you control options you don't have when it is merely cold.

Recipes always instruct you to process or mix the fat into the dry ingredients. The size of those fat pieces can change what your pastry will be like once it is baked. If you want a flaky crust, leave them in $1/2$-inch pieces. If you prefer a cookie-like crumbly crust, blend the fat pieces until they are the size of peas. Freezing the butter makes it easier to control the pieces' size.

Here is how to begin: Measure out the dry ingredients for your tart or pie crust into a freezer bag. Cut up the required fat into 1-inch pieces and add that to the bag as well. Be sure to note on the bag what liquids and flavorings you need to add to complete the recipe. Seal and freeze.

When you're ready to bake, turn the frozen mix into a food processor or bowl, and blend until the fat is the size you want. Finish the pastry by adding the liquids and gently pulsing or tossing with a fork. Once there are small clumps of dough that hold together when you press them between your fingers, the pastry dough is ready.

DARK AND MOIST GINGERBREAD

Serves 6 to 8 | *15 minutes prep time; 40 minutes oven time* | *Keeps 5 to 7 days, tighly wrapped, on the counter, and freezes beautifully*

Moist, dark, spicy, but not too sweet, this is classic gingerbread. The addition of black pepper has a historical hook: it was a common ingredient in gingerbreads of the past. We think it brings alive the other spices.

Gingerbread was one of the original baby foods. One of Germany's organic baby-food manufacturers evolved from a family of apothecaries. In their seventeenth-century shop, as in other "drugstores" of the time, gingerbread was dried until crisp and ground into a powder to which mothers added water or milk.

Gingerbread was considered a cure-all. It was said to settle stomachs, strengthen livers, and help mental powers—and we couldn't agree more.

2 cups minus 2 tablespoons **unbleached all-purpose flour,**
  organic preferred (measured by dipping and leveling;
  see page 307)
1 generous teaspoon **baking soda**
Generous ½ teaspoon **salt**
1 tablespoon **ground ginger**
¾ teaspoon **ground cinnamon**
¼ teaspoon **ground cloves**
¼ teaspoon fresh-ground **black pepper**
6 tablespoons **unsalted butter,** melted
¾ cup mild or dark **molasses**
¾ cup very hot **water** (190°F)
⅓ tight-packed cup **dark brown sugar**
1 large **egg**
Whipped cream, for serving

1. Preheat the oven to 350°F. Butter and flour an 8-inch square light-colored metal baking pan.

2. In a medium bowl, whisk together the flour, baking soda, salt, ginger, cinnamon, cloves, and black pepper. In a large mixing bowl, beat together the butter, molasses, hot water, and brown sugar. When the mixture is almost frothy, beat in the egg, and gradually add the flour blend. Stir until thoroughly blended, but no more.

3. Pour the batter into the pan. Bake for 35 minutes, or until a tester inserted in the center of the cake comes out clean.

4. For a moist gingerbread, cool it in the pan on a wire rack. For a drier consistency, cool the gingerbread in the pan for 10 minutes; then turn it out of the pan and set it on the rack to cool.

5. Serve warm if possible, with whipped cream. Don't forget to eat this for breakfast; it's even better the day after it's baked.

When you use an organic "dark" molasses in this recipe you get an intense, nearly chocolate-brown gingerbread with a tart edge. A supermarket "mild" molasses gives you gentler character and a warm caramel color.

Variation
APPLE CHUNK DOUBLE GINGERBREAD

Prepare the recipe as above, but blend into the dry ingredients 2 tablespoons fine-cut candied ginger and a Granny Smith apple that has been peeled, cored, and cut into 1-inch chunks.

Variation
DARK AND MOIST GINGERBREAD WITH CHEESECAKE POCKETS

Before starting the gingerbread, beat together 1 large egg, 4 ounces cream cheese, ¼ cup sugar, 2 teaspoons fresh lemon juice, and ½ teaspoon vanilla extract. Set aside.

Make the gingerbread batter, but pour only half into the pan. Drop spoonfuls of the cheese mixture over the batter. Then cover with the remaining gingerbread mix. Bake as directed. The cake may need another few minutes in the oven.

LITTLE FRENCH FUDGE CAKES

Makes 6 cupcakes, and doubles easily | *15 minutes prep time; 20 minutes oven time* | *Wrapped, the cakes keep well in the refrigerator for up to 5 days*

If you can melt chocolate and stir, you can make these cakes, and no commercial mix has chocolate as good as this. Quality chocolate is like breeding: it always shines through. Gooey chocolate pockets stud the cakes, while the cake itself is nearly as dense as fudge.

There is a real bittersweet edge here. For the kids add another 3 tablespoons of sugar. For yourself, keep the adult attitude, put the young ones to bed, light the candles, and pour two glasses of port.

You could turn this recipe into a cake by baking it in a 9-inch springform pan lined with parchment. Increase the cooking time to about 35 minutes.

One 3.5- or 4-ounce **bittersweet chocolate bar** (Lindt
  Excellence 70%, Valrhona 71%, Scharffen Berger 70%,
  or Ghirardelli 70% Extra Bittersweet, in order of our
  preference), broken up
1½ ounces **unsweetened chocolate**, broken up
5 tablespoons **unsalted butter**
1 teaspoon **ground cinnamon**
1½ teaspoons **vanilla extract**
2 large **eggs** plus 1 **yolk** (for a double recipe, use 5 eggs)
½ cup plus 2 tablespoons **sugar**
⅛ teaspoon **salt**
3 tablespoons **unbleached all-purpose flour**, organic
  preferred (measured by dipping and leveling; see
  page 307)
Half of a 3.5- to 4-ounce **bittersweet chocolate bar**, broken
  into bite-sized pieces

(recipe continues)

1. Preheat the oven to 375°F. Butter a dark metal 6-cup cupcake tin.

2. Combine the broken-up bittersweet and unsweetened chocolates with the butter in a medium-sized microwave-safe bowl. Melt them for 2 to 3 minutes at medium-low power. Check by stirring, as chocolate holds its shape when microwaved. Or melt it in a heatproof bowl over simmering water.

3. In a medium to large bowl, whisk together the cinnamon, vanilla, eggs and yolk, sugar, and salt until creamy. Stir in the flour to blend thoroughly. Then stir in the chocolate/butter mixture until smooth. Finally, blend in the bite-sized pieces of chocolate. Pour the batter into the cupcake pan, filling each three-quarters full.

4. Bake the cupcakes for 18 minutes. Insert a knife into the center of a cupcake. It should come out with some streaks of thick batter. If you have any doubt about doneness, press the top of a cupcake to see if it is nearly firm. Remove them from the oven. Cool the cupcakes in the pan on a rack for 5 to 10 minutes to serve warm, or for 20 minutes to serve at room temperature.

{ COOK to Cook }

The pan you choose will change the baking time of this and other recipes. Here, the dark pan called for gives you fudgy cakes in 16 to 18 minutes; shiny pans lengthen the baking time by a few minutes more. We use a dark (not black) nonstick metal pan for this recipe.

After eating chocolate you feel godlike, as though you can conquer enemies, lead armies, entice lovers.

—Emily Luchetti, pastry chef and author

Buying Chocolate
PLAYING THE PERCENTAGES

Could it be that one day we'll have more chocolates to choose from than coffees? Single bean, single origin, single pod, handpicked by nuns—some say overpriced hype, others say bravo for the choices. But for the baker the most important factor, aside from taste, is the percentage of chocolate in your chocolate bar. Percentages have always mattered, yet until recently American chocolate makers have not put them on labels.

The higher the percent number on the label, the more chocolate (called cacao, or cacao mass) and the less sugar in the bar. For instance, bittersweet chocolate ranges from 60 to 75 percent cacao. Semisweet runs from about 50 to 65, and milk hovers anywhere from 30 to 65 percent. Now you see why it's so important to use the type of chocolate called for in a recipe.

If the exact percentage called for isn't to be had, adjust the recipe's sugar by a few teaspoons one way or the other.

FARMHOUSE PANNA COTTA

Serves 6 to 8; doubles easily

10 minutes prep time; 4 to 72 hours refrigerator time

Make panna cotta 4 to 72 hours before serving. Store in the refrigerator for up to 3 days.

Culinary reputations have been built on this recipe. It is as lush and as memorable as any sweet you can conjure. Yet, essentially panna cotta is nothing more than jelled cream, and it is so simple it's almost mindless. This first appeared in a previous book of mine, but it became such a standby for everyone who made it that I wanted to offer it again.

Unlike other panna cotta recipes this one is far closer to a soft ice cream than to a quivering gel.

2 tablespoons cold **water**
1½ teaspoons **unflavored gelatin**
3 cups **heavy cream**
½ cup **sugar**, or more to taste
Pinch of **salt**
1½ teaspoons **vanilla extract**
1 cup (an 8-ounce container) **sour cream**

1. Put the cold water in a small cup, and sprinkle the gelatin over it. Let it stand for 5 minutes.

2. Meanwhile, in a 3-quart saucepan, warm the cream with the sugar, salt, and vanilla over medium-high heat. Do not let it boil. Stir in the gelatin mixture until thoroughly dissolved. Take the cream off the heat and cool for about 5 minutes.

3. Put the sour cream in a medium bowl. Gently whisk in the warm cream, a little at a time, until it is smooth. Taste the mixture for sweetness; it may need another teaspoon of sugar. Turn the panna cotta into a serving bowl or into eight ⅔-cup ramekins, custard cups, or coffee cups, filling each one three-quarters full with the cream. Chill for 4 to 72 hours.

4. Serve directly from the serving bowl. Or if you used ramekins, either unmold the individual servings by packing the molds in hot towels and then turning each out onto a dessert plate, or serve the panna cotta in the containers.

Variation
SWEET HERB PANNA COTTA

Prepare the recipe as above, but when combining the cream and sugar in the saucepan, add a fresh herb (for instance, 1 tight-packed tablespoon fresh basil or lemon verbena leaves, or 2 teaspoons fresh tarragon or rosemary leaves, or 2 tablespoons fresh fine-chopped lemongrass). Heat the mixture to just below boiling. Remove from the heat, cover, and let stand for 10 minutes for the herbs to steep. Then strain the cream, turn it back into the saucepan, reheat, and finish the recipe as written.

Variation
SAFFRON-ORANGE PANNA COTTA

Prepare the recipe as above, but when combining the cream and sugar in the saucepan, stir in a generous pinch of saffron threads and 1 teaspoon grated orange zest. Continue with the recipe as written. You don't have to steep or strain this variation.

Variation
PUMPKIN PIE PANNA COTTA

Prepare the recipe as above, increasing the gelatin to a full envelope (2 teaspoons) and soaking it in ¼ cup cold water. When you combine the warm cream mixture with the sour cream, add 1 cup cooked and pureed pumpkin or butternut squash. Spice the mixture to taste with allspice, nutmeg, and grated fresh ginger. Chill as described.

{ **COOK** *to* Cook }

Use organic cream if possible, and be sure the sour cream contains only cream and culture, no other additives. As written, this recipe unmolds with a soft, creamy finish, like softened ice cream. For a firmer panna cotta, increase the gelatin to 2 teaspoons (1 envelope).

SALLY'S COCONUT MACAROONS

Makes 30 cookies

8 minutes prep time; 25 minutes oven time

These keep for 3 to 5 days in an airtight container on the counter. They freeze well and are excellent eaten straight from the freezer.

The best recipes have backstories—at least, Sally's always do. Here she gives the lineage behind these macaroons.

"My mother had one mean sweet tooth. She would be the one begging to drive the ten miles to the nearest Dairy Queen, where she would always order the biggest sundae. We kids simply couldn't keep up. So it's no surprise that she was a great baker. These cookies were something we would often do in my teen years at about nine p.m. as a snack before bed. They were even better for breakfast."

2 large **eggs**, well beaten
½ cup **sugar**
Generous pinch of **salt**
1 teaspoon **almond or vanilla extract**
3 cups **sweetened shredded coconut**

1. Preheat the oven to 350°F. Spread a sheet of parchment paper over a large cookie sheet, or butter the sheet.
2. In a large mixing bowl, whisk together the eggs, sugar, salt, and almond or vanilla extract. Blend in the coconut until it is completely moistened. This is not supposed to be a batter, but rather well-moistened clumps of coconut.
3. Drop generous teaspoonfuls onto the baking sheet, and bake them for 20 to 25 minutes, or until the macaroons are golden brown with crisp edges. Transfer them to a rack to cool.

(variations follow)

Variation
EASTER BUNNY NESTS

Once the macaroons are on the cookie sheet, tuck a jelly bean or two into the top of each one before baking.

Variation
CHOCOLATE MACAROONS

Prepare the recipe as above, adding 3 to 4 tablespoons unsweetened cocoa powder to the egg mixture; or, alternatively, blend in ½ cup chocolate chips with the coconut.

Variation
RAINBOW MACAROONS

Nothing is better for a little-kid party than tinted macaroons. Imagine Day-Glo pink, electric blue, kelly green, and taxicab yellow. Add 2 to 3 drops of the food coloring of choice to the coconut. Toss to evenly color the strands before adding it to the rest of the ingredients.

Variation
COCONUT NUT MACAROONS

Prepare the recipe as above, adding ½ to ⅔ cup nuts—from coarse-chopped almonds, to pistachios, to hazelnuts—to the coconut mixture.

Variation
GINGER-SPIKED MACAROONS

Prepare the recipe as above, adding ¼ cup fine-chopped candied ginger to the coconut mixture.

These macaroons have more personalities than Madonna—elegant with demitasse, plush dipped into Old-Time Bittersweet Hot Fudge (page 323), perfect as snack food, and lovable as kid treats.

THE MAN
WHO TASTED SHAPES

Ever bite into a cookie and see a color or hear music in your head?
You could have a touch of synesthesia.

Synesthesia is a quirk of the human brain. The word means "joined sensations," as in someone who is born with senses hooked together. For instance, you would not only hear a voice, you would see it, or taste it, or even feel that you could touch it.

When we interviewed neurologist Richard E. Cytowic, a synesthesia expert, he explained, "For synesthetes the sensation is like fireworks. There is an explosion and then it falls away. Synesthetes are often very surprised that there is a name for this syndrome; they think no one else feels it."

Dr. Cytowic beguiled us with the story of the first time he dined at his friend Michael's house. After a few bites Michael said, "Oh no, there aren't enough points on the chicken." Dr. Cytowic realized he was a synesthete. Unusually, Michael had taste and smell combined with touch. He felt things mostly in his face and hands, explaining, "With an intense flavor a feeling sweeps down my arms, into my hands and I feel texture, weight, and temperatures as if I was holding something."

Michael was a skilled cook. Dr. Cytowic said, "He cooked according to the shape of things. He loved prickly pointed and round smooth shapes. He could also discriminate incredibly well. Bitter was smooth; sweetness tended to have curvature. He was wonderful to eat with. He would pause and reach his hand out over the table as if he were touching something. It would only last a second or two."

BUILDING THE LIBRARY

THE MAN WHO TASTED SHAPES
BY RICHARD CYTOWIC
(MIT PRESS, 2003)

Next time you bite into a piece of chocolate mint pie, think about how Michael tastes it: "I can reach out in the distance and stick my hands among twelve smooth glass columns. I can feel the coolness and curvature and it's all so deliciously smooth."

Always serve too much hot fudge sauce on hot fudge sundaes. It makes people overjoyed, and puts them in your debt.

–Judith Olney

OLD-TIME BITTERSWEET HOT FUDGE

| Makes close to 1½ cups | 10 minutes prep time; 10 minutes stove time | Store the fudge sauce in the refrigerator for up to 5 days; you will find it is excellent cold, straight from the jar |

Can a family survive without handy hot fudge? Can *anyone* survive without hot fudge? Why try? It is as necessary to a kitchen as garlic. Serve this warm with anything that doesn't move.

Microwave ovens vary. When melting the chocolate, start at medium-low power and check after 1 minute. If necessary, go to a higher setting.

10 ounces **bittersweet chocolate** (Lindt Excellence 70%, Valrhona 71%, Scharffen Berger 70%, or Ghirardelli 70% Extra Bittersweet, in order of our preference)

1 ounce **unsweetened chocolate**

2 tablespoons **unsalted butter**

½ cup **heavy whipping cream**, plus 2 tablespoons extra if needed

6 tablespoons **light corn syrup**

1 teaspoon **vanilla extract**

1. Combine the two chocolates and the butter in a small microwave-safe bowl. Begin melting them in a microwave oven set at medium-low power for 2 to 3 minutes. Check how the melting is progressing by stirring often. Chocolate holds its shape when microwaved, so it can be deceiving. When the chocolate is fully melted, set it aside.

Alternatively, melt the chocolates and butter in a bowl set over simmering water. When melted, remove the bowl from the water and cool for 5 minutes.

2. In a 2-quart saucepan, stir together the ½ cup cream, the corn syrup, and the vanilla. Stir as you bring them to a simmer over medium-high heat. Remove the pan from the burner and cool for 2 minutes. Whisk in the chocolate-butter blend until smooth. If the sauce is too thick, add the remaining 2 tablespoons cream.

3. Serve the hot fudge immediately, or rewarm it in a bowl over simmering water to preserve the silky consistency.

EDNA LEWIS'S SUGARED RASPBERRIES

| *Makes about 2 cups* | *5 minutes prep time* | *These will keep for a year or longer in the refrigerator* |

The legendary Edna Lewis—a granddaughter of slaves, raised on a farm in Freetown, Virginia—brought a conviction and honesty to her food that few have touched.

Late in life she started working with young chef Scott Peacock; together they co-authored *The Gift of Southern Cooking*. On the show Scott told us about this old method for preserving fruit, which keeps its taste fresh because there is no cooking involved.

Scott wrote in their book, "Miss Lewis gave me a jar of sugared raspberries—the first I'd ever seen—when I visited her one springtime. The following December, at my birthday dinner, I served them as an accompaniment to roast chicken and yeast rolls—very Southern and very delicious."

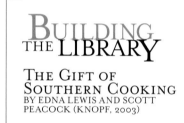

BUILDING THE LIBRARY

THE GIFT OF SOUTHERN COOKING
BY EDNA LEWIS AND SCOTT PEACOCK (KNOPF, 2003)

You can prepare strawberries or blackberries the same way, but raspberries seem to do and taste best.

2 cups (about 1 pound) fresh, unblemished **raspberries**
2 cups **sugar**

1. Carefully pick over the berries, removing any leaves, foreign objects, or spoiled berries. Put the berries in a mixing bowl, and pour the sugar over them. Use two large forks or a potato masher to mash the sugar into the raspberries until they are liquefied and no trace of whole berries is left. (A blender is not good for this, because it will pulverize some of the raspberry seeds, which should remain intact.)

2. Transfer the mashed berries to jars and refrigerate for at least 2 days before using. Stashed in the refrigerator, these berries are manna from heaven in January. Eat them straight by the spoonful or on bread, cake, or ice cream.

MARIE ANTOINETTE'S
Pleasure Dairy

Art and food historian Carolin Young introduced us to a side of milk we'd not known: the concept of the pleasure dairy. In the moments leading up to the French Revolution, the fashion at King Louis XVI's court was to build little garden follies as "pleasure dairies." Temples of femininity and motherhood, these were places for the nobility to literally let their hair down and play at farming.

Milk seemed to be at the center of the romps—milking cows, churning butter, and making cheese were favorite parts of the role-playing. The most famous milkmaid of them all was Marie Antoinette. At Versailles her pleasure dairy was part of a little rustic getaway spot called the Queen's Hamlet. There she dressed up in peasant muslins and performed plays, pretending to sell her milk and cheese.

Carolin explained that this trend was an offshoot of the writings of eighteenth-century philosopher Jean-Jacques Rousseau, who believed modern life corrupted man's natural goodness and that a return to nature and simple living was essential. The nobles of the day, however, spun Rousseau's longing for the natural into a competition in artifice, turning his philosophy into a mere fad.

But Rousseau had spurred change; his writings were part of the foundation of revolutionary thinking. As Carolin Young observed, **"While nobles romped like peasants, the peasants were revolting. The revolution was right around the corner."**

Few pleasure dairies still exist, though Marie Antoinette's can be seen at Versailles, and a beautiful one is open to the public at the Château de Rambouillet, the summer residence of the president of France.

BUILDING
THE LIBRARY

APPLES OF GOLD IN SETTINGS OF SILVER: STORIES OF DINNER AS A WORK OF ART
BY CAROLIN C. YOUNG
(SIMON & SCHUSTER, 2002)

ROSEMARY FIGS WITH HONEYED FRESH CHEESE

Serves 3 to 4 | *5 minutes prep time*

"Figs are the only fruit that can make you blush when you're alone," says *Los Angeles Times* food writer Russ Parsons. Alone isn't a bad way to enjoy them, either. In this recipe fresh figs are cut in half, their blush discreetly covered with fresh cheese and slicked with honey and rosemary. Eat them with your fingers. Once you've had your primeval moment, you might decide to share.

Pair the figs with good apple cider, or with a sweet wine like Muscat de Beaumes-de-Venise or Moscato Passito di Pantelleria.

8 to 10 ounces ripe dark **figs** (Calimyrna, Brown Turkey, Mission, etc.)

4 to 5 ounces fresh **goat, sheep, or cow's-milk cheese**

3 to 4 tablespoons **honey**

1 teaspoon chopped fresh **rosemary leaves**

3 tablespoons crushed **salted pistachio nuts**

Halve the figs from top to bottom. Smear each half gently with about a teaspoon of cheese. Arrange the halves on a platter, and drizzle them generously with honey. Sprinkle with the rosemary and pistachios.

COOK *to* **Cook**

According to Russ, a fig is ripe when it has a slightly creased look to its skin and has a few glossy tears of moisture, especially from the hole in the fruit's base called "the eye." Since figs don't ripen once they are picked, buy them ripe and eat them as soon as possible. Waiting only buys disappointment.

Another tip from Russ is to opt for black figs. Their flavor is usually sweeter and more complex than that of green ones. Figs come into season in spring and fall.

Seduction
AND FIGS

One of the most memorable reads of the past few years was Monique Truong's novel *The Book of Salt.* The story is told from the perspective of an imagined Vietnamese cook working for Gertrude Stein and Alice B. Toklas in Paris in the 1930s. Life has given the cook the role of outsider, always looking with a critical eye, yet craving contact and love. It contains one of the most poignant seduction scenes, which Monique read for us on the air.

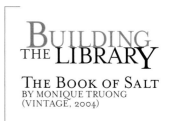

BUILDING
THE LIBRARY

THE BOOK OF SALT
BY MONIQUE TRUONG
(VINTAGE, 2004)

The cook has been sent to prepare a dinner in the home of a friend of Alice and Gertrude's. The friend turns out to be a beautiful young man; the home is his garret; and the cook begins to realize there are no guests. **The story begins in his voice:**

"Twenty-four figs, so ripe that their skins split.

A bottle of dry port wine.

One duck.

Twelve hours."

PINEAPPLE-GINGER SORBET

Serves 3 to 4

5 minutes prep time; 5 minutes processing

Best pureed and served right away

People mistake this for ice cream, which makes us both smile since there isn't a jot of cream in it, nor more than a few minutes of effort. Smooth, creamy yellow, and jammed with fresh fruit, this sorbet is one of those miracle concoctions that proves the ubiquitous frozen fruit found in every supermarket can become the classiest of sweets—dinner-party material as well as family food. All that is required is a food processor and a quartet of flavorings. Ginger, almond, lemon, and sugar are the miracle workers. Pineapple takes especially well to them.

One ¼- to ½-inch piece fresh **ginger**, peeled
One 16-ounce bag frozen **unsweetened pineapple chunks**;
    or 4 to 5 cups home-frozen fresh pineapple or other fruit
¼ teaspoon **almond extract**
Pinch of **salt**
5 tablespoons **sugar**, or to taste
Juice of ½ large **lemon**
3 tablespoons **water**, or more as needed

With the food processor running, drop the ginger through the feed tube. Process for 1 second. Then add the pineapple, a few chunks at a time. Finally, add the almond extract, salt, sugar, lemon juice, and water. Continue pureeing, stopping to scrape down the sides of the bowl as needed. Process until the sorbet is smooth as cream. If it is very stiff, add another tablespoon of water. Once the sorbet is smooth, spoon it into glasses or bowls and serve immediately.

Variation

RASPBERRY-PEACH SORBET

This is the remedy for flavorless frozen peaches. The mix of peaches and raspberries becomes a gorgeous magenta color.

Follow the recipe as above, omitting the ginger and substituting 1 pound frozen peaches and ½ pound frozen unsweetened raspberries for the pineapple. Serve as directed above.

Variation

TROPICAL FRUIT SORBET

Asian markets carry a selection of frozen fruits that we don't see in most supermarkets—mango, jackfruit, passion fruit, and the like. Substitute any of them for the pineapple. With these fruits, use fresh lime juice instead of the lemon.

Variation

FRUIT SORBET WITH CREAM

To any of these recipes, add ⅓ cup cold heavy whipping cream when the sorbet is completely smooth. The cream could streak the mix with a marbleized effect or be blended in completely. Coconut cream (available canned) can be used in the same way.

Be sure to leave the processor running until the sorbet is smooth. But you'll need to stop every so often to scrape down the sides.

THE ALMOND TRICK

Almond extract is one of those do-or-die flavorings. Too much and you think you'll never get the taste out of your mouth. Just the right amount and it's like salt on French fries—you don't know how you lived without it.

What salt does for the fried potato, almond extract does for insipid fruit. Insipid becomes engaging. Would that I could say this was my own idea, but I can't.

In the years when I spent much of my time buried in old cookbooks, one technique turned up repeatedly. Fruit recipes called for either bitter almonds or the little almond-shaped nuts from inside the pits of stone fruits. Both of these may be poisonous (the culprit is varying amounts of toxic prussic acid in the nuts), but their touch of bitterness could improve any fruit.

Today almond extract fills the role, with no danger of losing friends.

THE DUKE'S HOT CHOCOLATE

Serves 4 to 6

5 minutes prep time; 5 minutes stove time

Hot chocolate holds on the stove for an hour or longer, and can be stored in the refrigerator for 2 days

This hot chocolate has a pedigree. It dates from 1632, when the court cook to Bologna's ruling family, the Bentivoglio dukes, made it the fashion of the day. Scented with allspice, vanilla, and orange, this was the end product of one of Italy's earliest recipes for making chocolate from the cacao bean. Cook Giuseppe Lamma came up with other flavoring options, such as packing the chocolate in jasmine flowers for several days before melting it, or stirring ground amber into the hot drink.

Amber and jasmine notwithstanding, you can experience the chocolate as the ladies at court liked it: hot in winter, iced in summer. What a civilized late-night fix. Too bad they didn't know about marshmallows back then.

1½ teaspoons **ground allspice**

1 tablespoon **vanilla extract** (or the seeds scraped from the inside of a whole vanilla bean)

Generous pinch of **salt**

⅛ teaspoon fresh-ground **black pepper** (optional)

½ cup **sugar**, or to taste

Fine-grated zest of 1 large **orange**

3 cups **water**; or half water, half milk; or half water, half cream

10.5 to 12 ounces **bittersweet chocolate** (Lindt Excellence 70%, Valrhona 71%, Scharffen Berger 70%, or Ghirardelli 70% Extra Bittersweet, in our order of preference), broken up

1. In a 3-quart saucepan, combine all the ingredients *except* the chocolate. Bring to a boil, reduce the heat, cover, and simmer for 2 minutes.

2. Pull the pan off the heat, and let it sit for a few minutes. Then whisk in the chocolate until smooth. Taste the hot chocolate for sweetness and allspice. Serve hot.

Variation

HOT CHOCOLATE FLOAT

Top cups of hot chocolate with big spoonfuls of pistachio or vanilla fudge ice cream. Sprinkle with crushed pistachios.

Variation

ESPRESSO-CHOCOLATE HOT CUP

Reduce the liquid to 2½ cups, and increase the sugar to ¾ cup. With the chocolate, add ¼ to ½ cup brewed strong espresso coffee.

Variation

HOT CHOCOLATE TODDY

Add 1 ounce or more of dark rum to the chocolate. Garnish the cups with vanilla beans as stirrers.

Variation

HOT CHILE CHOCOLATE

In Step 1, add to the liquid mixture 1 generous teaspoon medium-hot ground ancho chile, or the hot and sweet Aleppo chile. Boil with the other ingredients.

Variation

THE DUKE'S CHOCOLATE GRANITA

Increase the flavorings to 2 teaspoons allspice, 4 teaspoons vanilla extract (or the seeds from 1½ vanilla beans), and ¾ cup sugar. Cool the hot chocolate and pour it into a shallow container. Freeze for 1 hour. Stir the hardened portion at the edges of the container into the center. Repeat two more times, until you have a shaggy chocolate ice. Serve the granita topped with nuts or cream.

Acknowledgments

Food is controllable while most of life is not. We want to give special thanks to the following people for their graceful and sometimes inadvertent contributions to this book.

Our original executive producer Tom Voegeli cashed in his not insignificant chips to get us on the air thirteen years ago, and has been a guiding force ever since. Thanks to American Public Media for years ago nurturing raw talent and their odd idea of a food show on radio.

Jennifer Luebke, Jennifer Russell, Judy Graham, and Amy Rea are our steadfast comrades in production and dear friends, who managed to keep all the balls magically and cheerfully in the air while our noses were buried elsewhere. Our "two Jens" took on the lion's share of production over the year it took to deliver this book. They did it with great style and joie de vivre and we are very grateful.

In addition to their existing jobs, Judy ruthlessly tested every recipe in this book, and Amy brought her editor's skills to proofing draft after draft. Never once did she raise her eyes to heaven as we incessantly asked, "How does this sound?"

"Eat me, I am gorgeous" photographs demand talent, craft, and attention to detail that can drive many around the bend. Photographer Mette Nielsen, stylist Carmen Bonilla, and Maggie Stoppera accomplished all that, and kept our photography marathons full of good cheer and on track. They even managed not to laugh out loud as two grown women argued over the amount of sauce on the noodles.

Our agent, Jane Dystel, is always there for us with clear thinking, great savvy, and a lioness's protective instincts. We had the great luck of finding editor Pam Krauss, who made this project fly with her inspiration and encouragement. Pam pulled together the forces that have made this book beautiful, and gifted us with designer Wayne Wolf of Blue Cup Design. We are indebted to him for taking our knapsack of elements and turning them into his playful take on elegance found throughout the book. Our thanks, too, to Clarkson Potter creative director Marysarah Quinn for her gentle, sound vision, and to Kate Tyler, Sydney Webber, Selina Cicogna, and the entire publicity and marketing departments for their tireless efforts.

At American Public Media and Minnesota Public Radio: Our thanks to Sarah Lutman, whose constant question, "What can I do?" is always asked sincerely; Tim Roesler, who single-handedly changed the fate of our program with his optimism and enthusiasm; Jon McTaggart, who backed us without hesitation when we said we wanted to turn the show into a book; and to Bill Kling, who takes public radio down paths few others even see.

Sincere thanks to the following people for making our work in public radio so fulfilling: Mark Alfuth, Mike Bettison, Norma Cox, Kathleen Davies, Chris Farrell, Mitch Hanley, Jeff Harkness,

Erica Herrmann, Nick Kereokas, Kate Moos, Rachel Riensche, Julia Schrenkler, Andrew Schumacher, Judy Skoglund, and Krista Tippett.

Great thanks to our radio family: Jane and Michael Stern, Joshua Wesson, Steve Jenkins, Christopher Kimball, Mike Colameco, Dorie Greenspan, Sally Schneider, Deborah Krasner, and John Willoughby. Their stories brighten these pages; and they make our jobs easy with their passionate, curious, and smart voices.

My thanks and my love to Patty Waters, Julie Hartley, and Marie Dwyer, three more open, loyal, loving hearts are not to be found. You continue to teach me how rich friendship can be.

My sister Nanine Swift, who never seems to doubt me and if she does, hides it very well; Denise Buelow, who single-handedly at times raised our children well; and the other nondoubters in my life: Sherry Guenther, Susette Swift, Lucy Rogers, Larry Grant, Deb Yanker Black, Jim and Gigi Voegeli, Kathleen Day-Coen, and Ruth Hadyn.

Where would I be without my Marine on St. Croix tribe? Always ready to eat and pick up stray children—my kind of people. Olivia, Maggie, and Will (hands-down winner of the most enthusiastic eater award), Raedeke, Karl, Tucker, and Ebbie Benson, Dorothy Deetz, Tod and Jay Drescher, Millie Kirn, Teri Kline, Colleen Peterson, and Anna Maakestad.

I would be remiss if I did not thank John, Eleanor, and Peter Yackel, who taught me what a family meal could be so many years ago, and Emily Allen, who served me my first balsamic on a warm summer night on Fremont Avenue.

And of course, for Tom, for whom a request to go to the herb garden used to be a sentence from hell. I hope I have given you a little more light on the path.

—SS

Great thanks to the colleagues I admire, and whose work spurs me on. Very special thanks to my dear sister in every way but blood, Cara De Silva, who is as obsessed with culinary scholarship as I am. For Marjorie, who is a true dear heart—a friend like no other; the Denver gang—Susan, Lisa, Alice, and Lu—wonderfully outrageous friends of a lifetime and great guinea piglets; for dear friends Ann and Tim, Bonnie and Al, Jane and Harry, Gayle, Tom and Ian, Steven, Kit, Nan and Sam, Eileen and Les, and all the people who have shared our table not realizing that they were test cases . . . and wonderful sports.

—LRK

Index

Note: Page numbers in *italics* refer to photographs.

WINE-BRAISED CARROTS WITH FRIED SAGE LEAVES (page264) WITH
TURKISH ALMOND SAUCE (page 241)
No-Cook Whole-Wheat Couscous (page 296)

CLASSIC CHICKEN NOODLE SOUP (page 49)
Crusty bread
Dressing-in-a-Bowl Supper Salad (page 14)
LITTLE FRENCH FUDGE CAKES (page 313)

PLUMPED GINGER-CARAMEL SHRIMP (page 227)
Dumbed-Down Rice (page 297) *with fresh basil leaves*
EDNA LEWIS'S SUGARED RASPBERRIES (page 324)

THAI CANTALOUPE SALAD WITH CHILE (page 41)
Goat cheese plate
GLASS OF NORTHWEST RIESLING OR APPLE CIDER

MOROCCAN GREEN BEAN TAGINE (page 126)
No-Cook Whole-Wheat Couscous (page 296)
ORANGE WEDGES WITH HONEY AND ORANGE-FLOWER WATER

FARMER'S TORTELLINI IN WINE BROTH (page 49)
Lynne's Retro Garlic Bread (page 179)
A VELVETY RED WINE LIKE ZINFANDEL OR SANGIOVESE

ALMOND CHUTNEY CHICKEN IN LETTUCE ROLL-UPS (page 113)
Sticky rice
PINEAPPLE-GINGER SORBET (page 328)

MIDNIGHT ASPARAGUS WITH CREAMY EGGS (page 110)
Boiled red potatoes
THE DUKE'S HOT CHOCOLATE (page 330)

CHEATER'S HOMEMADE BROTH (page 48)
Belgian Beer Bar Tartine (page 119)
BELGIAN GUEUZE BEER

SMOTHERED BROCCOLI WITH PEPPER, ONIONS, AND RAISINS (page 273)
Garlic and olive oil–rubbed bruschetta
SLICED PEARS WITH TALEGGIO CHEESE

CORIANDER-ORANGE-SCENTED RED LENTIL SOUP (page 74)
Pita bread with take-out eggplant puree
ROSEMARY FIGS WITH HONEYED FRESH CHEESE (page 326)